PUBLIC POLICY
AND PRIVATE ENTERPRISE
IN MEXICO

THIS BOOK HAS BEEN PREPARED

UNDER THE AUSPICES OF

THE CENTER FOR INTERNATIONAL AFFAIRS

HARVARD UNIVERSITY

Created in 1958, the Center fosters advanced study of basic world problems by scholars from various disciplines and senior officers from many countries. The research at the Center, focusing on the processes of change, includes studies of military-political issues, the modernizing processes in developing countries, and the evolving position of Europe. The research programs are supervised by Professors Robert R. Bowie (Director of the Center), Alex Inkeles, Henry A. Kissinger, Edward S. Mason, Thomas C. Schelling, and Raymond Vernon. A list of Center publications will be found at the end of this volume.

PUBLIC POLICY
AND PRIVATE ENTERPRISE
IN MEXICO

Raymond Vernon, Editor

STUDIES BY

Miguel S. Wionczek
David H. Shelton
Calvin P. Blair
Rafael Izquierdo

HARVARD UNIVERSITY PRESS

Cambridge, Massachusetts

1964

Foreword

BY EDWARD S. MASON FOR THE CENTER
FOR INTERNATIONAL AFFAIRS

This book is one of a series of studies of the relative roles of private enterprise and government in a number of developing countries. These studies under my direction are a part of the research program of the Center for International Affairs at Harvard. The countries have been chosen to give some notion of the rather wide spectrum of relations between the public and private sectors at different stages of development and in different areas of the world. Latin America is represented by studies of Mexico and Brazil; Asia by Iran, Pakistan, and Thailand; and Africa by Nigeria.

The first country study to be completed was *The Dilemma of Mexico's Development,* by Raymond Vernon, published by Harvard University Press in July 1963. The present book, *Public Policy and Private Enterprise in Mexico,* is a companion volume to the first. It includes an introduction by Professor Vernon and four case studies by other economists.

Raymond Vernon is Professor of International Trade and Investment in the Harvard Business School, and is also Director of the Development Advisory Service in the Center for International Affairs.

Miguel S. Wionczek is Head of Information Department at CEMLA (Center for Latin American Monetary Studies) in Mexico City.

David H. Shelton is Associate Professor of Economics, School of Business and Economics, University of Delaware.

Calvin P. Blair is Professor of Resources and International Business, Department of Marketing Administration, University of Texas (during the calendar year 1964 a visiting professor in the Harvard Business School).

Rafael Izquierdo is an economist in Mexico City, formerly with the U.N. Economic Commission for Latin America, now engaged in consulting.

Though the authors of the case studies assisted Professor Vernon in many ways during the years of his research in Mexico, this book should not be thought of as a joint product; each of the four authors has the responsibility for his own essay and for no other part of the book.

All of the studies in the public-private project are being financed largely by a generous grant from the Ford Foundation to the Center for International Affairs for research on the relation of government to private enterprise. The two Mexican books also were supported in part by the Division of Research, Harvard Business School, using funds provided by the Ford Foundation and the Associates of the Harvard Business School.

Contents

TABLES

Shelton, THE BANKING SYSTEM

Blair, NACIONAL FINANCIERA

Izquierdo, PROTECTIONISM IN MEXICO

INTRODUCTION

Public Policy and Private Enterprise

WHEN in 1959 my colleagues and I set out to try to understand the roles of the public and private sectors in the development of Mexico, we were only dimly aware of the size of the bite we had undertaken to chew. If our group could make any claim to expertise, that claim lay in the field of economics. Yet, throughout our studies, principles found in the study of history, political science, anthropology, and sociology kept vying with formal economics to provide an explanation of what we saw. In the end, each of us felt obliged to step outside the field of economics from time to time, even if it meant practicing in some fields of the social sciences without a proper license. It was in this uninhibited spirit that my recent book, *The Dilemma of Mexico's Development,* was written.

Broad interpretations such as one finds in *The Dilemma,* however, are a risky business. The process of economic development is complex; the level of abstraction necessary to describe it is sometimes distressingly high; so there is always a danger of losing touch with reality. But there are ways of hedging against that risk. One way is to take a series of borings in the landscape under study — in this instance, to explore in depth a number of aspects of Mexico's economy, looking for hypotheses which may apply more broadly and testing the hypotheses derived from other sources.

The four essays in this volume represent some of the product of this effort. Working independently, each of the authors explored some major aspect of the Mexican economy, probing for an understanding of the relations between the public and private sectors in his field of study. Fortunately, the preliminary results of these studies were available well before I had completed my work on *The Dilemma*. Although the interpretations presented in these essays are not always foursquare with the conclusions to which I myself was led, my own work was greatly enriched by the fact that I had access to the preliminary results.

EMERGENT RELATIONSHIPS

One cannot live long in Mexico without sensing the Mexicans' characteristic preoccupation with the history of their extraordinary country. The interest is easy to comprehend. Anyone who attempts to understand contemporary Mexico without much reference to its history courts major risks. This is certainly true of any effort to understand relations between the public and the private sectors in Mexico.

At the opening of the twentieth century, a decade or so before Mexico's historic Revolution, the country already had the beginnings of an effective national government and the nucleus of a modern private entrepreneurial class. But the functions of government were largely confined to those that seemed necessary to the maintenance of order; the engine of growth was thought to lie almost exclusively in the private sector, a sector dominated by foreign interests. Mexico's indigenous entrepreneurs, at the time, were few in number. Even they had, in the main, been grafted onto the Mexican economy from roots in Europe; and they were, to a considerable extent, oriented to regional communities such as Monterrey and Puebla.

By the early 1960's, both the public and the private sectors were utterly changed in capability and in quality. The government had built the apparatus of a modern state, including a civil service, a set of public banking institutions, an organization competent to design and build major public works, and an administrative machinery capable of directing a complex tax system, import controls, subsidies, and price controls. Meanwhile, the modern private sector, while still containing significant foreign interests, had become largely indigenous. What is more, it had discovered the concepts of modern entrepreneurship, including mass production and marketing, public financing, objective record-keeping, and corporate anonymity and continuity. The metamorphosis of both sectors was far from complete, but there was not much doubt as to the directions in which they were moving.

During the half century of change launched by the Revolution, there was a gradual and careful building up of habits of communication between the two sectors. In the 1920's the communication process was obscure, perhaps intentionally concealed by the leaders of both sectors from a public which had been conditioned to think of business as largely foreign, and of foreigners as largely exploiters. Some of the consequences of the interchange could be seen, however, in the quality of the government's actions — for example in its cautious, evolutionary approach to the expansion of the functions of the Banco de México; in its occasional gestures of conciliation toward the foreign utility and mining companies; in its restraint in the use of the taxing power.

Later on, the channels of communication between domestic businessmen and government were gradually broadened. Business groups were given official status in the apparatus of government. Their advice was sought from time to time by both formal and informal means, before major changes in government policy were instituted. Along with the labor and farm groups, they were given a day in court by presidents-elect as a prelude to the formulation of the presidential programs. In short, public communication between the two sectors became respectable in popular eyes.

There were, of course, a number of excursions and alarums in the evolutionary process. Foreign businessmen came to be distinguished from indigenous entrepreneurs and to be subjected to special pressures. But even indigenous entrepreneurs were not immune to occasional spasms of understandable uneasiness. Now and then a president with his eye to the propitiation of some other interest group in the Mexican economy was accused of neglecting the legitimate interests of the modern entrepreneurs. Sometimes the government stepped into a position of potential rivalry with the private sector or even pre-empted a field in which the private sector hoped to operate. Just as often, however, the government supplied some critical ingredient for the expansion of the private domestic sector: a riskless contract, a subsidized loan, an extension of the electric power or transportation system, a prohibition on imports, a curb on the operations of foreign-owned competitors producing inside the country. Besides, there was very little disposition on the part of either the public sector or the private indigenous business groups to elevate the problems that existed to issues of principle. Though some issues could be formulated in these terms, there was a willingness in the end to accommodate and compromise.

Why there should have been so few head-on clashes, so few hopelessly intransigent positions taken by the public and the private domestic sectors in this critical half century, is a problem that deserves the attention of the social psychologists. My own lay judgment is that, after the bloody phase of the Revolution ended, a mutual fear of the consequences of open conflict played a major role in inhibiting both sides.

The insecurities of the Revolution have laid their stamp on the style of all modern Mexican presidents. No Mexican president has felt secure enough to exclude all possibility of armed revolt against his regime. Therefore, Mexican presidents have rarely felt it worthwhile to go to the mat over issues on which the modern private sector (or any other significant group, such as the farmers or labor unions) could be expected to be united in hostility. By the 1950's, this tendency to temporize and compromise with the interests of any significant splinter of the Mexican body politic was an ingrained habit of operation. Indeed, even the process of presidential selection came to reflect this habit; the quality of neutralness became a critical prerequisite for any serious candidate.

The fear of the consequences of intransigence was not confined to the public side. It was also very much a part of Mexico's private business psychology. A revolutionary decade of lawlessness, insecurity, expropriation, and killing was not something easily to be forgotten. The insecurities of the turbulent 1930's kept these memories alive when they might have faded. And Fidel Castro managed to prolong the gnawing undercurrents of insecurity a good deal longer still. Accordingly, the private sector has been just as eager as the public side to find some basis for avoiding open conflict.

Compromise and conciliation are, of course, an indispensable element of responsible statecraft. A proper respect for the views of special-interest groups is required of any tolerable system of government. The disposition of Mexican presidents to be always sensitive to the needs and grievances of business, therefore, could be thought of as evidence of a mature political system. Certainly it seemed to favor Mexico's growth, at least until the latter 1950's.

All of which brings us to the theme developed at such length in *The Dilemma of Mexico's Development*. Bear in mind that the strategy of Mexico's presidents has required responsiveness not merely to the pressures of the entrepreneurs, but also to the pressures of labor, agriculture, the intellectuals, the politicians, the Catholic Church, the North and South, the cities and countryside. As the head of a party whose political philosophy parted company with no one, the president was a man whose ear could be legitimately commanded by every faction. And as the leader of a country whose history had never once recorded the peaceful and legitimate passage of power from an in-group to an out-group, he felt a special need to keep his lines of communication open to all dissidents. An unending concern to detect and conciliate opposition from every quarter became the hallmark of the Mexican presidency.

The problem is that a government wholeheartedly committed to such a pattern of operation may find it impossible to make the hard, painful, and unambiguous changes in policy that are from time to time demanded as a price in the process of growth; and this inability to produce the necessary changes for growth may bring the political machinery to grief. On the other hand, a government which *does* take the painful decisions required for growth may not survive the political risks of offending the opposition. As I see it, this is the dilemma that Mexico confronts. If it is obliged to seize one of the pointed horns, the relations between its public and private sectors may soon be undergoing another change.

Dilemma or not, however, some features of the relation between the two sectors seemed to serve very well indeed for a number of decades. Mexico, it appeared, had found the means for harnessing the creative energies of both sectors in support of the goals of economic development. Though public investment policies and programs sometimes led to protests on the part of the private sector, these programs seemed to be welcomed more often than not. And public regulation, extensive and onerous though it might appear, also garnered support at least as often as it provoked opposition from the private sector. Perhaps these results flowed from the fact that the Mexican government's activities in investment and regulation were not haphazard or unrestrained; most of them could be defined in explicit terms, relevant to the need to foster economic growth in the country.

PUBLIC INVESTMENT POLICY

Public investment in modern Mexico has usually amounted to a substantial fraction of annual gross investment in the country's economy — rarely less than one third, sometimes as much as one half, according to the infirm official data. As the essays of my colleagues demonstrate, public investments have fallen into a number of fairly distinct categories. The "natural monopolies" such as hydroelectric power generation have usually commanded a considerable part of the public total. In addition, however, there have been public investments of another kind, investments in ventures which could not hope to get a proper return through the price system, even though the economy as a whole might get a collective yield that amply justified the investment. Some of Mexico's investments in electricity *distribution* fall squarely in this category; the introduction of electricity to remote villages could not easily be justified on any calculus of private gain. Many of the country's investments in the distribution of water could not be defended in market terms; the rural buyers of water, it is assumed, could not be persuaded to pay an "economic" price. Yet those investments can conceivably be justified by the increased agricultural yields which eventually are captured by the nation in the form of higher living standards to farms or the cities.

Public investments in the "natural monopolies" and in activities which cannot pay out in private terms generally provoke little adverse reaction from the private sector in most countries. But some of the other categories in which the Mexican public sector has invested are more troublesome.

From time to time in the development of any country, there arises a near-indispensable demand for some single, indivisible production unit on a scale so large or in a field so unfamiliar as to exceed either the risk-taking proclivities of the private sector or its capacity to mobilize the capital for the venture. Even if the investment is attractive in private terms, the private institutions ready and able to make the necessary calculation — or ready and able to respond to the implications of the calculation when made — may not yet have appeared.

Problems of this sort can exist even in a relatively advanced country such as Mexico, with a well-defined entrepreneurial class already in existence. The fact that entrepreneurs exist in a country is not to say that entrepreneurs exist who are willing to look at investments of all types and sizes. Entrepreneurs, after all, come in types and sizes, too.

Psychologists have already gone a long way in undermining the economist's simplistic notion that the individual entrepreneur responds to an indifference schedule, with risk plotted as one variable and rate of return as the other. There are, so it appears, entrepreneurs devoted solely to low-risk situations and those who concentrate exclusively on high-yield ventures. There is no self-evident reason why an economy should provide entrepreneurs of various kinds in the combinations appropriate to the opportunities offered. From time to time, therefore, a developing nation is confronted with the question whether to fill the breach through an investment by the public sector.

The essays in this volume provide plenty of illustrations in which Mexico's public sector stepped in to fill a role which private entrepreneurs seemed unready or unable to assume. For example, Mexico's federal electricity commission, the Comisión Federal de Electricidad, made numerous extensions of the power-generating system at times when there seemed to be no private takers. The first great surge in steel-making capacity after the Revolution was achieved in the early 1940's largely through the support of Nacional Financiera, the public development bank. Five or ten years later, the private sector might have provided the funds; but in the early 1940's it was not up to the task. The country's experimental plunges into railroad-car building and into some branches of the chemicals industry also come close to the classic case of public risk assumed in apparent default of private risk-takers or private capital-mobilizers.

None of these cases is a simon-pure illustration of the indispensable role of the public sector in economic development. In each instance, special circumstances beclouded the question of risk-taking by the private sector. But one must resign himself to the fact that in a process as complex as economic development, there are few propositions for which history provides an unambiguous test.

Efforts to overcome the problems of risk and scale are also seen in other investment operations of the Mexican government. Nacional Financiera's willingness to borrow abroad for the purpose of re-lending to Mexico's private enterprises represents the public sector's way of dealing with some of these problems. The interposition of the government as a borrower through Nacional

Financiera has given the Mexican economy the cost advantage that accrues to large-scale borrowers; and the favorable interest rates which Nacional Financiera charges to private borrowers in Mexico have reflected some of that advantage. Besides, borrowing from Nacional Financiera presented less risk to the Mexican entrepreneur than borrowing directly abroad. Comparatively speaking, the agency was a friendly banker; at least it would hesitate to make a prompt foreclosure if a little accommodation would tend to avoid a ruckus inside the Mexican economy.

The Mexican government has used its investment powers in still other ways to cushion the risks of the private sector. One of the extraordinary features of Mexico's monetary policy has been the willingness of public-sector financial institutions to provide almost total liquidity both to public-sector obligations and to the obligations and equities of many important private issuers. Not only has outright failure become a thing of the past for large industrial enterprises and banks; even the whisper of strain, as reflected in the quotations for publicly held paper, has been muffled through timely interventions. Equity issues have been buoyed up by the public authorities as readily as bonds. In short, the risks of both lender and borrower, issuer and buyer, have been contained in a system of informal government guarantees against investment loss.

So far, we have dealt with investments of a kind which bears some reasonably clear relation to the development process. The investments of Mexico's public sector, however, are not all of this sort. The history of Nacional Financiera's operations is sprinkled with transactions whose contribution to national development seems fairly remote. Nacional Financiera has been used for the takeover of an ailing textile plant, at a time when textile mill capacity appeared to be in surplus; for the bail-out of an ill-conceived textile machinery plant; and for the absorption of several operating steel mills into the public system.

In each of these cases, a resolutely sympathetic observer could find some tie between Nacional Financiera's asserted development objectives and the particular transaction. For example, if private operators know that a rescue operation is possible *in extremis,* this knowledge may increase their propensity for risk-taking investment; if ill-conceived textile or textile machinery operations are bought up, the redeployment of the capital and labor force in the national interest may be achieved a little more quickly and easily; and if private operating steel mills could be added to public facilities to provide better technical "balance," steel output as a whole might benefit.

Though rationalizations of this sort come readily to hand, a certain proportion of the investment operations of Nacional Financiera and other government agencies has almost certainly been motivated by objectives other than development. An instrument of governmental power as potent as the power to invest is bound to be used for various purposes to which a responsive political machinery in any country is devoted. It will be used for the maintenance of uneconomic enterprises, when the swift dissolution of such enterprises would cause political unrest. It will be used for the redistribution of income among regions or classes, whether or not the redistribution would speed the national development process. It will be used for the generation of an image of protective self-respecting nationalism, when such a posture would add to the psychic income of the country and to the popularity and acceptance of the nation's political machine. All of these aims have motivated the Mexican government's public investment program at one time or another.

PUBLIC REGULATION

One can get some understanding of the relationship between the public sector and the private sector by looking not only at the patterns of public investment but also at the patterns of public regulation. But any outsider observing and interpreting the regulatory process in a culture other than his own is in danger of being misled by what he sees. Patterns of public law and regulation are the manifestation of a complex cultural process. The text of the final law or regulation, taken by itself, tells little about its implications for the economy. What the observer must know, among other things, is the intent and expectations of the parties in the application of the provisions.

The U.S. observer of the Latin American process is especially prone to this sort of error. His difficulties may begin with an imperfect understanding of the difference in legal systems. Constitutional provisions which in U.S. jurisprudence would have the force of law prove in Latin jurisprudence to be without force and effect until implemented by statute. Duly enacted statutes which in the U.S. system would create legal rights and liabilities, enforceable in the courts, prove under Latin legal systems to require executive regulations before they can have judicial effect. The requirement that the exercise of administrative discretion in individual cases should be subject to explicit statutory standards — a cardinal principle in U.S. legislative traditions — plays a very much smaller role in Latin jurisprudence. And the assumption that the courts will act as a branch of government wholly insulated from the executive — an assumption breached to some extent in every legal system that claims to honor it — clearly has less validity in Latin America than in the United States.

In Mexico, the most important single factor determining the outcome of any program of public regulation is the will of the executive. Accordingly, any given program of public regulation in Mexico tends to have somewhat more uncertainty attached to it than the U.S. observer would ordinarily expect. But one should not leap to the conclusion that a less discretionary system would be a clear improvement. To be sure, avoidable uncertainty is ordinarily regarded as a bad thing for developing nations; and it may be that this has been true for Mexico as well. But Mexico's presidents, at times, have turned their wide discretion to constructive advantage. Laws which have proved onerous or unpopular or unwise have been quietly disregarded. Regulations which have proved faulty have been administered as if the fault had been cured. The capacity for pragmatic accommodation and evolution, so evident in the history of Mexico since the Revolution, has been due in part to the ability of the executive to avoid the clutch of the law's dead hand.

The fact that Mexico's presidents have wide discretionary powers means that entrepreneurs are persistently concerned that the exercise of these powers should be consonant with their interests. A proper knowledge of the bureaucratic maze and the individuals who operate it is recognized, therefore, as an indispensable attribute of the effective Mexican entrepreneur.

The importance to the private sector of giving careful attention to the operations of the regulatory system has been due not merely to the flexible and discretionary aspects of the system, but also to its reach. In this respect, Mexico resembles the continent of Europe much more than the United States. Influenced by its mercantilist heritage, molded by various other cultural and historical forces which the U.S. did not share, Mexico has assimilated a pervasive system of government regulation more readily than the U.S. could have done. A Mexican government determined to exercise every facet of its statutory authority could control most of the critical aspects of the private sector's activities — as long as it remained in power.

In a regulatory system with these characteristics, entrepreneurs have little interest in battling over questions of purely ideological significance. The ideological overtones of any law and regulations, especially where they relate to so obscure, complex, and detailed an area as business transactions, are less relevant than the machinery for their application. Accordingly, the struggle over the machinery of control, not the question of the legitimacy of control, has provided the dominant issue in the regulatory relations between the public and private sectors in Mexico. In the field of import controls, the licensing power itself has not been seriously challenged; what has been fought over has been the relative powers of the two sectors to shape the decisions of the licensing apparatus. In the rationing of credit through the banking machinery, what is at issue is not the basic concept of selective credit controls and "discriminatory" credit allocations, but the earthier question of which borrowers are to be entitled to slices of the pie.

An effort to catalogue the public sector's objectives in the exercise of its regulatory process would be an effort in near-futility. Inevitably, the objectives have been multiple, evanescent, and conflicting. Controls over foreign trade illustrate the complexity of these objectives. The aim of restricting the expenditure of foreign exchange on imports and that of providing protection to domestic industry have coexisted in the same regulations, more or less comfortably. But in addition, foreign-trade controls have been shaped with an eye to their effects on public revenue; with a desire to hold down the purchase price of staple commodities; with a hope of discouraging exports in some areas and encouraging them in others; with an aim of squeezing back foreign-owned enterprises in Mexico and encouraging domestic ones; and with other ideas in mind.

Still, three main objectives have appeared persistently in the Mexican regulatory system.

The first such objective has been the forcing of industrial growth. This aim has been manifested not only through import controls, but also through credit allocations, tax policy, and other means. Here, the interests of the private sector and those of the public sector have not been in very sharp conflict. Private bankers, it is true, have preferred to do their own rationing of credit; and importers and distributors have felt their interests badly neglected. But the regulatory machinery and the political mechanism have usually allowed for some means of appeal and accommodation, if the offended interests were large enough and persistent enough. Besides, the speeding up of industrial growth has been consistent with the needs of the volatile labor force collected in the cities.

A second main aim of the regulatory system has been to deal with the problems of the agricultural sector — the demands for land, for credit, for markets, and for infrastructure. To stabilize and to improve the prices paid to farmers, the government launched a series of crop-support and marketing programs; and, in doing so, it managed to incur the enmity of the private merchants and distributors bidding for the crops. It is characteristic of the pragmatic basis of private-public relations, however, that eventually an uneasy truce was negotiated between the Mexican executive and the merchants, whereupon the private sector became the agents of the government in the execution of some of these programs.

The reaction of the bankers to the government efforts at redirecting credit toward the agricultural sector has been no more enthusiastic than the initial reaction of the merchants with respect to agricultural prices. In general, the bankers have doubted that there were many credit-worthy opportunities in agriculture not already covered by their loans. Nevertheless, they have lived stoically with the government's regulations, such as its selective credit controls, and have responded to these controls by looking a little more diligently for agricultural borrowers than they might otherwise have done. From the point of view of the private bankers, the results have not been entirely bad. Some bankers apparently managed to turn necessity into a profit-making opportunity, especially in the financing of export crops such as cattle and vegetables.

This may have been one of those cases in which lack of information and an exaggerated appraisal of risk on the part of the bankers were blocking the "economic" allocation of resources to the private sector. In an economy where credit is rationed, there is no strong incentive to ferret out new borrowers, however productive the opportunities they offer may be, as long as the more familiar borrowers readily pre-empt the lending capacities of the private banking institutions.

Once more, one is obliged to add that the regulatory efforts of the Mexican government in the field of agriculture were not singlemindedly devoted to the development goal, any more than the objectives of any responsive government can be single-minded in character. One administration after another has persisted in redistributing land into parcels too small for efficient farming. Every administration has followed its predecessor in espousing the collective *ejido* as the preferred channel of land distribution, despite the well-advertised weaknesses of that form of land tenure and the lack of progress in correcting those weaknesses. Exceptions to the redistribution pattern have been tolerated; there have been numerous instances in which the control of large land parcels has continued in apparent violation of the law. And there are no grounds for assuming that these situations have been tolerated in the interests of promoting economic development.

A third purpose of Mexican regulation has been to hold the foreigner in check within the Mexican economy. This thread running through Mexico's regulatory policy is clearly seen in our case studies. The thread has varied in strength over the years. It tended to be stronger in administrations that were generally disposed to give the public sector increased power, such as the administration of Lázaro Cárdenas; and it tended to be weaker in administrations that were disposed to increase the private sector's power, such as that of Miguel Alemán. But the correlation between pro-foreigners and pro-privateness was never perfect. And as Mexico's domestic businessmen grew in strength and versatility in the 1950's and early 1960's, the correlation seemed to weaken and even disappear. More and more frequently — in import policy, in tax policy, in government buying policy — one saw cases in which curbs upon the foreign private entrepreneur were intended in part to benefit the domestic private entrepreneur. Foreign private entrepreneurs were curbed not so much because they were *private* as because they were *foreign*.

Miguel Wionczek's essay on the electric power industry of Mexico repeatedly suggests the strength of the popular forces which obliged a responsive government to curb the strength of foreign enterprises in Mexico. As one reads the Wionczek essay, there are times when the unfolding plot seems to have the elements of classic Greek drama. Neither the Mexican officials who make government policy nor the foreign executives who direct the power companies seem to be free agents. In the end, the recapture of the quasi-public powers of the electric companies from the foreign hands which held them seems almost an inevitable step, ordained by some unwritten law of nationhood.

BEYOND MEXICO

Probably, much of what has been learned in this study of the relations between the public and private sectors in Mexico relates to the situation of only a few other countries. But some features of the Mexican situation may well apply more widely.

Once the desire for growth was fixed in the minds and programs of Mexico's leaders, it appeared inevitable that the public sector would widen its investment role and its regulatory aims. The increase was required in order to include a number of functions which economists have already identified, including the development of productive facilities whose social yield exceeded what could be recaptured in the marketplace; the creation of socially necessary facilities so large or unfamiliar as to be outside the capacity or interests of the private sector; the reduction of the private sector's risk in order to stimulate the private sector's willingness to invest in some inherently risky areas; and the nudging of the private sector to explore areas of investment in which initial ignorance or erroneous estimates of risk and yield existed.

A second proposition which may have wide application is that the widening of the public sector's role in Mexico was productive partly because the public sector did not often overreach. In general, the public sector's assumption of a new function only occasionally exceeded its capacity to exercise the function with some measure of responsibility. Though there was widespread inefficiency in the public sector as measured by the standards of more advanced countries, and though total fiascoes sometimes happened, the record of public performance was usually acceptable and sometimes even downright impressive. The public sector's restraint in undertaking little more than it was capable of performing may have been somewhat due to the desire to avoid open opposition from the private sector. Whatever the cause, the result seemed to serve the country well.

Still a third impression was the seeming inexorability of the movement to restrain the freedom of foreign private capital, a movement which seemed to flow out of the growing strength and internal resources of the Mexican economy.

Finally, one comes away from the Mexican experience with the conviction that no responsive government can be expected to exercise its powers with a total commitment to some single goal such as economic development. Even in the best of all possible worlds, the urge to cling to public power will be a compelling force that shapes the policies and actions of the governments of nations. However deep the commitment to economic development may be, therefore, governments will pause, backtrack, and detour from time to time as they weigh the political risks of undertaking hard development measures against the political hazards of losing development momentum. The disposition of governments to magnify the political risks of action while accepting the political hazards of stagnation may be one of the more pervasive errors of our time.

ELECTRIC POWER
The Uneasy Partnership

by
Miguel S. Wionczek

Chapter **I**

Origins of the Industry

MEXICO'S electric power industry, throughout the seventy years of its existence, has provided a battleground in which the interests of the private sector and of the government have continually met, clashed, and found a basis for compromise. In the process, the control of the industry gradually shifted. Originally owned and operated largely by foreign private investors, the industry found itself pressed little by little into a kind of partnership with the Mexican government. As time went on, the character of the partnership changed; the government assumed a more and more positive role while the companies found their room for maneuver more and more curtailed. By 1960, the industry was almost totally in public hands; an enterprise once owned by foreign private interests had been drawn into the domestic public sector. And thereby hangs a tale, which is the subject of this study.

The age of electricity came to Mexico with remarkable speed after its introduction into the United States and Western Europe.[1] By the late 1890's, only ten years or so after the widespread introduction of electric power in the more advanced areas of the world, Mexico also could claim to have entered the electrical age, in that a number of small Mexican-owned electric plants were turning the wheels of individual manufacturing and mining enterprises and lighting a few large urban areas. But it is in the first decade of the new century that the distance covered by the industry becomes truly impressive. Whereas in the United States a gross investment of some $275 million went into facilities for electric power generation and distribution between 1891 and 1900, British, Canadian, and United States interests spent about $75 million for the same purposes in Mexico's much smaller economy during the following decade. Almost 150,000 kilowatts — about four fifths from hydroelectric sources and the rest from thermoelectric plants — were added to the insignificant generating capacity that had been available in 1900; more than forty plants were built in major urban, industrial, and mining centers of the Republic; 10,000 people found occupation in the new activity; and the leading sectors of the Mexican economy received additional impetus from the substitution of mechanical power for human and animal energy.[2]

Between 1902 and 1906, five major British, Canadian, and United States companies entered the Mexican electric power industry, and for the next forty years these companies were to constitute the industry's backbone. Between 1905 and 1911 they built four major systems in different parts of the country. Most of the small Mexican-owned electric plants were bought up, integrated, and modernized — in some cases scrapped. By the end of the Porfirio Díaz era and the beginning of the Mexican Revolution in 1910, the foreign companies controlled the most profitable concessions for hydroelectric power generation, having either received these concessions directly from the Díaz government or bought them from their domestic owners.

The attraction which Mexico's large water resources had for foreign public utilities builders coincided with the interest of President Díaz and his advisers in bringing electric power into the country as an important component of the modern industrial structure. There are many proofs that the Díaz administration had kept very well informed about technological advances in the United States and Europe. In 1894, when the first large hydroelectric plants were installed in the United States, a decree was issued in Mexico supplementing an 1888 law on jurisdiction over transportation rights. This decree clarified the concept of federal control over national water resources and introduced for the first time the legal concept of "concession" with respect to the development of water resources. The 1857 constitution had left control over waterways partly to the jurisdiction of the states and municipalities; the 1894 decree not only extended federal control to practically all existing water flows, but gave the executive branch the explicit authority to grant concessions "for irrigation and production of power for industrial purposes." (State and municipal officials, who retained only the right to grant concessions for generation of electricity by steam, attacked the Díaz legislation as unconstitutional but got nowhere.) The same decree provided for tax exemptions to hydroelectric enterprises for a period of five years, tariff exemptions on imported equipment, and the right of the central government to expropriate (with due compensation) properties of potential value for private development as plant sites. It also made the determination of electricity rates dependent upon the approval of the central government.

In the last decades of the nineteenth century the British still held commercial and industrial pre-eminence in Mexico, and thus it was the British and the Canadians rather than the Americans who gave the initial impetus to the development of the country's power resources, while U.S. capital showed preference for mining and railroads. British-controlled capital probably accounted for close to 85 per cent of the total foreign investment in electric power generation and distribution between 1900 and 1910, as compared with 55 per cent in petroleum, 35 in railroads, and 15 in mining. The respective U.S. participation was somewhat over 5 per cent in public utilities, 40 in petroleum and railroads, and 60 in mining.[3]

In most cases, there was an identity of interests between the builders of the electric power industry and foreign investors in other segments of the rapidly expanding Mexican economy. Indeed, two of the most important men who entered the new activity already had wide interests in Mexico. Fred Stark Pearson, a Canadian and one of the founders of the Mexican Light & Power

Company, which operated in the central region of the Republic, was actively engaged in mining and prospecting in northern Mexico. Another Pearson, Weetman by name (later Lord Cowdray), the British national who built the public utilities in the oil-rich states of Veracruz and Puebla bordering the Gulf of Mexico, had long years of experience as a leading contractor for large public works undertaken by Porfirio Díaz in the final decade of the nineteenth century.[4]

People like the two Pearsons possessed very important personal qualities which may account for the speedy arrival and expansion of the electrical age in Mexico. They knew the country's physical resources and the psychology of the rulers and the ruled. Their access to technology and capital resources in their home countries was matched by their excellent personal relations with the governing elite in Mexico, whose attitude toward foreign capitalists was summarized in the following way in a well-known speech by José Limantour, the finance minister and intellectual spokesman for the Díaz administration: "Lacking, as we do, sufficient manpower and money to exploit the untold wealth lying in our soil, we should not fail to take advantage of those elements when they become available, simply because they come from abroad. Quite the contrary: the sum of benefits left in the country by every new industry or every increase in established industries contributes to providing greater well-being for those who reside therein, without distinction of class or nationality." *

Mexican historians, even though condemning the invasion of the new industry by foreign capital, agree that it was a natural consequence of the unavailability of domestic financial resources and entrepreneurial talent. A very nationalistic writer, thirty years

* Another passage from the Limantour speech is worth quoting: "The day will come, as has been seen in the history of other modern nations, when the population will have been enriched by an abundance of the things of life and better training for work; and those debts will be recovered little by little, and the bonds, stocks and securities of our most flourishing enterprises will be kept within national territory and never again allowed to depart." The speech is found in *Memoria de la Secretaría de Hacienda* (Mexico, D.F., 1906), pp. 336–337.

after the Díaz overthrow, explained the process in the following terms:

The inability of Mexican capital to create a truly national electric power industry is explained by the same reasons which allowed the country's principal economic resources to fall into foreign hands in the nineteenth century. The history of the metal smelting and refining industry, to name just one, developed in a fashion very similar to that of the electrical industry. In both instances a small group of Mexican capitalists launched and tenaciously developed an economic activity at whose head they could remain only as long as they did not have to face up to the problems of large-scale production. Modern and costly machinery were not within the reach of the scant resources of Mexican capital which was sorely harried by the land-tenure pattern, commercial anemia, monetary instability, and low purchasing power of the working masses. It would have been impossible by all odds to find Mexican capital to supply electricity for a city of 750,000 inhabitants, or undertake to stretch lines for more than 300 kilometers through the craggy mountain ranges encircling the central plateau.[5]

The administration of Porfirio Díaz, though not inhibited by any antiforeign feelings, did take care of its national supporters by distributing among them freely and under very liberal terms concessions for the exploitation of hydroelectric power. Of some two hundred concessions granted or confirmed by the central government between 1895 and 1910, the overwhelming majority were given to nationals, who speedily sold them to interested foreign parties. In the final years of the Porfirian period, speculation in these concessions reached amazing proportions. In many cases, concessions changed hands a number of times before reaching final users. Unlimited optimism about Mexico's economic future, shared by the Mexican elite and foreign investors, in some instances raised the final price of a promising concession to a level that was disproportionate to the cost of the other components of the investment and to the initial size of the market for electric power. (The excessive cost of original concessions was adduced by the companies in the late twenties as an argument against lowering electricity rates.)

At no time during the Díaz era was domestic capital more than a fraction of the total investment in the industry, and such capital was mainly in the form of small plants outside the main centers of economic activity. But, as this fraction declined, the reverse was happening as regards the participation of Mexican nationals from the Díaz entourage in the executive boards of the companies. Although the president himself and many of his closest collaborators were shareholders in the major foreign-controlled railway ventures,[6] they probably had no more than nominal financial interest in the electric power enterprises. One may surmise, however, that the presence of prominent Mexicans on the boards of the companies was another form of Díaz patronage, quickly accepted and even fostered by foreign entrepreneurs who were eager to have the assurance of friendly consideration by the government.

By 1910 some blocks of shares in leading electric power companies may have been purchased by Mexicans, but most of the capital resources were raised abroad. It is estimated that up to 1911 something over $60 million worth of bonds and common and preferred stock were placed in European, Canadian, and U.S. capital markets. There are no indications that it was difficult to raise this money. Not only were projects considered sound, but their promoters were widely known in their own countries as men of vision and financial acumen with profitable interests in Mexico and elsewhere in Latin America.

There is a good deal of controversy about the margin of profitability of public utility ventures in Mexico. Mexican sources claim that most of them brought fabulous profits from the beginning, whereas foreign historians who extensively investigated the companies' financial records refuse to share this opinion. According to one authority on the subject, British investment in Mexico "turned out to be less profitable than that in any other major Latin American country," and "this was especially true of the capital invested in government bonds, railroads, real estate and *public utilities*" [7] (italics added). Probably electric power industry investments under Díaz were less profitable than some ventures in mining and petroleum which brought really huge gains, but the power investments were also much less risky.

The fact that dividends on the outstanding stock were rather on the low side cannot be accepted as conclusive evidence of unsatisfactory profitability of the enterprises. One must remember that, as soon as concessions were acquired and sites for plants chosen, the companies had complete freedom of action, since the government's veto power over rates, set up in the 1894 decree, was never enforced during the Díaz administration. Companies were left free to set their rates and to negotiate contracts with private and institutional consumers. The demand for electric power was increasing so rapidly that in the final years of the period the companies were known to be unable in many instances to provide service to new industrial consumers in Mexico City and in the Puebla and Veracruz areas. It is true that some collection problems arose from time to time under contracts with municipal authorities, but public lighting services accounted for only about one third of the total energy sold, whereas much more was being used by mining and modern industrial enterprises which were owned in many cases by the same groups that controlled the public utilities. In this situation, low profit levels on the books of the utilities might be of little concern to these groups, so long as they were reaping a big harvest from the mining and industrial enterprises.

There is circumstantial evidence that these large consumers of electric power received preferential treatment and that, consequently, the remaining consumers in a sense subsidized the foreign-dominated industrial sector of the economy. That is a question that even an army of cost accountants could not solve. Nevertheless, small Mexican energy consumers were convinced not only in the Díaz time but until the government began regulating utilities companies in the 1930's that they were subsidizing foreign-owned economic activities in Mexico.

In any case it seems very probable that the low level of dividends was strongly affected by the companies' policy of reinvest-

ing a large part of their earnings. In the majority of cases, during
the Díaz era and even up to the Great Depression, electric power
companies operating in Mexico seldom went to the capital market
after the enterprises had been set up. Later expansion was financed
largely from their own resources; and this suggests that the over-
all profits were much larger than those shown in dividend payments.[8]

The peaceful and mutually satisfactory coexistence of the public
utilities and the Díaz administration was marred in the final years
of the period by conflicts that the companies had with two classes
of consumers whose shares of total demand were growing slowly
but continuously: municipalities and small business firms.

The first clashes between the companies and municipal authorities occurred at the time of negotiating the renewal of contracts
for the supply of public lighting services, originally fixed for a
period of five years. On a number of occasions between 1906 and
1910, during negotiations for renewal, municipalities bitterly complained about deficient services and high rates. It is difficult to
ascertain to what extent these accusations were a part of the
bargaining process, designed to offset the companies' complaints
about the poor paying record of the municipal authorities. Sometimes, strangely enough, attacks on the utilities were made jointly
with demands for new contracts of longer duration than the companies were willing to accept. Moreover, city officials in Mexico,
as elsewhere, were very well aware of the political appeal of their
arguments. Small industrialists and traders in Mexico were especially sympathetic to the cities' complaints since they were paying
the highest rates of all and were being treated as second-class
clients by the power companies, as the power supply and the distribution capacity fell behind the total demand.

Indeed, it was among these small and medium-sized domestic
capitalists, who were looking for their own place in the Mexican
economy at the beginning of this century, that the charge of the
exploitation of the Mexican consumer by a foreign-owned monopoly was first heard. The same language was to be used against

public utilities in Mexico three decades later by the first nation-wide organization of small and medium-sized industries in Mexico, the Cámara Nacional de la Industria de Transformación (CNIT). Municipal authorities and small entrepreneurs were not the only ones who were unhappy with the performance of the electric power enterprises under the Díaz laissez-faire regime. Intellectual dissenters during the Díaz regime began to express various misgivings, even during periods of rapid industrial expansion. In 1905 and 1906, Andrés Molina Enríquez, a prominent intellectual and member of the national Mexican agricultural society, made a detailed review[9] of the water resources legislation in force and suggested that it be strengthened. Defending federal control over all uses of water resources, Molina Enríquez found government policy toward the concessionaires too lax and too liberal and devoid of any clearly defined long-term purposes. He was particularly unhappy with the indefinite duration of concessions for electric power generation, excessive tax exemptions, and the absence of the regulation of rates. Consequently, he suggested that concessions should not extend to perpetuity; tax exemption should be made uniform; and rates should not only be regulated by the federal authorities, but revised every five years. He asked further that taxes be levied in proportion to the rate level and that some portion of the tax proceeds be used for subsidizing industrial development and irrigation. (Shortly thereafter, toward the end of the Díaz era, the first national irrigation plan was begun.) Molina Enríquez not only proposed that future rate policy should take into consideration actual power costs and regional income differences, but also urged the formulation of a national plan for the utilization of hydraulic resources.

Molina Enríquez was not alone in these views. New ideas about the need for changing the nature of the relations between the public utilities and the state were germinating in many places at the same time. In the last years of the Porfirian regime even Limantour's voice was heard among those criticizing the laissez-faire policies of the administration, and in 1908 the government

bought out a controlling interest in Mexico's main railroad lines.[10]
Shortly afterwards, from quarters closely linked with the *cientí-
ficos* surrounding Díaz, clear threats were addressed to the public
utility companies. On June 9, 1909, *El Economista Mexicano* had
these harsh words to say on the subject:

> The Mexican Light & Power Company has recently been the object
> of certain serious attacks by the Mexico City press that have convinced
> most of the population affected — who for that matter have more
> than one cause for complaint against the company. There is no doubt
> that the company is poorly managed and that its relations with the
> public are hardly governed by the desire to please a clientele that for
> the moment, at least, is not free to dispense with its services . . .
> The instances of the municipal take-over of the services in Glasgow
> and London have left the residents of those two cities completely
> satisfied. They should serve as very eloquent examples of the type of
> idea to which we have reference. All the foregoing leads to the
> thought that it might well be advisable to seek analogous means of
> solving a problem which involves everyone and which includes such
> large interests that they cannot be left to the caprice or turpitude of
> an enterprise that is at complete liberty to build itself up into a power
> capable of taking possession of society itself.

The Díaz regime took notice of the intellectuals' criticisms and
the consumers' rumblings. Surprisingly enough, new water resources legislation was passed in 1910 shortly before the old
dictator's fall. This legislation, following to some extent the ideas
of Molina Enríquez, tightened the conditions under which concessions were granted for hydroelectric purposes.

These first signs of hostility toward the public utilities were not
taken seriously by Mexico's leading companies, which continued
to count on the administration's benevolence. As in many other
countries at many other times, foreign capitalists in Mexico in
1910 believed that the era of enlightened dictatorship would never
end in a violent and abrupt way. The companies' confidence in the
future is indicated by the fact that many major additions and
expansions to existing generation and transmission capacity were
started as late as 1909 and 1910 and were continued after Díaz

fell and Francisco Madero took over the reins. In fact, contrary to what might have been expected, no major company stopped its expansion program with the fall of Díaz. The first growth period of Mexican Light & Power, operating in the center of the Republic, extended from 1905 to 1914; the Puebla–Veracruz and Guanajuato systems also did not stop expanding until 1914; Compañía Hidroeléctrica de Chapala (Chapala hydroelectric company), serving the Guadalajara region, terminated its investment program in 1912.

The companies, so deeply engaged in building up new capacity at the time of the Díaz overthrow, must have shared with other foreigners the belief that the economic growth of Mexico was consolidating rather than weakening the power of President Díaz. Even when Díaz fell, they must have thought that this was another Latin American palace revolution, changing the individuals at the helm but not the system as such. This at any rate was the opinion of the London *Economist*, which in its first comment on the outbreak of the Revolution, published on November 26, 1910, said that "the admirers of enlightened autocracy have had a rude shock," but that the events of that month were likely to lead to nothing more serious than "a temporary interruption of activities and a reduction of profits." This "temporary" interruption lasted more than a decade.

It may be an exaggeration to claim that public utilities promoters together with other foreign investors brought the blessings of modern civilization to a backward country at the turn of the century,* but it would also be unjust to condemn them without

---

* A picture of bringing electric power and light to Veracruz in 1905 is described in almost poetic terms by Weetman Pearson's biographer: ". . . Next, he formed the Vera Cruz Electric Light, Power & Traction Company, obtaining the necessary concessions from the Municipality, and quickly superseded the ancient mule-drawn trams with a finely equipped electric system with modern cars. Simultaneously, he took electric lighting in hand and brought a cheerful blaze of light into shops, cafes, private houses and promenades . . . it was small wonder that the people of Vera Cruz came to look upon the English contractor as a worker of miracles." J. A. Spender, *Weetman Pearson, First Viscount Cowdray, 1856–1927* (London: Cassell & Co., 1930), p. 109. A few years earlier, the press of

reservation. They came to Mexico in search of profits from their capital and skill and they took every possible advantage of the opportunities offered by a rapidly growing laissez-faire economy. Their behavior did not differ from that of the public utilities builders in the more advanced countries, about whose exploits an abundant although not too edifying literature exists.

It was not their business to concern themselves with the needs of the economy in which they operated, unless those needs coincided with their own objectives. Neither should they have been expected to accept the principle of public service, especially since the state was not aware of this concept either. They were experienced and cautious operators. They surveyed the country before launching their ventures, chose locations for generating plants carefully, and took care to establish major interconnected systems without delay. Although not economists, but engineers and financiers by profession, they were well aware of the various concepts that are decisive for the success of any productive venture, such as the savings to be gained from large-scale operations and from the availability of external economies, and such as an understanding of the respective advantages of capital and labor-intensive projects. They came to Mexico to stay forever — they thought — and in their own way they believed in Mexico's future.

The electric power industry, after the fashion of progress in other sectors of the Mexican economy, was initially a by-product of, or complement to, earlier large ventures in export-directed activities — mining and petroleum. But it soon became a part of a circular process of development which was advancing on many fronts simultaneously.

The foreign entrepreneurs, by erecting at great speed an industry that for their times was modern and efficient, not only made possible the expansion of the Mexican export sector in the first

---

Mexico's capital was thundering against the city's transportation services, complaining that the public had to wait for hours in rain for the arrival of tramcars and that they represented a danger to the lives of citizens and domestic animals.

decade of the century but added to the country's infrastructure which after the revolutionary upheaval was to serve as a physical basis for the next stage of Mexico's modernization, coinciding with the international prosperity of the twenties.

As long as relations between the private and public sectors in the Mexico of Díaz were limited to intercourse between foreign entrepreneurs and the national ruling elite, no serious problems of friction could have arisen. This marriage of convenience was profitable to all concerned. But precisely because of the speed of economic development in the second half of the Porfirian period — between 1895 and 1910 — new forces appeared on the scene whose interests did not necessarily coincide with those of foreign capitalists. The first clashes, occurring in the final years of the era, did not in any way affect the financial position of the industry which, because of the benevolent attitude of the state, was able to dictate conditions to those who sought its services. But already national consumers were finding allies among intellectuals, who had begun a broad attack upon the Díaz administration's political and social philosophy.

For fifteen years the Revolution that began in 1910 diverted Mexico's attention from such relatively minor problems as the relations between the foreign public utility monopoly and the consumers of their services to the larger issues of national existence. But the pattern for future battles was set. In post-Revolutionary Mexico, the two main participants with conflicting objectives — the companies and the public — were to continue in their respective roles. What was destined to change was the role of the central government. The state first became an arbiter between the two contending groups, later the co-participant in the productive activities, and finally — some sixty years after the arrival of the electric age to Mexico — the sole owner of the electric power industry.

Chapter 2

From Revolution to Depression

IT is difficult to discuss the relations between the private electric companies and the state during the two decades following the outbreak of the Revolution. If by the state we understand a centrally-directed administrative mechanism extending its power over the whole national territory, the state hardly existed in Mexico up to the early twenties. Then the post-Revolutionary governments of Alvaro Obregón and Plutarco Elías Calles were primarily occupied with other problems inherited from the Revolution that were more important and more pressing than electric power.

During the period of chaos, foreign interests in Mexico concentrated on one immediate objective — saving their physical assets from destruction. For this purpose all possible stratagems were used — for example, establishing a *modus vivendi* with anyone who even for a short period held effective power in the area of their operation; paying the necessary ransoms and bribes; and in case of direct danger to major properties, pressing their home governments to intervene.

Because of a fortunate combination of circumstances, the foreign public utilities were quite successful on the whole in preventing damage to their installations in Mexico. In the first place, the areas of major military operations did not coincide with the regions where the most important electric power facilities had been constructed; secondly, contrary to hostile propaganda abroad, the upheaval was not directed against foreign interests as such;

thirdly, the successive Revolutionary governments made conscious efforts not to provoke outside intervention and were perfectly aware that the destruction of alien property would only increase such a danger. Consequently, with a few exceptions like the damage wrought to the Mexican Light & Power Company property during the disturbances in the capital in 1912 and 1913, and a few armed assaults by marauding rebels in the countryside in 1915 and 1917, electric power facilities did not suffer much, if one takes into account the magnitude of the violence and destruction engendered by the Revolution.

Financial losses of the public utilities, however, were very substantial and they were doubly painful because most of the companies had incurred heavy obligations in connection with the construction and expansion programs which they started on the eve of the Revolution. The blows rained from several directions. Mining, one of the major customers of electric power, became paralyzed for extended periods in some regions. Municipalities, whose paying record had been poor even under the Díaz regime, went broke and refused to pay their bills. The remaining groups of consumers at best could pay for the companies' services in worthless paper currency, often printed locally by phantom authorities. Although Venustiano Carranza's government issued an order in 1917 that municipalities and other state agencies pay electricity bills in gold and silver, this had very little practical effect upon the companies' total receipts. One public utility after another was forced to suspend payment of dividends and service on its bonds. In the case of the Mexican Light & Power Company, losses were recorded from 1914 to 1921; Vera Cruz Light & Power suffered financial losses between 1913 and 1916; Guanajuato Power, between 1913 and 1918; and Chapala hydroelectric company, between 1913 and 1920.

The successful survival of the upheaval by the electric power industry is confirmed by many Mexican sources — both friendly and unfriendly to the foreign interests.[1] To some extent, it explains why, immediately upon the return of the semblance of order on a national scale with General Obregón's taking power in 1921, all the major companies again initiated ambitious construction and expansion programs and continued them without interruption right up to the early days of the Great Depression. The industry's executives correctly estimated the magnitude of deferred demand for electricity in post-Revolutionary Mexico and also assumed that additional demand would appear during the reconstruction period because of the resumption of the boom in export-oriented activities.

The optimistic attitude of the companies was further strengthened by the policy announcements of Obregón's successors, stressing the need to modernize and consolidate the economy within the new institutional framework. It soon became clear that, in the electric power field, the laissez-faire conditions under which the companies had operated before 1910 would continue in force, at least for some time. The companies had not been involved in the head-on clash between the Revolutionary groups and foreign capital over control of the land and the subsoil. They operated facilities indispensable for the modernization and expansion of the Mexican economy. And domestic interests, public or private, were too weak financially to go into such capital-intensive ventures as public utilities.

The great political debate which led to the adoption of the new constitution in February 1917 had not embroiled the electric power industry, which continued to be considered as one of the manufacturing activities fully reserved to the private sector. However, when defining *"bienes de propiedad de la Nación"* ("property of the nation"), Article 27 of the constitution included water resources among them. At the same time, the article granted to the federal government the exclusive right over such resources. In these respects, Article 27 was a reaffirmation of legal concepts already included in the water resources legislation passed in the last months of the Porfirian era. Another law of 1917, reorganizing the public administration in the manner periodically done in Mexico, confirmed the existing jurisdictional arrangements under which the Secretaría de Agricultura y Fomento had become recognized as having jurisdiction over water resources and concessions and the Secretaría de Industria y Comercio over the technical aspects of the electric industry. As far as public utilities were concerned, the framework for relations between the private sector and the state continued in force unchanged.

The electric power companies used this favorable situation to full advantage, and during the 1920's the industry probably grew faster than any other sector of the economy. Whereas the gross national product increased between 1920 and 1929 by some 20 per cent and the manufacturing output by about one third,* total installed electric power capacity almost tripled and total generation more than doubled. By 1930, per capita capacity was three times as large as in 1910 or 1920. About one fourth of the population (or some four million people) became actual consumers of electric power, a high enough proportion if one remembers the poverty of the inhabitants and their sparse distribution over a territory one third the size of the United States. However, per capita consumption apart from the mining and industrial sector's needs continued very low. It was estimated that in 1926 one third of the power generated was sold to mining and metallurgic enterprises, some 20 per cent was sold to other industries, and slightly over 45 per cent was used for public lighting, electric traction, agriculture, and home consumption.[2] And most of the home consumption was confined to the large cities and to the prosperous export-producing areas in the North and along the Gulf coast.

The power companies concentrated on expanding their existing facilities, which were geared to supplying electric power in traditional production centers and the larger urban areas. It is difficult to blame them for this. First, these companies formed a part of much larger enterprises operating internationally and were confronting a growing demand for electric power not only in Mexico

---

* These figures, based upon official sources, should be considered as very rough approximations only, in view of the extremely poor quality of Mexican economic statistics in that period.

but in other parts of Latin America as well. Secondly, because of the mountainous character of Mexico, investment in generation and transmission facilities in the less developed areas of the country was not attractive in profit terms. Nonetheless, the concentration of new investment in the fastest-growing areas was largely responsible for the first signs of dissatisfaction with the performance of the industry among the Mexican government technicians — the *técnicos* — and other intellectuals as early as 1920 at the end of the Carranza administration.

The scant Mexican literature on the electric power industry published in the 1920's is relatively free of attacks upon the public utilities as foreigners. Neither does the literature contain any forthright accusations that the monopolistic position of the industry made it possible in the absence of public regulations to dictate conditions to the consumers. Instead, the complaints of the 1920's seemed based upon the apparently sincere belief of the possibility of harmonizing the antagonistic interests of the companies and their customers through effective regulation. In the first study ever published in Mexico on the relations between the industry and the electric power consumers, Mexican *técnicos* declared that, "aware of the role played by electric power in the present economic world and convinced of its social implications, all the governments on earth in greater or lesser degree seek to encourage its development and regulate its application for the general good." This regulation should "combine maximum convenience for the public with the greatest possible protection for the firms." [3]

President Obregón's establishment of the Comisión Nacional de Fuerza Motriz (CNFM), or national power commission, in December 1922 was the first actual attempt to regulate the electric power industry in Mexico. The CNFM was set up as a permanent advisory body functioning as an agency of the two ministries, Agricultura y Fomento and Industria y Comercio, which continued to share jurisdiction in that field. The commission kept out of the field of thermoelectricity because the federal government lacked jurisdiction over steam plants, but in the hydroelectric field the commission's terms of reference were very broad. It was to make policy recommendations on such things as conservation of national hydraulic resources and coordination of their use for irrigation and industrial purposes; revision of the legal status of enterprises selling hydroelectric power to the public; regulation of electricity rates; and intervention in conflicts between the consumers and the companies.

The founders of the CNFM were extremely well informed concerning developments abroad.* They clearly had in mind the necessity of drawing up a national electric power policy and they considered the newly created body as a first step toward the early establishment of a national executive agency which would centralize federal control over all aspects of the industry. Hence, the commission was instructed to make a detailed study of foreign legislation covering public utilities; to analyze domestic policies and practices; to initiate special legislation aimed at federal control over concession grants, franchises, and electricity rate structures; and to prepare "over-all estimates of the industrial needs of the country and of the probable future demand for electric power in relation to the present state of development of national water resources." [4]

In operating terms very little came out of this first endeavor. The CNFM was handicapped from the beginning by the absence of any basic legal instruments with respect to regulation of the industry; by a shortage of funds and personnel; and by the general hostility of the companies, which, in defense of "the rights of private property" and "industrial liberty," generally refused to cooperate with the new official body.[5] But the contribution of the CNFM to electric power legislation in Mexico should not be underestimated, for this body drew up the legislation of 1926, which

* A lecture given in 1920 in Mexico City by José Herrera y Lasso, who was to be one of the founders, contained a detailed review of public utilities legislation in the U.S., Canada, Japan, and Western Europe; and articles and pamphlets published in 1924 and 1925 made numerous references to the proceedings of the World Power Conference, held in London in mid-1924.

for the first time spelled out a series of general principles to be applied by the government in its relations with public utilities.

By the mid-1920's Mexico found itself far behind the more industrialized countries in the regulation of the electric power industry, and there is little doubt that the decade of revolution was mainly responsible for this. The pressure for putting the relations between the state and the industry on a modern basis had made itself felt as early as the Carranza regime from 1915 to 1920 and it continued to grow as the country returned to normal.

Historians generally agree that one cannot speak of normal conditions in Mexico before the administration of Plutarco Elías Calles (1924–1928); the year 1925 is often considered a watershed between the Revolution and Mexico's contemporary history. During this year, which witnessed growing tensions in the relations between Mexico and its northern neighbor and the maturing of the conflict between the state and the Church inside Mexico, intellectuals and *técnicos* close to President Calles found enough time and energy to introduce a number of important economic policy measures, critical for the future growth of the Mexican economy. Because of his insistence on land reform, his implementation of the 1917 constitution with respect to foreign property rights, and his conflict with the Church, Calles was regarded abroad as an example of rabid radicalism, a kind of Castroism in the Latin America of the 1920's. A perusal of statements made by Calles and his closest collaborators in 1924–1926, primarily for Mexican consumption, makes it evident that this was not the case. Calles' radicalism was limited to agrarian and labor questions that were the logical consequence of the Revolution. On other economic issues he represented a mixture of strong nationalism and of middle-class hopes that a new liberal society could be built on the ruins of the past, on the basis of the country's rich potential resources.[6] In 1925 the country's central bank, the Banco de México, and the national farm credit banking systems were established; the national irrigation commission was created; and an ambitious program of public works was launched to improve and expand the antiquated and badly damaged transportation and communications systems.

In the footsteps of these major economic reforms came the adoption of the Código Nacional Eléctrico (national electric code) on April 30, 1926. The probings by the CNFM had provided confirmation of the complete legal chaos and anarchy in relations between the government and the private utilities, a situation which according to *técnicos* was due in part to the lack of understanding within federal, state, and local administrations of the "operating techniques of the industry and its eminently public-interest features." [7] The probings also confirmed the existence of the widespread abuses of consumers, other than large mining and industrial enterprises. In 1925 rates for small and medium consumers were found to be as high as before the Revolution; the supply of electric power was erratic; transmission facilities were dangerous to the lives of the companies' technical staffs; and meters and other equipment installed on the clients' premises were faulty.

The legal chaos and the nature of the companies' behavior toward their clients were adduced by *técnicos* as decisive and urgent reasons for the adoption of legislation intended to fulfill these major purposes:

1. to extend federal control to all stages of hydroelectric power generation and distribution, rather than just to the establishment of new plants; and

2. to find a legal formula for federal jurisdiction over the thermoelectric plants, which were still operating under state and municipal concessions and franchises.

The national electric code included a declaration of principles which would govern the industry. It said, among other things, that all regulation and control of the generation of electric power for industrial and commercial purposes was to come under federal jurisdiction exclusively and that the power industry itself was to be considered a "public utility." The code also contained a long series of technical rules on the industry's operations, designed for implementation by a special new office (later a department) of the Secretaría de Industria y Comercio. All this represented progress, but very limited progress. No clear precepts were established as to how regulation and control would be exercised by the authorities. In fact, the jurisdiction over the industry continued to be divided among federal agencies; the *técnicos* had unsuccessfully advocated a single central regulating agency — a goal that even to this day has not been reached. Nor was the *técnicos'* view accepted to the effect that any legislation should be preceded by an amendment to the 1917 constitution, whose Article 73 limited Congress' authority in economic matters to mining, commerce, credit institutions, general means of communication, postal services, and water resources. Bitterly criticizing the 1926 legislation in its final form, one of its original drafters, José Herrera y Lasso, wrote a few years later:

> Instead of proceeding resolutely to the constitutional amendment which was essential in order to provide a solid foundation for the new law, recourse was had to the handy artifice called on in the excesses of legislative fever that are so common in our country, consisting of making the substantive part of the law a simple declaration of principles and of ill-defined administrative goals . . . The procedure has the shameful features of not offending the fetishistic scruples ordinarily attributed to the constitution; of eluding the thorny points of difficult practical application by putting them off for the subsequent regulatory provisions; and of softening up the opposition and calming the natural alarm that all new legislation creates in interested circles.[8]

The lack of clarity and coherence in the 1926 legislation may have been due to the fact that the politicians in the Mexican Congress were not aware of all the intricate legal and technical problems that lurk in the relations between the state and the public utilities. But there is also a possibility that the matter was not pressed further because of political considerations of which the *técnicos* were not necessarily cognizant and which had very little to do with the electric power industry as such. The year 1926 was a very difficult one for the Calles administration, which, in trying to enforce the 1917 constitution on many fronts at the same time, ran into the simultaneous opposition of the landowners, the Catholics, the foreign oil companies, and finally the United States government. Consequently, it may well be that the President and his advisers decided not to complicate further their already complicated life by incurring the enmity of the foreign-owned public utilities, and left the matter open for further consideration at a more opportune time.

Such a decision would also partly explain why the entering into force of the 1926 legislation was delayed for more than two years. Whereas in countries with Anglo-Saxon law, statutes tend to be self-operative, the Mexican legal system provides that no law may enter into force unless followed by a supplementing regulation — a *reglamento* — issued by the executive branch. It was not until August 1928, shortly before the end of the Calles administration, when the tensions over petroleum and foreign property rights had disappeared and an armistice was achieved with the Church, that the implementing regulation to the 1926 electric legislation was issued. Even this document would not immediately result in action, but at least, on paper, it was clear and concise and contained a series of important innovations which two years earlier had mysteriously disappeared in the Congress from the original draft of the law drawn up by the *técnicos*. It extended federal authority to all commercial aspects of the electric power companies and explicitly called for the governmental regulation of rates; it established a federal system of concessions for thermoelectric enterprises and provided for the possibility of revision within a year of all concessions granted to the companies by state and municipal authorities. Furthermore, the Secretaría de Industria y Comercio was empowered to revise and approve the rate structures of all the companies operating in the country, and was given the right to demand access to the companies' books. The rates must be reviewed at least every five years. Herrera y Lasso commented that the *reglamento* "is as far reaching and explicit as the precepts of the law are ambiguous and vague; to such an extent that one might validly inquire whether the regulations are not rather a new law which repeals the former one . . ." [9]

Just as political considerations may help to explain the Calles administration's delay in bringing some sort of order to the relations between the state and the public utilities, the decision to do so in the summer of 1928 must have been in response to the appearance on the scene of a new force. This new force consisted mainly of small industrialists and merchants, who during more than a quarter of a century had considered electricity prices in Mexico as unreasonably high. By the mid-twenties this class not only had grown substantially in numbers, but had started to organize itself, first on a local and later a regional level, for the purpose of creating a counteracting power in national political and economic life against other pressure groups, especially against organized labor.

With the return of security in the country, Calles' public works programs and the secondary effects of international prosperity upon Mexico speeded the emergence of this new national entrepreneurial class. Sooner or later the new group was bound to find a common issue on which to test its strength. Cheap power was a perfect issue on many counts. First, electricity rates still were widely considered to be exorbitant.[10] Second, despite all the secrecy surrounding company records, the disparity between prices paid by large and small consumers had become widely known; the ratio between prices on electric power sold in block to large mining and industrial consumers and those charged to commercial establishments, small industrial plants, and domestic consumers ranged from 1-to-15 to 1-to-25. In the 1950's it was about 1-to-5. Third, no known substitute for electricity was then available in the country. Fourth, the owners of the industry were foreigners who were reputedly harvesting large profits from their operations and in addition had easy access to external financial resources — a situation contrasting with that of national entrepreneurs who were persistently short of investment funds.

The fight for cheap electricity seems to have originated with the textile industry, the biggest single consumer of electric power in the 1920's with the exception of mining and petroleum. The first organized movement against prevailing rates dates back to 1921, when the textile producers (whose over-all situation was then very difficult) succeeded in organizing a consumer league in various industrial towns, whose members were pledged not to pay electricity bills until the companies reduced the rates. Centering around the cities of Puebla and San Luis Potosí, the two traditional strongholds of the growing entrepreneurial class, the movement received support from the Cámara Nacional de Comercio (national trade chamber), which on various occasions intervened with the federal authorities and invited industrialists and merchants to organize pressure groups on the state level. The press of the period relates a number of cases in which governors of the various states tried to intercede with the companies on behalf of the local business community and met with very limited success. Writing letters to the local dailies to complain about high electricity prices and allegedly poor service became very fashionable in the mid-twenties, and such complaints provided the dailies as well as trade and industry papers with material for editorials having a broad popular appeal. Thus, in the summer of 1928, a month before the *reglamento* to the 1926 electric power legislation, an organ of the Puebla merchants had this to say on the subject of electricity rates: "We have fallen into a bog of permanent crisis. Production costs are high because of the high price of motive power. This is a question of life or death for the national economy. The electric power company has become an enemy of Puebla's progress." [11] In strictly economic terms, the cost of power plays an insignificant role in total production costs for an industry such as textiles, but more than economics was at work here; the bitterness of the complaints of the industrial electricity users in Mexico must have been somewhat related to the especially vulnerable position of the foreigner who exercises monopoly power in a highly nationalistic environment.

The companies, however, did not take seriously the growing

expressions of dissatisfaction. Neither did they seem to be gravely concerned over the new federal legislation, which, as both they themselves and the *técnicos* knew, would be open to challenge in the courts as long as Article 73 of the constitution stood in its original form. Some companies, in fact, started court action against the 1926–1928 legislation and refused to accept the new powers of the Secretaría de Industria y Comercio; others chose the road of cooperation — if not in the spirit intended, at least formally. But all this must have been considered simply a nuisance in a situation where over-all business was not only good but getting better every year.

In many respects the behavior of the companies between 1926 and 1930 reminds one of the good old days toward the end of the Porfirian era. In these years preceding the Great Depression, the sky seemed to be the limit for the companies' executives in Mexico. Not only did the generating capacity of all the major systems increase by about 50 per cent in comparison with the level of the mid-twenties, but the whole structure of the industry was changed by the arrival on the scene of a large volume of new capital, brought in by a newcomer to Mexico, the American & Foreign Power Company, the Latin American subsidiary of the Electric Bond & Share system in the United States. During 1928 and 1929, immediately before the outbreak of the world economic crisis, American & Foreign Power bought three of the five large electric systems then operating in Mexico, for a sum estimated at over $70 million; in addition, it acquired individual thermoelectric plants in seven medium-sized industrial centers. As a result of this financial operation, the biggest in the history of Mexican public utilities until the industry's nationalization in 1960, American & Foreign Power became the owner of all major generation and transmission facilities in Mexico outside the Mexico City area.

The optimism of American & Foreign Power is indicated by its purchase, between 1923 and 1929, of electric, gas, telephone, ice, water, tramway, and ferry companies in eleven different Latin American countries. One author, with long years of service in a foreign-owned public utility in Mexico, mentions two reasons for these investments: relatively high rates of profitability and threats of increased utility regulation in the United States.[12] In Mexico the company not only continued all the expansion plans started under the previous managements, but immediately set additional programs in motion. Thus, whereas the Mexican Light & Power Company's second stage of expansion ended in 1930, the American & Foreign Power Company continued to add to its generation and distribution facilities for a couple of years more, and in the case of the Puebla–Veracruz system even up to 1935, the year in which the self-financed growth of the private electric power industry in Mexico was destined to end forever.

Chapter 3

The Conflict

IN the fall of 1928 neither the *técnicos* in the government nor the private power companies — nor, for that matter, anyone else inside or outside Mexico — foresaw that the next twelve months would basically change the nature of the relationship between the state and private enterprise in the Western world, including Mexico.

The Great Depression had a profound effect on both Mexico's government and Mexico's electric power industry. The onslaught was felt almost immediately in Mexico, and paralysis spread with great speed to all sectors of the economy. Between 1930 and 1932, Mexico's gross national product declined abruptly. Mining output fell off in three years to the volume observed in 1907. In the same period manufacturing production declined in volume by some 15 per cent and in value by one third; and by 1932 gains made by that sector during the entire previous decade were wiped out.* Exports decreased in volume by one third and in value by over 45 per cent.

Strangely enough, the trend of domestic prices did not reflect the breakdown of the economy. Whereas in the United States wholesale prices declined in the 1929–1932 period by over 30 per cent, in Mexico the drop was only 18 per cent. This phe-

---

* The literature on the behavior of the Mexican economy in the twenties and during the Great Depression is very scant and the statistics are extremely weak. The estimates presented here are taken from various scattered sources and should be considered as general approximations only.

nomenon may be subject to a variety of interpretations, but it suggests that the real income of the majority of the underemployed population suffered comparatively more than in the industrial countries.

In electricity prices for middle and small consumers, there was simply no change. This phenomenon was easy to explain from the power companies' viewpoint. The demand for electric power in the mining and metallurgical sector, which at the outset of the depression still accounted for close to 40 per cent of the total demand for electric power in Mexico, suddenly dwindled. Between 1929 and 1932 employment in mining was halved, dropping from 90,000 to 45,000 workers; output of silver declined by 35 per cent, lead by 45 per cent, and copper and zinc by 60 per cent. Thus, revenue from the sale of electricity to middle and small consumers increased in importance to the utilities. For their part, those consumers, who had complained about the high cost of electricity during the economic recovery of the Obregón and Calles administrations, felt even more abused when the rates continued unchanged during the depression.[1]

The conflict between electric companies, on the one hand, and the consumers and *técnicos,* on the other, was building up toward an eruption. Consumer behavior became increasingly violent. In some states, for example, consumers who were cut off because they had not paid their electric bills were reconnected by "defense squads" organized by consumer leagues. By mid-1932, the companies still showed no willingness to make concessions to the public clamor for lower rates. And the central government still was not ready to enter upon the scene energetically. The *técnicos* were obviously frustrated by the inaction of their political superiors in the governmental hierarchy. The federal government did not provide the regulatory agencies with the necessary personnel and funds for enforcing the existing code. Nor did it take steps to initiate the long overdue reform of Article 73 of the constitution, without which the legislation of 1926–1928 was on legal quicksand. Consequently, in an atmosphere tingling with emotion which was heightened by the foreign ownership of the companies, the consumer resistance movement spread throughout the country. It culminated in the establishment in late 1932 of the Confederación Nacional Defensora de los Servicios Públicos (national public service defense confederation), a nation-wide organization in which *técnicos* and intellectuals joined forces for the first time with small industrial, commercial, and private consumers.

The Mexican consumers' direct action against the companies, although it abounded in violence, was not, one should remember, an isolated phenomenon in those times. Furthermore, it was fed to some extent by widely circulated press reports of similar though perhaps more peaceful expressions of dissatisfaction by U.S. electric power consumers.[2] The spectacular crash of the gigantic Insull system in 1929 and the bankruptcies of other large U.S. private utility systems only added strength to the attacks of the Mexican consumer leagues, which by 1932 were styling themselves as the avant-garde of the "historical awakening of a weak and exploited nation fighting against blood-thirsty octopuses." [3]

It is not easy to explain the inactivity of the central government in the disputes between the consumers and the utilities during the years from 1929 to 1932. In the few instances in which the central authorities intervened in the electric power conflicts during those years, it was only in individual cases and only when the matter was about to get out of hand because of the direct threat of the consumers to power-company property. The rest of the time it was left to the consumers and the companies themselves to solve their problems as best they might. This neutral position must have been due to the interaction of a series of complicated factors. The country was not only passing through a severe economic crisis, but through a political one as well. The political scene bore small resemblance to the relatively peaceful conditions of the first and final years of the Calles administration. Although Calles himself stayed as the power behind the throne after 1928, his influence did not go uncontested. Besides, the conflicts with big foreign interests which seemed to have been solved in the final years of Calles' presidency proved not to have been finally settled, as witness the sudden deterioration in United States–Mexican relations in 1930–1931 during the term of office of Pascual Ortiz Rubio, Calles' successor and protégé. In addition, there are reasons to believe that the bureaucracy (as distinguished from the *técnicos*) stood in the way of federal intervention. In part, the bureaucrats' unsympathetic position was due to the novelty of the problem of public utility regulation. In part, it may have been the result of collusion between the companies and lower-echelon government officials — a phenomenon not entirely unknown on the state and local level in the United States during the 1920's.

But the *técnicos* continued to urge the consumers on, using devious routes to keep the protests alive. Their major objective, it appears, was to wrest from the companies the privileges they inherited from the pre-Revolutionary era, and to prevent the extension of company control over the water resources not yet incorporated in the large private generating systems. Since the industry apparently could not be effectively controlled and since it could not be induced by legal incentives and persuasion to implement programs which the *técnicos* considered vital to the development of the national economy and welfare, they apparently concluded that the only way to deal with the companies was to limit their access to the new resources needed for the generation of power. As far as the *técnicos* were concerned, the country should control not only its exhaustible resources such as petroleum, but also its renewable resources such as water. But the *técnicos* feared that once the companies got hold of the remaining choice water resources, it would never be possible to dislodge them. If access to this potential wealth could be denied, according to their view, either the state or domestic private capital might one day be in a position to exploit these resources for the country's benefit.

An opportunity to put this thinking into practice was offered by a law which had been passed in August 1929, the first revision of water legislation since the Revolution. The new "Ley de aguas de propiedad nacional" (national water resources law) and its *reglamento,* issued a few months later, considerably tightened federal control over water resources and clearly sought to eliminate the possibility of private companies' getting hold of concessions for "future use." From that time forward, temporary permits were issued instead of concessions; the eventual issuance of a long-term concession was made contingent upon satisfactory completion of the undertaking covered by the temporary permit. Even the long-term concessions were limited in various ways. There was provision for the return to the nation of all water resources upon the expiration of concessions, which could not in any case remain in effect for more than seventy-five years; provision for the government's right to modify concession terms without indemnity, in case of the need to use water resources for any purpose related to land reform legislation or the encouragement of "better utilization of these resources"; provision for the state's right to buy out the concessionaires, should such action become necessary; and, finally, provision for the direct use of water resources by the nation, if this became necessary. The same legislation defined priorities for the utilization of the water resources and put their use by private electric power companies at the very end of the list.[4]

By the end of 1932, pressures for direct government intervention in the electric power industry were getting out of hand. By that time, it was no longer simply a question of lower rates. A wave of nationalistic radicalism had affected the country and had undermined the faith of post-Revolutionary intellectuals in the feasibility of building the country's economy along liberal lines with only moderate state intervention. Whatever ideological pressures for the new order may have been lacking in the 1917 constitution and in the writings of the Revolution's leaders were abundantly provided by events outside Mexico. The Soviet experience with the first five-year plan, officially announced in Moscow as completed at the end of 1932, was showing to eager listeners in Mexico that neither industrialization nor economic development was possible without abundance of electric power and that the development of electric power demanded that the problem be handed over to the state — that is, the *técnicos*. Moreover, voices raised in the United States lent support to all the worst suspicions in Mexico regarding the antisocial behavior of private utilities in all countries.

Political circles now realized that the electricity issue could not be ignored. The annual State of the Union Message delivered to the Congress by President Abelardo Rodríguez on September 6, 1932, referred to the problem at some length. This portion of the official document was drawn up by the minister of industry and commerce, who reviewed legislation on the electric power industry and water resources in the preceding five or six years. The statement affirmed that the ministry had already begun to implement that part of the legislation applicable to its area of jurisdiction, particularly in the field of rate control. High electricity rates, it was argued, not only harmed consumer interests but also increased the demand for other sources of energy and consequently weakened the nation's natural resource base.

Following this declaration, the minister of industry and commerce invited the power companies to submit their rates for downward revision, and by the end of 1932 he was able to inform the press that in various localities the companies had accepted the ministry's suggestions and had cut substantially their prices to small and medium consumers for the first time in the thirty-year history of the Mexican industry. Not all the companies agreed to cooperate with the government, however. The largest one, Mexican Light & Power, known as Mexlight, successfully delayed any rate-lowering action for almost two years by arguing in the courts that the legislation passed under Calles was unconstitutional. (This company's rates in the capital and central Mexico were revised downward in July 1934, eighteen months after some smaller companies accepted the government's suggestions.)

The administration not only took action on rates but also, at long last, addressed itself to the constitutional issue. In December

1932, President Rodríguez asked the Congress for an amendment to Article 73 of the constitution that would expressly mention the electric power industry as being under the jurisdiction of the federal government.

But all this — the government's initiatives and the companies' willingness to sacrifice some of their diminishing profits — was too little and too late for Mexican public opinion. In early 1933, the Confederación Nacional Defensora de los Servicios Públicos called for nationalization of the power industry, observing that the Congress had delayed action on the constitutional amendment.

The confederation's hand was considerably strengthened by the appearance in March 1933 of Franklin D. Roosevelt's *Looking Forward*, a compilation of his articles and speeches. The book was hurriedly translated and published in installments within less than two months in a widely read weekly journal, *El Economista*, the intellectual organ of the young generation of economists and other *técnicos,* many of whom had easy access to the highest government circles. The very first installment carried the part of the book dealing with the public utility scandals in the United States and Roosevelt's program in the field of electric energy (even though this was the eighth chapter of the book). The editors of *El Economista* declared in the prefatory note: "These statements demonstrate that any thesis of economic liberalism [laissez-faire] in the governmental practices of our great neighbor to the north may be considered as out of order . . . A modified state socialism is presently in the making in the United States."

Judging from the Mexico City press, one must assume that the impact of Roosevelt's book was very considerable. The debate on the respective advantages of laissez-faire and statist economic policies in a modern society raged throughout the summer of 1933, with supporters of Roosevelt's stand widely and enthusiastically quoting his attacks on the political power of the U.S. financial "trusts," and specifically on public utilities.[5]

That Roosevelt's views were discussed in the highest circles is shown by an interview that was granted that summer by President

Rodríguez to Ezequiel Padilla, a well-known young economist who was to become foreign minister in the early 1940's. The text of the interview, as published in *El Economista* on August 10, 1933, contains the following illuminating passage:

Ezequiel Padilla: "With respect to electrification, this forms the fundamental basis for all modern economic structures. Lenin captured the enthusiasm of the Russian people with his electrification program. Roosevelt, in his book 'Looking Forward,' affirms: 'An important part of my policy will be the collective appropriation of hydraulic resources by the people. This policy will be as radical as American liberty, as the Constitution of the United States. The Federal Government will under no circumstances relinquish these resources and the control thereover as long as I am President.' " *

Abelardo Rodríguez: "In Mexico a project for the nationalization of all free electric power resources is awaiting Senate approval. One cannot conceive of modern life in the absence of the use of electric power potential to organize an independent economy. The Six-Year Plan will be able to include perfectly reliable forecasts on the utilization and step-by-step development of electrical energy which, as is common knowledge, belongs almost entirely to foreign companies because of the lack of foresight and the capacity of our disorganized economy."

By this time the central government seemed to be finally ready to move in. But since doubts still existed among the leaders of the movement for the nationalization of the electric power industry, they had decided to use the highest possible trump in the game — to seek direct support from General Calles, the "Jefe

---

* This of course is a translation from the Spanish of the *El Economista* article. Actually, Roosevelt's book as originally published in the United States said something not quite so radical. After stating that "the nation, through its Federal Government, has sovereignty over vast waterpower resources in many parts of the United States," Roosevelt declared: ". . . we shall forever have a national yardstick to prevent extortion against the public and to encourage the wider use of that servant of the people — electricity. As an important part of this policy, the natural hydroelectric power resources belonging to the people should remain forever in their possession. This policy is as radical as American liberty, as radical as the Constitution of the United States. Never shall the Federal Government part with its sovereignty and control over its power resources while I am President of the United States." Franklin D. Roosevelt, *Looking Forward* (New York: John Day Co., 1933), pp. 153, 154.

Máximo de la Revolución Mexicana," the man who still held the
ultimate power in the country.

In mid-July, the Confederación Nacional Defensora sent ?
memorandum to Calles who was watching the national scene closely
from semi-retirement in his native state of Sonora. Calles was
asked to support a program for

> a definitive solution of the electrical industry problem which has
> arisen because of the lack of appropriate legislation in the field and
> the absence of effective official control of the operations being con-
> ducted by the electric power firms — from their vantage point as
> unassailable monopolies — on the basis of serious abuses, dangerous
> deference and very high rates, thereby effectively and continuously
> obstructing development of industry, leading to prohibitive expense
> in connection with domestic services and constituting a substantial
> cause of economic disequilibrium owing to the exodus from the
> country of many millions of pesos each year in the form of excess
> profits obtained by these businesses from their ignoble exploitation
> of our natural resources.[6]

Demonstrating that the memorandum was the work of people
well versed in world developments, the document went on to
draw Calles' attention to the fact that "the problem at hand is
not one that affects our country, exclusively, since the influence of
those powerful trusts that corner the world's most important
markets in China as well as in Japan, in Europe, in the United
States, and in Latin America, has through sharp speculation and
unfair dealings cultivated a general *malaise* and set up a systematic
obstruction to the liberal utilization of that basic element of prime
necessity, electricity in its multiple applications."

With its memorandum the Confederación Nacional Defensora
enclosed: a translation of the appropriate chapter of Roosevelt's
Looking Forward; certain of the confederation's earlier statements
presented to the authorities of the official party, then called Partido
Nacional Revolucionario; and a copy of a speech on the subject
of public utilities, delivered in Mexico City by the new U.S. ambassador, Josephus Daniels, shortly after his arrival.[7]

Calles must have reacted positively to the memorandum. In

the second half of 1933 things started happening. First of all, the official party document that outlined the economic policies of the government for the period 1934–1939, known as "El plan sexenal" (the six-year plan), and approved by Calles, included a section on the electric power industry, declaring this industry of "inherent social interest for the national economy" and setting two basic conditions for its development:

1. The supply of electric power, instead of being governed by the companies' profit considerations, should be effected at a price low enough to enable agricultural and industrial enterprise to be developed by electric power.
2. The distribution system for said power should branch out through our territory, so that new regional producing nuclei will be developed and the formation of new industrial centers will be facilitated.[8]

The six-year plan, ratified by the party in December 1933, added that in order to effect an adequate supply of electricity throughout the country, "the government will look to the formation of a national system of electric power generation, transformation and distribution, composed of semiofficial enterprises and consumer cooperatives."

That this was not supposed to be just another declaration of principles may be gathered from the following developments in the winter of 1933–1934, within a few weeks of publication of the plan: A tax on the generation of electric power was introduced; the automatic five-year exemption from profit taxes for newly established electric enterprises was rescinded; Article 73 of the constitution was amended to extend federal authority to all phases of the power industry, including thermoelectric plants; and the president asked for and received Congressional authority to establish a Comisión Federal de Electricidad (CFE) — that is, a federal electricity commission — after going through the necessary legal and technical preliminaries. This new agency, whenever established, was to study appropriate planning programs for the national electrification system; undertake all types of operations related to the generation, transformation, and distribution of electrical energy (including the acquisition of personal and real property, shares, and securities); organize semiofficial regional and local electrical concerns to produce, transmit, and distribute electric power at fair prices; and set up cooperatives of electricity consumers with a view to effecting supply under more favorable terms.[9] In point of fact, the CFE was not established until 1937, but the way for the government's entrance into the electric power industry had been cleared.

On December 20, 1933, the same day that President Rodríguez asked the Congress to give him authority to set up the CFE, another very novel presidential proposal reached the legislative branch of the Mexican government, seeking authority to establish a petroleum company, to be owned equally by the government and Mexican nationals, "for the purpose of exploring and exploiting the country's oil resources and assuring the domestic market, and especially the government and railroad system, an ample supply of oil and its derivatives." It was not mere coincidence that, on a single day, the legal foundation was laid for direct state intervention in oil exploitation and in electric power generation and distribution, two fields in which the Mexican state is today the sole owner and operator. What seems to be unusual and is often overlooked is that all this took place a year before Lázaro Cárdenas became president in December 1934, and under the aegis of two Mexican statesmen who were conservative by any standards — General Plutarco Elías Calles, the real ruler of the country in 1933 and 1934, and President Abelardo Rodríguez, a rich industrialist from Baja California.

Chapter 4

Enter the Government

BETWEEN 1932 and 1935 the private electric power companies completed the expansion programs conceived in the 1920's. Thereafter, in contrast to the public utilities in the developed countries, Mexico's power industry remained in a state of semistagnation until the end of the Second World War. From 1936 to 1945 something less than 100,000 kilowatts were added to the country's total generating capacity of 610,000 kilowatts (including plants owned by industrial and mining enterprises for their own use). Of this new capacity, the private utility companies created some 30,000 kilowatts in the single year 1939; and another 40,000 kilowatts came from the first installations put into operation by the Comisión Federal de Electricidad (CFE) in 1944 and 1945. The average annual growth rate of the power industry over the whole 1936–1945 period was scarcely more than 1 per cent; and only by pushing generation to the utmost limits of available capacity was an annual increase in output achieved.

As a result, by the end of the war Mexico faced a critical power shortage. In the words of high government officials in charge of electric industry regulation during the Avila Camacho administration, Mexico had fallen into "a dangerous situation consisting of the inability to supply the electricity service needed in order to guarantee the economic development demanded by the nation." [1]

The unavailability of foreign-produced industrial equipment during the war period accounts only in small part for the near standstill of the Mexican electric power industry during the years 1936–1945. The real cause was the cold war between the state and the companies from the mid-thirties on. The role of the private utilities in the Mexican economy became a part of the much larger issue of the relationship between foreign capital of all sorts and the Mexican government. This relationship, in turn, was seriously endangered and almost completely severed by the conflict between the country and the international oil companies, which culminated in, but did not end with, the oil expropriation of March 1938.

The oil dispute during the Cárdenas administration of 1934–1940 has been discussed so extensively by Mexican and foreign scholars that there is no need to dwell on it here. It should be stressed, however, that during the unfolding of the great drama that led to expropriation, international oil interests committed every error of judgment imaginable because they did not believe that the government of a weak and underdeveloped country beset with international problems would ever dare to take over their properties. What started as a purely legal contest, a conflict between oil unions and the companies, soon became an issue of national sovereignty versus the economic interests of foreign groups. The oil companies were unwilling to compromise; the state faced the alternatives of surrender or expropriation; despite all the risks, it chose to expropriate.

During a political struggle of such magnitude, it would have been too much to expect that other foreigners present on the scene would go unharmed. The Mexican public, which had for some time been accusing the electric power companies of unfair treatment, now looked upon their foreign owners and executives as part and parcel of the "international conspiracy" led by the oil companies. The power companies, for their part, regarded the Mexican administration as class enemies and expected the worst possible treatment.[2]

Forces were working inside and outside Mexico to localize the oil conflict, even when the controversy was at its height. Otherwise it is quite possible that, under the pressure exerted by Cárdenas' leftist and nationalistic entourage, the electric power industry also would have been nationalized in 1938. The tranquilizing forces were: the U.S. government, which refused to get directly involved on the side of the oil companies; President Cárdenas himself, who after having been forced to nationalize the oil companies was anxious to avoid reaching a point of no return in his relations with the United States and other industrial powers; and the power company executives, who wisely adopted an attitude of nonparticipation in the conflict.

We have seen that the framework for the true regulation of public utilities in Mexico was established shortly before the Cárdenas administration, under the direct pressure put on Calles and his successors by a coalition of *técnicos,* intellectuals, and electric power consumers. But the new administration demonstrated at an early date that it considered electricity a field of considerable urgency. In the autumn of 1936, less than a year after ex-President Calles had been forced to drop his active behind-the-scenes role, the new president instructed the Secretaría de Economía Nacional (the new name for the Secretaría de Industria y Comercio) to draft a federal law on electric energy along the lines suggested in the six-year plan, that is, a law to consolidate federal control over the industry and to replace the national electric code of 1926–1928. The first draft of what was called the "Ley de la industria eléctrica" (the electrical industry law), completed before the end of 1936, was subsequently submitted for comments to the electrical unions, which together with the rest of organized labor constituted the president's main political backing at that time. This gesture could scarcely have provoked a sympathetic reaction on the part of the private utilities which remembered only too well Cárdenas' tacit support of the electrical unions during a 1935–1936 labor conflict. Nor could it have escaped the companies' notice that shortly before the new bill was announced the president had submitted another legislative proposal to the Congress, providing for new regulations on the expropriation of private property. Existing expropriation laws dated back to 1905, in the Porfirio Díaz regime. The proposed regulations were in accordance with Article 27 of the 1917 constitution.

Foreign scholars give credence to President Cárdenas' claim (in answer to insistent queries from Washington) that the expropriation bill meant exactly what it said and had the sole aim of modernizing the legislation in force.[3] But in view of earlier conflicts between the Calles administration and the oil companies over the interpretation of the constitutional clauses on federal-owned properties, public utility executives became understandably suspicious. Their doubts regarding the administration's intentions increased when the trade unions summarily rejected the draft of the electric power law as too friendly to management.[4] The companies probably were also aware that the expropriation bill, on the other hand, seemed to suit everybody except the foreign interests. This legislation was speedily enacted before the end of 1936 and was applied for the first time in June 1937 as the vehicle by which the Mexican government acquired total ownership of a railroad system, Ferrocarriles Nacionales Mexicanos, which accounted for more than half of the nation's railroad facilities. Majority ownership in this line had been held by the Mexican government since the days of Porfirio Díaz.[5]

The political scene in 1937 was dominated by land reform and by the growing conflict between the oil companies and their unionized workers. Land reform led to prolonged absences from the capital on the part of President Cárdenas. The president toured the country with a large court of advisers, whose special fields were not necessarily limited to agriculture. It was in the summer of that year, on a trip to Yucatán, whose electric energy facilities were entirely confined to a few main cities, that the Comisión Federal de Electricidad (CFE) finally was born. In his decree the president charged the new agency with "organizing and directing a national system for electric power generation, transmission and distribution, based on technical and economic principles, on a nonprofit basis, for the purpose of obtaining the greatest possible output at minimum cost, for the benefit of the general interest." [6] This language went much further than the intentions expressed in the enabling decree of three and a half years earlier.

The authorship of the new presidential decree was ascribed to a small but vocal group of electrical engineers educated abroad, who since the late 1920's had been the standard-bearers of the movement to nationalize the public utilities, had participated actively in the early 1930's in the establishment of the Confederación Nacional Defensora de los Servicios Públicos, and had later helped draft the electric power sections of the six-year plan. It was not surprising, then, that the decree gave the CFE extremely broad powers:

to study the over-all planning of the national electrification system and the bases for its financing; to perform all types of operations related to electric power generation, transmission, and distribution; to organize concerns devoted to the production and distribution of electric power at fair prices; to organize concerns devoted to the manufacture of apparatus, machinery, and materials appropriate to generating plants and electrical installations; to properly channel the organization of electrical energy associations; and, finally, to intervene and, where appropriate, decide on the electrification activities that official, semiofficial, or private institutions plan to undertake.

As made clear by these terms of reference, the fathers of the CFE intended to create more than a state-owned electric power company. Their aim was to establish a centralized agency which would take upon itself the task not only of electrification but of overseeing and directing the activities of private companies in the electric energy field whenever such action seemed advisable.

The men responsible for the birth of the CFE did not seem to worry much about the fact that the financial resources put at their disposal were insignificant. (The commission's initial budget for 1938 amounted to a paltry 50,000 pesos.) Although they were probably looked upon by the management of the private firms as impractical dreamers or inexperienced bureaucrats, they proved in fact to be seasoned and realistic politicians. Their strategy provided for promoting their plans by stages: they correctly estimated that in the political climate prevailing in the country, once the legal foundations for the CFE were laid the means to run it would be found. They believed that the magnitude of these means would depend as much upon the private companies' behavior as upon the CFE's effort and the federal government's financial resources. One should not even exclude the possibility that some of the *técnicos,* aware of the forthcoming and inevitable head-on clash between the oil companies and the state, hoped for an extension of the conflict to the public utilities field. They must have known of the convenient presence of the new expropriation law, well suited to take care of such a situation. The *técnicos* further believed — and here they were right — that they were riding the wave of the future. At best they would take over the whole public utility field; at the very worst they would have one foot in the door opening eventually to the same goal — the absorption of the power industry by the state.

The establishment of an agency with a budget smaller than the salary earned by a single public utility executive did not create much excitement among the electric companies. What worried them far more was the steady worsening of the oil conflict and its possible side effects for other foreign interests in Mexico. The utilities officials in 1938 considered their nationalization at any moment a serious possibility in the aftermath of the oil expropriation.

The companies' position was complicated by the complete breakdown of communications between the resident foreign businessmen and the Mexican government at that time. It had always been possible for foreign companies in Mexico to win some friends and influence some people in the intricate government apparatus, but in 1938 no one in official circles could be won over or influenced for fear of being branded a traitor to the country.

In August the nightmare of the possible expropriation of the electric utilities was dispelled. Instead of expropriation, the government proposed to pursue the goal of power industry regulation through a new and tightened-up draft of the Ley de la industria eléctrica, under discussion since 1936.

As far as the private companies were concerned, the threat in the new bill had to do with the rate-regulation mechanism and the concept of fair return on investment, points which in the opinion of the companies were not adequately defined. At the companies' instigation these and many other features of the bill were harshly criticized in the Mexico City press by the principal organization of businessmen, then known as Confederación Nacional de Industria y Comercio. Shortly afterwards, the Secretaría de Economía Nacional, acting in the name of the chief executive, rejected all the business group's observations as "baseless and contrary to the legal and social principles which served as the guide for the elaboration of the draft bill." With regard to the main criticism — the absence of any concrete guarantee of *minimum* profits for the electric power companies — the ministry had this somewhat unresponsive observation to make:

Those who are criticizing the bill want the legislator to fix the amount of those profits at the outset. What they propose is inadvisable because the profits of an enterprise should always be proportionate to the gross earnings obtained at a given time by capital invested in the country. The establishment of a fixed per cent of profit is unacceptable because such a step would either be contrary to the interests of the consuming public by imposing a higher rate than that which the power company should legitimately receive at a given moment, or prejudicial to the concessionaire by virtue of being lower than the profits that would rightfully be admissible in accordance with prevailing economic circumstances.[7]

In this situation the companies' only recourse was to take up the matter with President Cárdenas. This was attempted through Ambassador Josephus Daniels, who received instructions from Under Secretary of State Sumner Welles to help the power companies in their difficulties. Daniels took care not to become personally involved in the matter, but in November 1938 he arranged for an interview between the president and Curtis E.

Calder, head of the American & Foreign Power Company. That Daniels did not completely support the companies' position is evident from his subsequent communication to Welles:

I have examined the measure, and while I would not say so to any Mexican or utility officials, it seems to me in the main to be a wise method of regulating public service corporations. If attention is called to the provisions that are unwise, by utility officials, they might secure their deletion from the measure before passage . . . If the United States had enacted somewhat the same legislation (omitting some features) when light and power companies were in their infancy, we would have escaped the Insull scandals and Roosevelt would not have been compelled to wage a hard fight to secure legislation which, in a sense, could do no more than lock the stable after the horse was gone . . .

Mr. Calder is in effect asking our Government to step in and tell the Mexican Government what sort of utility laws it should put upon its statute books. That is going far beyond any request that has heretofore been made by American investors in this country.[8]

There is no record of the details of Calder's interview with Cárdenas, nor is it known whether other company executives were able to gain the president's ear. Despite all the preliminaries, after Congress had approved the Ley de la industria eléctrica with slight amendments at the end of 1938 and the implementing regulations had been issued, the companies seemed reasonably content.[9]

The law, modified in some respects once again at the end of 1940, became the basic legislation in the field until the industry was nationalized in 1960. Designed to control and regulate all aspects of the power industry and to promote its development as well, the law specifically provided for:

1. granting concessions for the generation and distribution of electric energy for not more than fifty years;

2. limiting the issuance of new concessions to Mexican companies only and subjecting them to prior approval of the CFE;

3. compelling the concessionaires to undertake construction programs needed to meet the demand for electric power;

4. submitting all new construction projects and related financial arrangements for government approval;

5. establishing the property value base as of December 31, 1941, and providing for the evaluation of new investments at their actual cost, for the purpose of calculating the companies' authorized return;

6. introducing a uniform accounting system;

7. fixing rate structures for periods not in excess of five years;

8. revising rates only in the event of basic changes in the economic factors upon which the rates previously in force were based;

9. transferring all technical matters to the Dirección General de Electricidad (bureau of electricity) in the Secretaría de Economía Nacional; and

10. establishing the Comisión de Tarifas (rate commission), a decentralized agency over which the ministry of national economy would hold broad veto powers.[10]

There is circumstantial evidence that the year 1939, following the issuance of the law, witnessed some relaxation of the tensions between the state and the power companies. The companies, remembering their earlier uncertainty about the future, felt that the worst had been avoided and that the way to mutual accommodation had probably been found. Thus, for example, the 1939 annual report of one of the American & Foreign Power subsidiaries had this to say on the subject: "The law states that the company shall have a 'reasonable' profit and the proposed Regulations in addition to establishing a form of procedure to be followed in the matters pertaining to changes in rates, permit companies to apply and show cause for rate increases when justified and, in general, seem to be designed along constructive lines and to give the industry some much needed relief." [11]

Thus it came about that the larger companies responded to the growing demand for electricity by making minor additions to their generating capacity and transmission facilities in various parts of the country. The year 1939 was the only year in the 1936–1946 period when the two big companies, Mexican Light & Power (Mexlight) and American & Foreign Power, made new investments in the country. Their expansion plans were abruptly suspended, however, when the results of the first practical tests of the new legislation became evident in 1940.

Upon publication of the electric industry law, the power companies had immediately asked for increases in rates, which had been lowered at the beginning of the thirties. Certain rate boosts were speedily granted in the late summer of 1939 by the deputy minister of national economy, but suspended in 1940 by the minister himself on order from the president. The case of the Mexlight petition[12] clearly showed that rate setting was, and would continue to be, governed by political and not economic criteria. In justification of his order to suspend the increases that had already been granted, the minister of economy explained to Mexlight that

the order for suspension . . . was in response to observations made by various groups of public opinion concerning the new rates and the very natural desire of the President of the Republic and consequently of this Ministry to have sufficient time to study these observations and, as necessary, to review the documentation on which the rate calculations are based. In addition, further objections to the imposition of the rates have been received, and this Ministry's time is currently occupied in examining and weighing the merits of the new arguments. This attitude is moreover perfectly justified; whereas the Ministry concedes that the regulation of public service enterprises is primarily a technical function, it must not fail to recognize that government action in this area is directly connected with the public weal since the effects of the regulation are felt throughout every part of the community served by the power companies.[13]

It took another six months and a change of administration to get Mexlight a reversal of the suspension order and rate increase amounting to approximately 30 per cent. These concessions were made conditional on the investment of the additional proceeds in the expansion of generating facilities in Mexico City, where industries were already suffering from acute power shortages. But the relations between the state and the electric companies had been damaged beyond repair. For the companies, the 1939–1940 incident confirmed their suspicion that there was "a deliberate governmental policy to keep rates down, so that the Federal authorities could eventually nationalize all the foreign private power interests." [14] On the other hand government circles, as well as large sectors of public opinion, regarded the controversy as further proof that the companies' sole aim was to drain the country of its wealth by exacting exorbitant profits.[15]

In the meantime, the Comisión Federal de Electricidad, or CFE, was enlarging its operations. Its budget was augmented, at first by bigger federal appropriations and later by additional proceeds from a special 10 per cent tax on the consumption of electric energy all over the country. The CFE took upon itself two immediate tasks: the construction of small plants in the outlying areas devoid of electric power facilities, and the development of the largest untapped reservoir of hydroelectric power in central Mexico, where in the early thirties private unexploited concessions had been rescinded. The year 1944 marked the inauguration of the first major unit of the new facilities which soon, under the name of the Miguel Alemán System, were to become the largest single generating system in the whole country. By the end of 1945 the commission had a generating capacity of close to 50,000 kilowatts. Two large plants in the States of México and Veracruz accounted for over 80 per cent of this total; twenty-two smaller plants in ten states, with an average capacity of 350 kilowatts, accounted for the rest.

The first CFE plant was explicitly mentioned as a high priority project in the second six-year plan elaborated in 1940 by the *técnicos* during the final year of the Cárdenas administration. This plan for the period 1941–1946 was much more specific with respect to the country's electrification needs than the first six-year plan had been. The new plan provided for federal intervention in this field through:

1. executing new electric power projects in order to complete the national electrification program;

2. giving priority for generating facilities that would serve the greatest number of inhabitants per unit of investment;

3. continuing study of the demand for electricity in the various regions so as to undertake necessary projects in the event these were not opportunely taken care of by private enterprise;

4. mobilizing budgetary resources, private savings, and all other means of financing in support of the promotion of the country's electrification.[16]

The CFE entered the 1940's in a setting which appeared to its directors particularly conducive to the expansion of government-produced electric power. The five large systems owned by foreign interests had ceased to grow, and by not offering service to new customers they were restricting the electric power supply. In fact, one of these, the Compañía Hidroeléctrica de Chapala, which served the region around Guadalajara, the second biggest industrial center of Mexico, went bankrupt and was bought by the federal government from the U.S. owners in 1940.

The future of the country's industrial development was seriously endangered. The large expansion program needed to cope with deferred and expected demand was beyond the financial possibilities of the private companies. Even if they were able to mobilize the necessary resources, which the *técnicos* estimated at more than $100 million for the decade of 1941–1950, this, in the opinion of the CFE, would involve an excessive outgo of foreign exchange in the form of interest, royalties, and profits. Thus, the only alternative, as the *técnicos* saw it, was to mobilize domestic resources to finance an expansion of facilities. If private savings were not forthcoming, they proposed to use the savings of the public sector supplemented by official external borrowing, presumably from U.S. government sources. Since private savings were not attracted to this particular activity, the CFE felt itself to be the logical choice as the agency to conduct the national electrification program.[17]

The private companies could hardly be expected to work up any enthusiasm over these outlines of future CFE policies as endorsed by the commission's highest officials. What seemed to bother them most of all was the CFE's trespassing on what they considered their own geographical preserve — the broadly defined regions in which the companies had operated since the end of the nineteenth century, particularly in the central region of the Republic and the Gulf states. According to the companies' interpretation, the commission had been created to supply power only in areas that had not been developed by private interests. As a long-time official of one of the large companies, Robert P. Wolfangel, complained in 1961, after nationalization: "Rural electrification was to be one of the responsibilities of the Comisión Federal de Electricidad . . . This was the task to which the Commission should have been dedicating more time, effort, and money. Instead, although not a general rule, it was trying to win a psychological battle with the populace over the private power companies. When the Commission should have been electrifying new areas for the social motive, it started to invade the concessions already being exploited by the power companies." [18]

The introduction of political considerations in rate setting by the federal authorities, the general tightening of regulatory activities, the CFE's announcements about its future policies, and the companies' general distrust of the government thus led to the standstill in electric power expansion on the part of the private utility companies. Besides, the establishment of new facilities — public or private — was hampered by the tight controls which the U.S. government imposed on exports of capital goods because of strategic war needs. Also, the CFE, though long on plans, was short on funds until the mid-forties. Consequently, well before the end of the war, serious shortages of electric power appeared all over the country notwithstanding the overloading of generation and transmission facilities and the mushrooming of small private service plants in manufacturing establishments.

By late 1945, the shortages of electric power had become so bad that for the first and last time in Mexico's modern history the government had to seek emergency technical help from foreign engineers. These were recruited from among the experts who had directed the war effort in electricity in the United States between 1941 and 1945. The mission was headed by Edward Falck, former chief of the U.S. Office of War Utilities Administration.

Mimeographed documents prepared in 1946 in connection with the work of this foreign mission make very interesting reading. Intended for official circles only, they analyzed with great frankness the developments that had led to the dangerous stagnation of the electric power industry at the end of the war. One of the papers, drawn up not by the foreign engineers but by a Mexican government official, Oscar R. Enríquez, director of the bureau of electricity in the Secretaría de Economía Nacional, presented the following description of the relations between the state and the private companies from the early thirties until the end of the war:

> Because of the lack of experience in the regulation and control of public services, the first legal provisions issued by the government [in the late twenties] to exercise control over the electric industry were not based on the study and analysis of existing conditions in that industry in Mexico but, following the line of least resistance, represented a translation of the technical administrative measures in effect in the United States. This led to the Código Nacional Eléctrico which remained in force until the year 1939.
>
> Notwithstanding the existence of the Código, the regulation of the industry involved no well-defined principles on which the official electricity policy could be based. These policy considerations consisted of complete adherence to rules issued at the discretion of successive ministers of industry and commerce who were directly responsible for controlling and regulating the domestic power companies.
>
> Under such a government system numerous deficiencies were bound to arise, at times to the detriment of the electrical industry, and at others imperiling the vital interests of the nation . . .
>
> As a result of the system adopted by the government [during the period from 1926–1939] and probably motivated by abuses or arbitrary action on the part of the public utility firms, the authorities felt called on to adopt a harsh policy (perhaps too extreme) to control company earnings, limiting them to an extent that was more than likely inadvisable . . . During the period from 1932 to 1939 power companies operating in the country considered the government's treatment of

them extremely severe and as a result of this feeling apprehensively gave up all ideas of promoting electrical development *thus abandoning to its fate one of the most essential items in economic life* [italics in original].

To determine the degree of responsibility that the power companies, largely financed by foreign capital, should assume for the present critical situation in which the country finds itself is not the most important when one studies the causes that have deterred electrical industry development in the past. Those firms in any case, as subsidiaries of foreign organizations, did nothing more than comply with provisions that did not originate in Mexico but were based on decisions made in New York, Montreal, Toronto, and Brussels.

. . . most of the blame for the present state of Mexico's electrical services rests on the authorities and officials who did not have sufficient foresight to measure and accurately evaluate the effects that the issuance of measures to control and regulate foreign firms would be likely to have on the nation . . .[19]

The question arises whether the problem as posed at the end of the war by a high government official was really that simple. Neither the state nor the private electric companies were the free agents they thought they were. In the immediate prewar period neither party was in a position to fulfill the conditions asked by the other. In view of the oil conflict and the generally depressed economic conditions, which were pushing the Mexican society to the left, the state could hardly have created a "favorable climate" for foreign investors, especially in a field where previous abuses by the companies were common knowledge. On the other hand, not only were the companies asking for what they believed to be a fair return on their actual investment, but they were seeking long-term political security for future foreign investors as a whole. Their attitudes were clearly expressed in a leading U.S. financial journal in the summer of 1940:

Hence, even if the rate and labor problems of the utilities were settled, foreign capital could not be counted upon in adequate amounts to finance the very urgently needed extension of Mexico's utility industry unless assurances were forthcoming that these properties will not be confiscated by the Government.

An ultimate solution of the utility problem confronting the country, which takes the form of an increasingly acute shortage of power, requires a modification of Mexico's policy with regard to foreign investments generally. By showing respect for the legitimate interests of foreign capital that has been invested in all productive enterprises within the country, and refraining from expropriation except where full and prompt payment may be made, the way would be paved for a renewed, urgently needed flow of funds from abroad into the vital electric light and power industry, which has been starved of capital, comparatively speaking, by the policies pursued during recent years.[20]

The inability of each side, with its own vested interests, to fulfill the other's demands was only part of the picture. Additional complicating elements were the lack of government experience in the regulatory field and the traditional characteristics of the Mexican legislative structure, which confers broad discretionary power on individual high officials.

Under normal conditions the regulation of private economic activities amounts to seeking a reasonable compromise between the fairly well-defined but partly conflicting interests of society and of the private entrepreneur.[21] The conditions under which the electric industry functioned in Mexico in the thirties and forties were abnormal in the extreme, and thus no reasonable compromise could have been reached. Still, from the standpoint of economic development needs, the state had at that time no alternative to a compromise. One must keep in mind that even if the government had foreseen the companies' refusal to invest and had tried to do something about it, as suggested by the 1946 official report, it was powerless to do so. Neither domestic private capital nor budgetary resources were available for the country's electrification. The concept of foreign developmental aid had not yet emerged, and international financial institutions simply did not exist. Thus, during the war Mexico could do little but stand by and watch the stagnation of her electric power industry while her *técnicos* were drawing ambitious plans for the future. But, at the end of the war, Mexico, unlike most other Latin American republics, no longer had to rely solely on foreign-owned companies for an adequate supply of electrical energy.

Chapter 5

Beginning of the End

AFTER 1945 there was a great and sustained expansion of electric power generation and distribution facilities, comparable in terms with the final years of the Porfirio Díaz era which had ushered in the electric age in Mexico. The modernization and expansion of the power grid brought supplies of electricity not only to urban centers of the country but also to many outlying rural areas. Between 1945 and 1960, the installed electric power capacity increased from 700,000 kilowatts to about three million. Annual power generation increased in the same period from 3.1 billion to 10.8 billion kilowatt hours.

The result of this growth was greatly to reduce the relative importance of the foreign-owned power companies. Between 1945 and 1960 the CFE added more than 1,000,000 kilowatts to its initial capacity of less than 50,000 kilowatts. The two large foreign companies, Mexlight and American & Foreign Power, increased their capacity by about 500,000 kilowatts. The rest of the industry, consisting of small local public service plants and of power stations established by numerous industrial enterprises for their own use, contributed an additional 700,000. In 1945, the two large private companies had controlled 60 per cent of the total installed capacity; the CFE had accounted for 5 per cent; and the rest of the industry 35 per cent. By 1960, the CFE controlled some 40 per cent of the total capacity; the two foreign companies together around 33 per cent; and the small public and private service plants about 27 per cent.

In money terms, it can be estimated roughly that out of the total 1945–1960 investment in the electric power industry selling to the public, equivalent to some 600 million U.S. dollars, a little over two thirds (about $400 million) was mobilized by the state-owned sector and the rest (less than $200 million) by the two foreign private companies. More than half of the investment in the public sector came from the federal budget, over one third from external sources (mainly the International Bank for Reconstruction and Development), and only one tenth (some $50 million) from current revenues of the CFE and from other state-owned plants. Mexlight and American & Foreign Power obtained their financial resources for investment in three approximately equal parts: from undistributed profits and depreciation reserves, loans granted by the government's financial institutions, and credits from the International Bank and the Export-Import Bank of Washington.[1]

The basic postwar change in the structure of ownership of the installed capacity was not followed by similar changes in power distribution. The explanation lies in a working agreement between the state and the private power companies, whereby the CFE plants served the private companies first. Only after their needs were met did the CFE sell directly to power consumers. In fact, many of the new publicly owned plants were built at locations in which the private companies *had* to be the major customers of newly generated power because they controlled the distribution systems there. From the inauguration of the first major CFE generating plant in 1944 until 1959, the energy purchases of the two foreign companies from the commission averaged 75 per cent of the commission's annual output. Although this percentage declined somewhat in the late fifties, the relative importance of the CFE-generated energy in the total volume of business transacted by the two private utilities was increasing sharply all the time. Whereas in 1950 their energy purchases from the commission were equal to some 15 per cent of their sales to end-users, ten years later, on the eve of nationalization, they were equal to nearly 50 per cent.

Between 1945 and 1960, electric energy consumption increased at nearly 11 per cent a year, a rate almost double that of the increase in gross national product. The diversification of the economy and the shifts in the location of certain economic activities visibly affected the pattern of power demand. The demand for energy to supply irrigation, public lighting, and commerce was more than enough to offset the sluggish consumption needs of two stagnant sectors, mining and traditional agriculture. At the war's end, industrial consumption accounted for 60 per cent of the total, and residential and commercial consumption another 20 per cent. By 1960 industry's share declined to 45 per cent while that of the two other principal end-users increased to 30 per cent. (Industry's declining share was due not only to the faster growth of demand in some other sectors, but also to the increasing substitution by industry of cheap oil products for electricity.) At the same time, changes in the pattern of industrial power consumption proved that Mexican industrialization was progressing on all fronts. In 1945, the manufacture of capital goods had absorbed only 30 per cent of the power bought by the industrial sector as against 70 per cent used in the manufacture of consumer goods. Fifteen years later, these proportions were reversed, partly because a new and important customer group emerged in the manufacturing sector — the chemical producers. By 1960, the chemical industry alone accounted for one fifth of the energy consumed by Mexico's industrial activities.

It is clear that through much of this period of expansion the inability of the power industry as a whole to make profits and to mobilize additional resources in the domestic and foreign private capital markets seriously limited the expansion programs. In the case of the CFE, growth depended upon the availability of federal funds, for which all the rest of the public sector was strongly competing, and upon the International Bank's willingness to lend. The private electricity industry also depended on the good will of

Mexican and foreign credit institutions. In the late fifties the international financial agencies started taking an increasingly dim view of the capital structure of the electric power enterprises, and of the official rate structures which had not kept pace with inflation. And, at the same time, the state was forced into adopting more conservative financial and monetary policies. Thus the two main lines of financial support for the industry were weakened and necessarily exerted a braking action on expansion programs. This phase lasted until the private companies were nationalized and rate policies were completely overhauled.

The state's responses to the difficulties of the power industry were complicated and equivocal. There was no single statement of policy reflecting an official view of the relation of rate levels to changing levels of direct and indirect costs in the power industry. Nevertheless, the postwar administrators made it perfectly clear that, on political grounds, they rejected a radical revision of the rate structure and the constant upward adjustment of electricity prices to conform to the general inflationary trend. At the same time, however, attempts were made to compensate the private sector of the industry for inadequate rates. These measures were many and varied. The companies were given unrestricted access to CFE-generated power under very favorable pricing conditions; at the time of periodical collective contract negotiations, the government persuaded the electrical trade unions to restrain their demands; through Nacional Financiera, the Mexican government's development bank, the firms received sizable medium-term domestic credits carrying an interest much below the current market rate; and finally, the government acted on behalf of, or jointly with, the private companies in obtaining foreign loans, and extended its unconditional guarantee to all the major loans granted them by international agencies.

Though all this may not have satisfied the private companies, two points must be made. First, the low prices fixed on power sold in large blocks to the private companies were in all probability the main reason why the CFE had little or no profits during the

entire decade of the fifties. Secondly, two thirds of the total investment made by the private companies between 1945 and 1960
either originated with the Mexican public banking system or was
mobilized abroad with the government's indispensable support in
the form of a guarantee.

The government's indirect financial assistance to the private
companies, in combination with the large transfers of budgetary
resources to the state-owned sector of the power industry, was
tantamount to subsidization by the rest of the economy of one
of the activities vital to the country's development. Such a policy
had tremendous advantages: unsophisticated public opinion was
not aware of its cost; and the latent hostility of the Mexican society
toward the foreign owners of the utilities was held in check. But
the policy also suffered from two major shortcomings. In the first
place, the subsidy had to be covered out of the proceeds of a less-
than-ideal tax system. Secondly, policies of this type were doomed
in the long run because the private companies regarded whatever
they received in the way of special consideration as too little,
whereas the state considered its concessions as more than ample.
Very soon the patterns of mutual disappointment emerged. Once
again, as in the thirties, the state, or rather many individual high
officials, started looking upon the foreign-owned utilities as completely unresponsive to the country's needs. The companies, for
their part, coined a special name for the years 1946–1960, indica-
tive of their attitude. For them, the postwar era was the period
of the "great deception."

Although relations between the state and the private power
companies under the Miguel Alemán administration (1946–1952)
were probably better than they were before or since, the marked
impetus given the electric industry in that period was due less to
a successful give-and-take between the two parties than to the
government's willingness to provide ample financial support for
developmental activities, including electrification, without any very
great regard for internal monetary stability or the balance-of-
payments position. It was the job of Alemán's successor, Adolfo

Ruiz Cortines (1952–1958) to swing the pendulum back and to implement austere monetary and financial policies as a means of combating inflationary pressures without bringing the country's economic development to a standstill. The success of such policies depended on putting many economic activities vital to development on a more self-sustaining basis, with a view to diminishing their growing dependence upon domestic and external credit.

The electric power industry was obviously one of the first candidates for such a reorganization, especially in view of the fact that the state had learned, through the experience acquired by the CFE, that sustained development of electric power resources required very heavy investment, much greater than the state itself could handle. Consequently, in October 1953, before the new administration was a year old, a Comité para el Estudio de la Industria Eléctrica Mexicana (committee for the study of the Mexican electrical industry) was established, consisting of officials drawn from the various governmental agencies concerned. This group, known as CEE-MEX, was instructed to study ways and means of financing the country's electrification and to present the federal authorities with a program for action, aimed at putting the electric power industry on a sounder financial footing and bringing a greater measure of order to relations between the public and private enterprises operating in this field.

It took CEE-MEX about four years to fulfill its assignment. Only shortly before the end of the Ruiz Cortines administration was its voluminous and extremely competent report completed.[2] However, its proposals have never been acted upon. A basic disagreement among the public agencies involved was never effectively resolved. Indeed, the CEE-MEX report was circulated among interested state officials only after it was acknowledged that the CFE representative on the committee had not been in agreement with many of the opinions expressed in the document.

The majority report analyzed the history of the industry and its relations with regulatory agencies since 1942 and confirmed what the interested parties had already known intuitively: existing laws and their regulations dealing with the financial aspects of the electric power industry, although similar to the regulatory systems in many other countries, simply did not work in Mexico. According to the document, this situation, which was endangering the future of the power industry as a whole, was due to a combination of institutional, historical, and general factors that could not be overcome without a complete overhaul of the regulatory mechanism and a radical departure from the practices followed in the past by everyone concerned.

The assumption that the state could underwrite the financing of the industry's expansion was found to be completely unrealistic on both economic and political grounds. It was concluded that: "There is no possibility of finding a satisfactory solution to the financing of the power industry under the present regulatory system. At the same time the urgent problem must be tackled of substituting this system with another that, utilizing Mexican and foreign experience, can permit the realization of the industry's investment programs in a manner offering new advantages (or fewer disadvantages) for the general interests of the country." [3]

CEE-MEX estimated the total cost of electrification programs for 1954–1963 at nearly U.S. $400 million, evenly divided between local currency costs and foreign exchange expenditure. But whereas some 50 per cent of the electric power investment during the ten-year period 1944–1953 had been financed out of federal subsidies, including domestic public credits, it was now recommended that the net financial contribution by the state to the development of the industry be cut to a nominal proportion (5 per cent) of the total outlays. The committee assumed that once the regulatory laws were overhauled, electricity rates drastically raised, and the financial structure of the private companies improved, obstacles to loan operations with the international institutions would disappear. The committee asserted, therefore, that the necessary funds should be mobilized by raising new private domestic capital, by reinvesting profits, and by procuring foreign loans.

For all this to happen, however, in the opinion of the committee majority, the following general conditions would have to be fulfilled: the text of the new legislation would have to give firm assurance of adequate returns to all the segments of the industry, including state-owned enterprises; confidence would have to be instilled regarding the continuity of such a policy; the level of returns would have to follow trends of interest rates in the domestic capital markets; and specific financial instruments would have to be created to permit domestic private investors to participate in the power industry.

Since such a policy was hardly possible under the existing legislation, CEE-MEX outlined in detail the characteristics of a new regulatory system to supersede the one established in the late thirties under the Ley de la industria eléctrica. The new legislation, the experts insisted, would have to be written with the greatest possible clarity, thus making it unnecessary to issue additional regulations or to make frequent modifications in the law itself. It was also deemed vital that direct federal intervention in the regulatory process be eliminated except in cases of national emergency. The regulatory control of the whole power industry should be given to a new autonomous agency, the Comisión Reguladora de la Industria Eléctrica (electrical industry regulating commission), whose members would be designated by the president. The Comisión Reguladora would act independently; its rulings would be subject to veto by the executive branch (through the Secretaría de Economía Nacional) only in the event the agency should breach statutory levels of the industry's net returns, as set by the proposed new law. The committee estimated that net profits of the industry after taxes should be fixed at 12 per cent of its capital assets, thus enabling two thirds of the profits to be distributed to shareholders and the rest made available for reinvestment.

The massive report prepared by CEE-MEX resulted in a few secondary improvements in the relations between the state and the private power companies. It paved the way for the reorganization of the American & Foreign Power properties under Mexican corporate law and the introduction of some measure of order into the companies' accounting procedures, which had been the subject of perennial controversies with the regulatory agencies. In addition the mere knowledge that such a study was under way may have stimulated the companies' investment plans in the mid-fifties and helped the country in its Washington negotiations for international power development loans. But after its completion in 1957, the report was quietly shelved and subsequently forgotten.

The majority members of CEE-MEX would have been guilty of considerable political naïveté if they had believed that their proposals had a ghost of a chance of being translated into action. The fatal shortcoming of the inquiry was the same as that found in many other august official investigations in Mexico and elsewhere. The majority members of the committee brought purely economic and technical points of view to bear upon the issues involved. It is true that the document, addressed to the highest state officials, discussed with considerable candor the many non-economic factors that were largely responsible for the failure of the regulatory process and for the uneasy relations between the state and the foreign-owned utilities. Unfortunately, however, the CEE-MEX study considered these problems as only secondary.

To most of Mexico's high officials, the CEE-MEX recommendations must have seemed little short of political dynamite. The implementation of the proposals would have resulted in a steep upward revision of electricity prices, followed almost automatically by annual rate increases in line with the rise in the industry's costs. If the state did not consider it politically feasible to put such government-owned enterprises as the railways and the petroleum industry on a sound financial footing by increasing the prices charged for their services, how could it be expected to launch a much more difficult operation involving sizable increases in the profits of foreign-owned companies and real or imaginary hardship for millions of electricity consumers? After all, the committee estimated that by way of incentive for the private companies to launch expansion programs commensurate with the country's needs, their annual profits would have to be increased to some $12 million a year in the 1954–1963 period, compared with only $3 million annually in the early fifties.

As the private industry's unofficial spokesman, Robert P. Wolfangel, admitted after the companies were nationalized: "Increased rates, no matter how small the increment, always brought adverse public reaction in Mexico. They could even lead to a political crisis which could cause foreign capital to look for a more stable environment." [4]

A sharp upward revision of rates would have brought more than the eruption of public hostility toward the foreign owners of the utilities. The *políticos* in the government knew that it would have also led immediately to the emergence of strong pressures in the electrical unions for the revision of collective contracts. Once the workers' demands were granted, the industry's cost would have increased once again and the process of continuous rate-wage adjustments would have picked up speed. Since the position of the electrical workers in Mexico is similar to that of the steel and automobile workers in the United States, union gains in the power industry would affect the general industrial wage level. In short, the implementation of the CEE-MEX proposals might have created more problems than they were meant to solve.

The committee's somewhat cavalier dismissal of some of the critical factors obstructing a reasonable *modus vivendi* between the state and the private power companies was not the only weak feature of the CEE-MEX recommendations. In their otherwise commendable attempt to put the power house in order, the authors of the inquiry invaded a field where no trespassing was tolerated. Not only did they regard the CFE as just another producer of electric power, on a par with the private companies, but they even suggested that the CFE be deprived of what the CFE itself and large sectors of public opinion considered one of the agency's most important *raisons d'être:* the function of planning, coordinating, and implementing national electrification programs and policies.

Only a belief in miracles would have led one to expect that almost twenty years after its inception, the CFE would be willing to relinquish its role of national power development planner, to deny itself free access to federal funds, and to accept the resurgence of the private companies as powerful and threatening competitors.

Besides, the CFE had powerful allies throughout the nation. These allies, the sworn enemies of foreign-owned utilities and foreign investment generally, were no less vocal during the postwar period than the coalition of consumers, *técnicos,* and trade unions that had pressed for the power industry's regulation back in the thirties. There was a basic difference, however. Before the war the campaign was led by *técnicos* and other intellectuals; but now the leadership was taken over by the newly organized class of smaller industrialists, grouped around the Cámara Nacional de la Industria de Transformación (CNIT), a business association established during the war, and carrying considerable political impact. The CNIT's attacks upon the private power companies represented one of many fronts on which the battle of nationalistic young entrepreneurs was fought against the older well-entrenched business groups that had cooperated with foreign capital. The two CNIT slogans in this particular field were "cheap power for national industry" and "electric power development by the state." In view of the political motivations of the group, it was absolutely irrelevant that, as a number of technical studies disclosed, electric power costs in the manufacturing sector were less than 1.5 per cent of total production costs and that increases in electricity prices could easily be passed on to the consumer.

The thesis of the CNIT, presented at its annual meetings and in innumerable books and pamphlets[5] issued during the period in which CEE-MEX was quietly pursuing its technical study, may be summarized as follows. The Mexican economy, especially the manufacturing industries, was suffering greatly because of continual increases in electricity rates, which boosted prices of domestically produced industrial goods and depressed the real income of its potential consumers. Electricity rate scales were the result of a secret bargaining process conducted between the powerful private companies and the federal regulatory agencies, in which neither consumers nor "national" industrialists were adequately represented. The CNIT maintained that the representation of consumers in the rate commission by the two national federations of industrialists and merchants (CONCAMIN and CONCANACO) was nothing but a practical joke.[6] Consequently, the CNIT insisted, the existing rate structure was set up without giving any serious consideration to income inequalities and the urgent need to provide cheap energy to nationally owned industries that were producing for a very limited domestic market. The steady increase in power prices was due mainly, if not exclusively, to the voracious appetites of the foreign-owned companies. Their profits were being repatriated under the curtain of secrecy, thus seriously limiting the availability of financial resources not only for the expansion of the electric power industry but for the country's industrialization as well. Thus, a circular process was set in motion, in which the interest of the Mexican state, industrialists, and individual consumers were constantly being sacrificed for the benefit of a small group of foreign monopoly capitalists.

Although a broad measure of agreement existed among CNIT leaders with respect to the diagnosis, opinion was quite divided concerning the policies to be followed to ensure an adequate supply of cheap power for the country. Most of the CNIT advisers, recruited in the main from professional engineering organizations, agreed on a number of secondary and sometimes internally contradictory points. They insisted that no solution could be had unless the climate of secrecy surrounding the real financial position of the companies and their relations with the CFE was destroyed and the consumers through CNIT given a voice in the industry's regulation. They maintained further that the rate structure should be revised in such a way that the well-to-do consumers would subsidize industry and the poorer classes. At this point unanimity tended to break down. The more radical people in the CNIT were calling for immediate confiscation of the private companies' property, on the grounds that their profits over the years exceeded many times the initial investment. Other industrial leaders were pressing for increased federal assistance to the public power sector and centralization of federal control and regulation. The last group also demanded an immediate inquiry into the reported abuses by the companies and the inefficiency of federal regulatory agencies, with a view to arriving at an early decision as to the source and manner of providing financial resources for the country's electrification.

Throughout the CNIT campaign against the private companies, which reached its peak around 1955, the CNIT argued that the electric power industry should serve the development of the country not only through the general supply of cheap electricity, but also by buying its capital equipment and supplies in Mexico. The country should without delay build a heavy electrical equipment industry, and the power plants should be forced to use more equipment of domestic manufacture. The CNIT leaders can hardly be taken to task for disregarding the inflationary implications of their own proposals; for, after all, they were not searching for logical solutions; they were presenting an action program meant to carry the widest possible national appeal.

It is highly problematical whether in the face of such a well-managed and articulate campaign the private power companies would have been able to restore in the eyes of public opinion the image of respectability lost in the thirties. In any case, they did not try very hard to do so. This was probably due to three somewhat contradictory reasons: First, the foreign-owned utilities underestimated the force of the appeal of their enemies to a larger sector of the Mexican society; secondly, they wrongly believed that the state was immune to such pressures and could dictate policy at will; and finally, because of the misfortunes and difficulties they had encountered in many other Latin American countries, they were prone on occasion to take a fatalistic attitude concerning their business future.

Thus, the main line of the private companies' counteroffensive took the dual form of direct pressure upon the regulatory agencies and the higher echelons of the state mechanism (in the expectation of obtaining more satisfactory rate rulings), and of lobbying in Washington, where external credits were negotiated. In addition, very prominent Mexican and foreign personalities were brought into the boards of directors of Mexlight and the American & Foreign Power Company, and financial advisory committees and other rather unorthodox public relations techniques were also employed.[7] All this, however, instead of bringing satisfactory results, provided the companies' enemies in Mexico with highly effective political ammunition and contributed to building resentment within the government itself. During interviews with the writer, Mexican officials with long experience in the utilities field recalled that whereas in the thirties, the Roosevelt administration allegedly vetoed a visit to Mexico on behalf of expropriated oil companies by an ex-U.S. Ambassador to Mexico, in the fifties another ex-U.S. Ambassador to Mexico was the honorary chairman of the board of one of the electric companies, and the board itself included a number of individuals who had held high office in the previous U.S. administration. The same Mexican officials complained about the relentless activity on behalf of the companies, conducted privately by many members of the U.S. Congress during periodic "good neighbor" visits to Mexico.

Relatively late in the day more sophisticated methods were introduced, and the art of public relations as known in the more developed countries was applied by the companies operating in Mexico. For this purpose, the Cámara Nacional de Electricidad, a national chamber of private electrical firms, languishing for almost two decades within the CONCAMIN (Confederación de Cámaras Industriales), was resuscitated and entrusted with a broad publicity campaign, aimed at convincing public opinion that the privately owned sector of the power industry was not necessarily one of Mexico's worst enemies. The chamber made a considerable effort to transmit to all its members a message to the effect that the interests of the large companies were identical with those of a few hundred owners of small private generating plants in the outlying provinces. The results of this campaign, accelerated in the late fifties, were meager, however, since by that time a number of small owners were in the process of selling their plants to the CFE.

Thus, in spite of its efforts, the role of the Cámara Nacional de Electricidad by the end of the fifties was reduced to that of a rather unwieldy forum, in which once a year real and imaginary complaints against the government and the CFE were aired. In these periodic sessions, formal appeals were made to the government to cease giving priority to the CFE in the field of new concessions for power generation, to grant adequate power rates and establish a climate favorable to private investment in the power industry, to eliminate the red tape in the regulatory agencies, to revise labor laws so as to deprive the electrical trade unions of the right to strike, and to extend the duration of collective contracts beyond the legally authorized two-year period.[8] However, participants in the chamber's annual meetings undoubtedly thought of themselves as only going through the motions, for never during the whole postwar period did the chamber actively participate in an organized way in the formulation of the electrical sector's policy vis-à-vis the government.

By the end of the fifties it became clear that the recommendations of the long-awaited CEE-MEX report would not be acted upon. The last large foreign credit for power expansion before the 1960 nationalization was granted to Mexico by the International Bank in 1958, and utilities circles were aware that the CFE was preparing a new loan application for presentation to the Bank covering a still larger sum to be devoted to financing its 1959–1965 program. Well-informed people were reporting from Washington that the international and U.S. agencies would require that any new loans be contingent upon the complete overhaul of the rate structure. But government action on this front was not forthcoming. The private companies, which in the mid-fifties had also drawn up new expansion plans, were marking time and drawing more and more on energy generated by the CFE. The process of periodic rate adjustment was dragging along as before, and the state and the foreign-owned companies had come to a total impasse.

It was at this moment, in the words of a well-informed observer, that "the big power companies seriously began to think in terms of selling out everything to the Mexican Government, provided a fair sale value would be agreed upon." [9]

Chapter 6

The Final Act

THE nationalization — or as Mexicans prefer to call it, the "Mexicanization" — of the two important private companies was consummated peacefully within less than six months between the spring and the fall of 1960. It consisted of two separate financial operations, involving the transfer, upon mutually agreed terms, of property with a book value of some $400 million. Then, as a final touch, the government in 1961 bought out the remaining privately owned generating systems of marginal importance.

The first of the two major steps came in April 1960 when the government acquired from the American & Foreign Power Company all of its properties for a price of $65 million. Other assets bought, including materials and supplies, fuel, and construction in progress, brought the total transaction to $70 million. At the same time, Nacional Financiera, the official development bank, which took over the administration of the acquired properties, assumed all outstanding debts of the American & Foreign Power subsidiaries amounting to $34 million. The purchase price of $70 million was substantially the same as the value which previously had been approved by the authorities as a basis for rate-making. The contract of sale provided for a down payment of $5 million. The remainder, including payment for construction in progress, was made payable in Nacional Financiera dollar obligations guaranteed by the government, maturing semiannually over a period of fifteen years and carrying an interest rate of 6½ per cent tax-free. American & Foreign Power agreed to reinvest in Mexico in non-utility enterprises the amounts received from these Nacional Financiera obligations as they came due. For this purpose a new investment company owned by American & Foreign Power was established after the conclusion of the deal. (This company's first industrial investment in Mexico took place in 1960; it consisted in minority participation in a $16.5 million aluminum smelter in association with Mexican investors and with the Aluminum Company of America.)

In the late summer of 1960 the properties of the Mexican Light & Power Company changed ownership, but in a somewhat different way. By agreement, the government acquired directly from the Belgian holding company Sofina and from individual investors 90 per cent of the outstanding Mexlight shares for a total of $52 million. This reflected a price somewhat higher than the stock exchange quotations before the beginning of negotiations. In addition, the Mexican government assumed the Mexlight medium and long-term debt amounting to $78 million. It is understood that the government's initial cash outlays in both of these huge transactions were financed out of a loan granted to Mexico in March 1960 by the Prudential Insurance Company of America, the first long-term credit, since the Porfirian era, granted by a private foreign financial institution to the Mexican government without any conditions attached to its use.

The purchase of the two power companies was hailed in Mexico as a step comparable only to the land reform of the early Revolutionary era and the expropriation of the petroleum industry by Cárdenas in 1938. During the celebrations in September 1960 following the consummation of the agreement with Mexlight, the country was covered with posters reading:

LAND — 1910

OIL — 1938

ELECTRIC POWER — 1960

The President of the Republic himself, Adolfo López Mateos, set the tone to these national festivities by announcing in his 1960 State of the Union Message to the Congress:

I must inform you of the policy implemented by the executive branch of the government under my responsibility regarding a matter of vital importance to the country, whose import and significance go beyond the fiscal year or a presidential term, embracing the future of Mexico, its development, and the generations which will succeed us. This policy is directed — *as in the case of petroleum* [italics added] and solid, liquid and gaseous hydrocarbons — to assure that the generation, transformation and supply of electric power will be carried out by governmental institutions, organs of the Nation, through which, as always, the Mexican people — as ultimate authority — will be present . . . On definitely Mexicanizing the electric power industry of the country, no harm was done to any legitimate rights or interests, and the procedures employed were in accordance with our general development.

The companies themselves hailed the transfer as a fair, just, and equitable deal. The American & Foreign Power Company's annual report to the stockholders explained its sale of Mexican properties in the following words:

This agreement is based on the belief that conversion of the Company's investment from the power business to industrial and commercial enterprises would result in improving earnings and would be beneficial to the Mexican economy. The Mexican Government was already predominant in the electric energy business, and it was apparent that the Government's share of the electric business in areas heretofore served by the Company's Mexican affiliates was necessary. Integration of the Government's properties with those of the Foreign Power affiliates could result in substantial economies of operation, and facilitate the raising of capital for future expansion as necessary.[1]

Mexlight executives, somewhat less enthusiastic, also paid tribute to the Mexican government's fairness, at the same time explaining their decision as a sheer necessity. Speaking at a time when secret negotiations had already begun, General Maxwell D. Taylor, then chairman of the company, had recalled that Mexlight was competing at a disadvantage in the money markets for new capital required for its construction program because its earnings in the previous years ran at about 6 per cent on the book value of common share investment, a return "substantially below" the percentage earned generally on common share equity by U.S. public utilities. Taylor gave to understand that under these conditions, the company was exploring all other alternatives, including, presumably, the sale of its properties to anyone willing to take the burden off its shoulders.[2]

Very little has been officially disclosed about the considerations which led to nationalization. There is, however, more than circumstantial evidence to the effect that the initiative came not from the state but from the foreign utilities themselves. The idea of selling their properties to the government did not occur to the companies suddenly in 1960. It is known, for example, that American & Foreign Power, just before undertaking its expansion program of the early fifties, had been contemplating such a move.[3] But when executives of that company arrived in Mexico in the latter part of March 1960, with an offer to negotiate the sale of its properties to the Mexican government, their decision was based on something more than the inability to get adequate profits from their investment in Mexico. It was a consequence of a much broader decision to get out, if possible under favorable conditions, from the utility business in most of Latin America, since the company's problems and difficulties in the whole region seemed to be growing to unmanageable proportions.

During the late fifties American & Foreign Power, with its properties in ten Latin American republics other than Mexico, was in serious conflicts with the authorities and the consumers in at least four of these countries. In Argentina, litigation was being fought in the courts about the amount of compensation to be paid for its properties transferred to public ownership in 1958. In Brazil, the State of Rio Grande do Sul took over the company's plants in Porto Alegre in May 1959. In Colombia, although the company filed rate increase applications in 1958, the matter was still dragging along in 1960. In Cuba, the American & Foreign

Power subsidiary was seriously affected by a law of August 19, 1959, reducing rates by over 20 per cent. In such circumstances, the company's executives obviously had to share the widespread opinion expressed in a leading U.S. utility journal in mid-1960: "For many years now the handwriting has been on the wall for foreign operators of electric power and other utilities in Latin America. It is believed in many quarters that in due time about all electric power supply will be government-owned and operated south of the Rio Grande and as far as Punta Arenas." [4]

The company's proposal to the Mexican government came at an appropriate moment because Mexico's access to public foreign loans for electric power expansion was blocked by the government's unwillingness to revise (and the political impossibility of revising) rate schedules as much as the companies sought. This does not mean, however, as the power companies claimed, that the federal government had planned for years to take over the industry. True, the minority parties of the extreme left (the Communist Party and the Partido Popular) included in their election platform of 1957–1958 a call for the industry's nationalization; and the left wing of the PRI (the government party), composed of intellectuals grouped around ex-President Cárdenas, asked for the elaboration of plans for eventually taking over the public utilities by the state. But neither the presidential candidate nor the official platform itself ever raised this issue. The declarations of the PRI leaders in 1958 were confined to assurances merely that the next administration would foster the electrification of the country as a part of over-all development policies.[5]

These attitudes did not change — at least on the surface — even after the purchase of the American & Foreign Power properties. The handling of the negotiations with that company indicates that the authorities wanted to keep the matter outside the political context, probably aware that the disclosure ahead of time would have created strong pressures from many sides for using the company's handicapped position to get the property at a bargain price. A source very close to the private electric power interests reported in 1961 that the negotiations were handled by the finance ministry and that: "In spite of the fact that the volume of annexes which accompanied the memorandum of offer made it physically impossible for anybody to thoroughly review them, it was from one day to the next that the net basic sale price was fixed at $65 million." [6] It is common knowledge that the highest officials of the Comisión Federal de Electricidad were not aware of the negotiations (a fact which may have been partly due to the government's intention not to transfer the newly acquired properties to the CFE). The breaking of the news to the public was handled in a perfunctory manner, the purchase of the American & Foreign Power plants being presented as a routine business operation. Finance Minister Antonio Ortiz Mena, in his opening speech to the 1960 annual banking convention, which started a day after the disclosure of the purchase, disposed of the matter in less than ten sentences.

All this makes a convincing case for an interpretation of the American & Foreign Power transaction as a fairly spontaneous deal in which the interests of the seller and the purchaser coincided for different, but mainly economic, reasons. It was probably only upon the conclusion of the negotiations that the government became aware that it might be desirable, not only on economic but also on political grounds, to solve the remaining part of the problem by buying out the Mexlight properties. Mexlight itself seemed to be caught by surprise. The over-all position in Latin America of the Belgian Sofina utility interests, to which Mexlight belonged, was much better at the time than that of American & Foreign Power. Mexlight's directors apparently did not make a decision immediately. On the surface, at least, life continued as usual. In early May of 1960, after the sale of the other company's plants had already been disclosed, Mexlight filed with the authorities a new rate application to compensate it for increased labor costs resulting from the revision of the labor contract earlier the same year. Nevertheless, the Mexlight executives evidently were impressed with the government's reasonable behavior in the earlier transaction. The government meanwhile came under certain pressures because of developments beyond the control of anyone in Mexico. Thus negotiations were not long in beginning. And their speedy conclusion was facilitated by the new developments affecting the government.

These developments had to do with Cuba. In the summer of 1960 Mexico was dragged into the crossfire of the U.S.-Cuban conflict. In the final week of June, the Castro government seized the Western-owned oil refineries and the U.S. retaliated by canceling the Cuban sugar quota and taking the matter of its speedily deteriorating relations with Cuba to the Organization of American States. All this was interpreted as a sign that the U.S. was finally getting tough and that it had decided to seek the establishment of a common hemispheric front to isolate the Castro regime. In the midst of political and diplomatic maneuvers preceding the meeting of the Western hemisphere foreign ministers in August 1960, the political temperature in Mexico rose almost to the boiling point. Not only on the Mexican left but in the governing party as well, the opinion prevailed that the Cuban regime was being persecuted mainly because of its hostility to the powerful private foreign interests and not because it represented any danger to hemispheric security.

The fact that the toughening of the official U.S. attitude coincided with the expropriation of the oil companies in Cuba reminded many Mexicans of their own country's conflict with the oil companies in 1938. In the Mexican Congress voices were heard from influential political figures to the effect that in these difficult times Mexico's duty was to stand by the side of Cuba. These statements, considered by the conservative domestic elements as a sign of an official turn to the left, shook the country and threatened the political equilibrium skillfully fostered by the successive presidents since the end of the Cárdenas administration. It seemed at times, during that summer of 1960, that things were getting out of hand and were leading toward the polarization of political forces into two powerful blocs led respectively by the pro-Cuban radicals and the anti-Cuban conservatives.

At this moment, the situation seemed to demand the restoration of national unity around a bipartisan issue, cutting across the lines of emerging and antagonistic political groupings. Such an issue had to fulfill a number of conditions: it had to have the broadest nationalistic appeal; it had to be in line with the traditions of the Mexican Revolution; and, obviously, it could not be an issue considered provocative by the U.S. government or public opinion in the United States. The nationalization of the electric power industry was probably the only available issue which could have helped to restore the badly needed feeling of national unity without greatly antagonizing anyone inside or outside the country. In taking over by peaceful means this sector of basic importance for economic development, the government would be able to show the public that it was continuing the policy of political and economic independence proclaimed in 1910; to prove to the left that it was unswervingly bent upon fulfilling the long-time objective of reducing the encroachments of foreign economic interests in the country; and to demonstrate to conservative domestic and foreign circles that what had to be done would be done in a legitimate and equitable manner, with concern for the interests of private investors.

It was clear to the officials involved that the success of a political maneuver of such magnitude depended to a considerable extent upon the behavior of domestic business groups, which in the past had never looked with enthusiasm upon the expansion of state participation in the economy. The government's fear of such a reaction may have played a part in the secrecy surrounding the negotiations with American & Foreign Power. But, with few exceptions, the reaction of the private sector to the purchase of that company's properties in the spring of 1960 was surprisingly mild. The domestic private sector, which only a few years back was bitterly divided between friends and enemies of foreign private investment, now looked upon the taking over of major foreign properties as unobjectionable in principle.[7] In the first place, the nationalization took place in a "basic" industry; and in the second, Mexican business had not played a major role in this field and had no desire to do so. Thus, the assurance of a favorable reaction on the part of the Mexican capitalists and entrepreneurs made the operation appear politically riskless.

The favorable reaction to nationalization by the major political groups from the extreme left to the extreme right vindicated the government's expectation. During the weeks and months following the taking over of the electric power industry, the image of national unity reappeared. There was no Mexican who at that time did not feel in a way proud that, in the midst of the Cold War extending toward the shores of the continent, the political leaders of his country were able to achieve a major national objective without having to push the country to the brink of a domestic or external conflict.

According to the statements of the finance minister on taking over the Mexlight properties, the nationalization of the industry had been dictated by a number of considerations.[8] First, said the minister, generating facilities would have to be doubled within the next eight years to match the increasing demand; private companies had no plans for making any sizable investment in power generating facilities, and hence the burden of financing the industry's expansion would fall upon the state. In addition, the absence of adequate planning in the electric power industry in the past had been due in part to the existence of two incompatible segments of the industry; hence this incompatibility had to be ended. Finally, because of deficiencies in the legislation in force, the concessions of the private companies had been of practically indefinite duration and thus the only way left to take over the industry was to buy out the private concessionaires.

The spokesmen of the government hoped that nationalization would make it possible to integrate the generating and distribution systems on a national scale. They hoped that financial outlays by the government would be unnecessary, since the reorganized power companies would be barred from access to federal resources to offset operating deficits. Although the purchase of the private utilities represented a heavy foreign-exchange cost, it was argued that this was a once-and-for-all transaction which would stop a continuous drain on the balance of payments, represented by transfer of earnings and sizable administrative expenses and substantial salaries to the foreign management.

Official declarations neither spelled out any details of the future structure of the integrated industry nor threw any light upon the role of the Comisión Federal de Electricidad in the new setup. At least for the time being, the two purchased companies were to continue to function as separate entities — one to be managed by an undersecretary of the finance ministry and another by an undersecretary of the ministry of industry and commerce, both released from their federal posts.

Whether or not the authorities had clear ideas at the time of the nationalization on how the state-owned industry should be run, the *técnicos* inside and outside the CFE were in general agreement that the needed operative efficiency could be achieved only if the separate entities were integrated into one centralized agency and the principal transmission systems were interconnected and merged into one national grid covering the whole country.[9] They believed that electricity rate structures would have to be modified for the purpose of fostering access to cheap electricity for the rural areas and that labor conditions would have to be made uniform through the establishment of a single national electrical trade union.[10]

Circumstantial evidence suggests that the taking over of the private companies by the state did not lead to a sudden disappearance of past problems — and even that new ones thereafter emerged. These new problems are directly related to the weight of the electric power industry, taken as a whole, within the Mexican economy and within the Mexican public sector. Prior to nationalization, relations between the state and the foreign-owned segment of the industry were shaped by the interaction of the different government interests and labor, consumers, foreign investors, and managers. Nationalization did not bring a new unity of interest among the government, labor, and consumers. It created a new conflict in the relations between the managers of the new nationalized industry and the rest of the federal government. After 1960, the government had to cope with the tendency of the *técnicos* within the CFE to try to create a state within a state.

Although the nationalized electric industry of Mexico accounts for only about 1 per cent of the gross national product, its relative importance in the economy has to be measured by the fact that it absorbs about one eighth of total public investment, and that its labor force exceeds 40,000 people. In addition, because of the high priority given to the country's electrification, the relative role of this industry will grow with the passage of time. Though political power is highly centralized in the office of the president in Mexico, public enterprises have always shown an incredible ability to escape effective federal control.

Accordingly, the government has not found it easy to make a decision centralizing the electric power industry under one agency. The decision has probably been rendered still more difficult by a desire to assure political equilibrium between the forces of the left and the right. Among conservatives, the management of the CFE — the only group that could run an integrated industry — has been regarded as a concentration of left-of-center nationalists with strong statist tendencies. The government, therefore, has been slow to move on this front.

Just as the integration of the industry, long urged on economic and technical grounds, has been held in abeyance by political considerations, the integration of the labor force into a single trade union also has become quite difficult. At the time of nationalization, the electrical unions were organized into three separate groups, covering the three major segments of the industry: Mexlight, American & Foreign Power, and the CFE. The first two groups had a long tradition. Their political role reached its apex under the Cárdenas administration, and they succeeded in wresting from the foreign power companies wages and fringe benefits unknown in other industries. Consequently, their prestige was high in labor circles and among the general public for the successful defense of their interests in the face of "the onslaught of the greedy foreigners." The union of the CFE workers came later; and though it became more than twice as strong numerically as the two older unions, it trailed behind in winning wage concessions and other benefits.

Successive administrations had considered it a useful policy to give free rein to the Mexlight and American & Foreign Power workers so that the government could count on their support in conflicts with the companies. But in the case of the CFE the government was the employer. Here, a too liberal policy could easily lead to unrest in other parts of the labor world. Consequently, the policy of the CFE union leaders was to get assurances from the government that the economic and social gains of its members would not remain too far behind the advances obtained in a somewhat less peaceful way by the workers in the private power companies.

The purchase of the foreign utilities stirred the labor unions to action. The objectives were to create a single labor body and to bring the contracts in the plants of the CFE and American & Foreign Power in line with the conditions prevailing in the Mexlight properties. Even more radical demands were heard in late 1960 — for sizable increases in wages and fringe benefits in view of the fact that "the industry now belonged to the nation," and for workers' participation in the management of the industry. All these suggestions were flatly rejected as demagogic outbursts of irresponsible union leaders. The expected growth of the industry, it was said, would result in automatic improvement of the economic and social conditions of the workers, but for the time being sacrifices were expected from everyone concerned. Since the nationalized industry did not aim at operating at a profit, there was no justification for the unions' demands. As far as the workers' participation in the management was concerned, it was declared out of the question. "The federal government," according to a newspaper report, "has not forgotten past experiences, particularly in regard to two activities which were the headaches of their time, the railroads and the petroleum industry. The government did not purchase the electric companies at a cost of 600 million pesos in order to turn them over to the workers. From the experience gathered over the years the government has recognized fundamental errors in this system or practice which was followed in the Ferrocarriles Nacionales and presently in Petróleos Mexicanos." [11]

When the pressures of the union leaders did not subside, the managers of the nationalized enterprises adopted a progressively tougher line, warning the workers in the future not to expect any more than existing labor legislation required. The new collective contract negotiations between the nationalized Mexlight and the Sindicato Mexicano de Electricistas in late 1961 differed very little from the pattern of the previous bitter negotiations with the foreign management. Mutual recriminations and accusations were heard — alleged sabotage committed by the workers and alleged exploitation by the management — and the final settlement was reached only through the intervention of the labor ministry.[12] As a result, existing misgivings against merging the three separate electrical unions hardened, and the idea of unification was dropped.

All this should not obscure the fact that one of the most important problems confronting the industry found a rapid solution within little more than a year after nationalization. Immediately after the purchase of the foreign power companies, flat denials had been made that the rates would be increased in the near future. In mid-1961, however, the first cautious official voices suggested that a rate revision would be necessary because of the need to mobilize large resources for the expansion of electric power facilities vital to the country's development. But even then, the work of a special committee which had been set up to study the financial implications of the nationalization was kept secret. It was only in late 1961, when that body had its recommendations ready, that the authorities entered into consultations with organizations in the private sector. When the rate changes were made public early in 1962 the spokesmen for business, labor, and consumers declared them just, necessary, and unavoidable.[13] Such protests as occurred were narrowly based and short-lived.

In mid-January of 1962 the electricity rate system was completely overhauled along the lines recommended by the special committee. The new national rate structure put an end to the situation existing in this field since the thirties. At the time of the rate overhaul over 150 different rate structures existed, based upon generation and distribution costs in individual plants, with regional differences for similar services of as much as 300 per cent in extreme cases. In general, the highest rates were charged in the least developed areas where, because of the scarcity of demand, the lack of water resources, and the obsolescence of the thermal plants, the unit costs were usually the highest. With the change in rates, the country was divided into three broad areas, and within each area an appropriate median for all types of services was fixed. This led to a considerable increase in rates in the low-cost regions such as the industrial center of Monterrey, a slight increase in the metropolitan area around Mexico City where more than half the total generated power of the country is consumed, and sizable reductions in the backward states of the South and Southeast.

At the same time the government managed to do for itself what it could not permit the private companies to do, namely, to increase the over-all level of rates. The over-all upward revision of rates amounted to some 17 per cent and was estimated to increase the industry's annual revenue by some 400 million pesos, eliminating the operating deficit of the CFE and bringing the annual net profits of the power industry as a whole to 5 per cent of invested capital. The system of applying different rates according to end-use was retained, but the pattern was altered considerably. Residences and industrial plants bore the brunt of the changes. In the case of residences, the fixed contract charges were cut down for the benefit of small consumers, and a system of rates that had clearly benefited the larger consumers was abandoned in favor of a straight-line rate schedule. Industrial rates were increased in most cases by about 40 per cent and commercial rates by somewhat less. Agricultural rates, primarily for irrigation purposes, were left unchanged, presumably for future adjustment; and the subsidized rates for small industrial establishments which mill corn and produce *tortillas*, the staple food of the low-income groups, were also kept at the previous very low levels.

The upward readjustment of rates reopened to Mexico the door to external public borrowing for electrification. Less than half a year after the new rate schedules were put into effect the International Bank granted Mexico the equivalent of 130 million U.S. dollars to finance foreign-exchange expenditures on a four-year investment program elaborated by CFE *técnicos* for the whole industry. The program called for a total expenditure of $435 million for the construction or expansion, before the end of 1965, of thirteen thermal plants and ten hydroelectric projects with a total capacity of 2.4 million kilowatts, equivalent to all the generating capacity added in the country between 1945 and 1960. It appeared in 1963 that the foreign-exchange expenditure under the program would exceed the $130 million loan and that the authorities expected additional credits from the Export-Import Bank and exporters of heavy electric equipment in Europe.

Looking back at the circumstances surrounding the purchase of the private electric utilities in 1960 and its consequences, one comes to the conclusion that although the nationalization led to a heavy drain on the country's external resources and did not result in the reorganization and integration of the industry as suggested by the *técnicos*, it was a wise undertaking in more ways than one. In terms of internal politics, the 1960 operation not only helped to preserve domestic peace endangered by Cuban developments, but instilled in the Mexican people an additional measure of self-respect as once more they demonstrated their ability to run efficiently a technologically complex industrial activity.

The challenge of new problems arising from the nationalization was met by the state with the astuteness characteristic of seasoned politicians. The economic advantages of the recommendations made by the *técnicos* were carefully weighed against the potential political dangers arising from the integration of the industry's management and labor unions into nation-wide blocs. The final decisions in these fields were postponed *sine die,* but where decisions could not be postponed, as in the case of the rate revision, they were framed in a manner which coincided with the popular conception of the public interest.

Even the style in which the 1960 deal was done yielded major benefits to Mexico. There is no doubt that because of the difficult — if not hopeless — position of the companies in the late fifties the Mexican government could have arranged the transaction on much more favorable terms. Clearly it would have been possible to save many millions of dollars by putting the purchase offer on a take-it-or-leave-it basis; but such a saving might have been costly to Mexico in terms of future hostility on the part of foreign business interests. The Mexican state did not consider it advisable to provoke the enmity of two powerful foreign enterprises and was eager not to destroy its good relations with international public and private financial centers. The power companies, on their side, performed equally well. No complaints were issued publicly by them; on the contrary, ample publicity was given in the United States, Canada, and Europe to the gentlemanly behavior of Mexico. To the extent that Mexico's liberal attitude toward the companies helped to retain confidence in the country's political and economic future among foreign investors and in international financial circles, the price paid was well justified. Access to international financing resources was now restored and the basis for future expansion of electric power facilities vital for Mexico's sustained economic growth was assured.

Chapter 7

Epilogue

DURING the sixty years or so of foreign-owned utilities operations in Mexico, relations between the state and the private power companies passed through a number of stages which step by step encroached on the companies' "sovereignty" and brought about the ascendancy of the public sector in the field. Beginning with the 1930's, when utility regulation was first introduced into Mexico, all interested parties — the state, the electrical unions, and the consumers, on the one hand, and the foreign utilities, on the other — regarded their mutual relations as a condition of warfare. Consequently, a large part of the Mexican public was convinced that the 1960 nationalization measure was the inevitable victorious outcome of battle with the companies, whereas the owners and managers of the privately owned utilities regarded it as the final step of capitulation to a government long bent on capturing them.

A thorough investigation of the historical record does not support these views, though it does strongly suggest that the government takeover of the electric power industry was a logical solution of the impasse reached in this field in the postwar period. The reasons for nationalization were actually more complicated than the warring parties themselves realized. Their hostile relations were dictated not only by their partially conflicting immediate interests but by a series of other factors over which neither had full control. Efforts at accommodation, such as those essayed in a half-hearted way in the 1950's, faced overwhelming odds. Such accommodation would have been possible in the long run only under two conditions: if the regulation of the utilities in Mexico could have been applied efficiently and rationally; and if the long-term objectives of the private companies had coincided with the state's economic development goals.

Utility regulation is a highly complex legal and administrative process. Even in advanced countries it has encountered serious difficulties because of conflicting pressures exerted by the utility owners and the consuming public. Since the regulatory process involves not only the establishment of fair, rational, and coherent laws, but also their fair, rational, and coherent implementation, the process faces formidable problems in an underdeveloped country fraught with political and social tensions. The matter is further complicated by the nationalism of developing societies in which the foreign-owned utility operates under monopolistic or quasi-monopolistic conditions, and by the inflationary pressures which accompany the development process and call for frequent revisions of electricity rates.

As we have seen, the difficulties inherent in utility regulation in Mexico had their roots in a clearly contradictory but probably unavoidable situation. All attempts to regulate the electric power industry since the late 1920's were patterned after the legislation in force in the more advanced countries, whose experience had only very limited application to Mexican conditions. Regulatory legislation in the advanced countries left only limited discretion to the enforcing authorities, but the margin of discretion left to the regulating authorities in Mexico was so great that the controls soon bore little resemblance to those in operation in other areas of the world. The regulatory system of Mexico was reduced to a bargaining process in which clearly political considerations on the part of the state were, as a rule, made to prevail over the confusing letter of the law. Keeping in mind the abuses claimed by Mexican consumers of electricity prior to the establishment of the regulatory mechanisms, the consequent general hostility toward foreign-owned utilities in Mexico, and the continuous attempts of the companies to influence the enforcement of the law, one cannot but wonder how utility regulation could have been expected to work.

The second and even more important difficulty had its origin in the impossibility of reconciling the companies' profit-maximizing objectives with the government's developmental objectives, among which the country's electrification held a very high priority. The foreign power companies came to Mexico at the end of the past century, convinced that Latin America offered very attractive prospects for investment in utilities. Because of the nature of their operations, however, they were the only group of foreign-owned firms subject to regulation in the interwar period. The profit performance of the utilities was held in check at a time when investment activities in other sectors were bringing excellent financial results. The private companies wanted their rates increased, and they wanted the assurance that the state would not intervene in the generation and distribution processes. The state, at the same time, was demanding that the companies contribute to national development by expanding generating capacity everywhere — not only within the major consumer centers but in other areas as well. But neither of the two sides could deliver what was needed for a mutually satisfactory *modus vivendi*.

It seems obvious in retrospect that the Mexican government was not in a position to allow foreign companies to adjust their rates upward, in view of their monopoly position and the formidable strength of Mexican nationalism. Nor was it possible to tailor rate revisions to conform to national interests; for such a modification would have had to entail not only a continual upward adjustment of rates, but also regional differentiations based on national development goals or simply on social equity. As a consequence, the companies refused to invest, particularly outside the traditional centers of demand for electric power. The state — aware of the importance of electrification for the over-all development of the country — had to move into the generation and distribution field.

Thus, by mid-1960 the only practicable solution to the impasse from the standpoint of Mexico's long-term interest was to place the entire electric power industry under direct government control. So ended the relations between the Mexican state and the private electric power industry.

THE BANKING SYSTEM

Money and the Goal of Growth

by
David H. Shelton

Chapter **I**

Mexican Finance Today

No part of the Mexican economy has a record of public-private intermingling which is more curious and provocative than that of the financial community. This record contains the germ of a Mexican answer to the ubiquitous riddle of public policy: will public initiative be servant, master, or partner of private initiative? In no Mexican field has the relationship been the subject of more experimentation and probing than in banking. My purpose is to survey the evolution of banking and related institutions as a case study in the more general history of public and private enterprise in Mexico.

As has been true with so much of the nation's economic life since the late nineteenth century, a great part of what has happened in its financial sector can be understood only in the context of Mexico's intense desire to end centuries of humiliation and poverty. The goal of economic development makes comprehensible much of the tortuous history of money, credit, and the institutions most closely linked to them in modern Mexico. For almost a century, Mexican leaders have sought financial entities and financial mores which would advance the national struggle for economic growth and social justice, however these happened to be conceived at the moment. The choices they made have gradually produced an indigenous Mexican approach to creating the "right" financial milieu for progress.

That which has emerged from Mexican experience with financial institutions is neither complete nor wholly consistent. It may or may not be permanently viable, and it may or may not have applicability to the problems of other nations. But Mexico has now played the game of growthmanship in banking for longer than most other underdeveloped nations, and she has played it with considerable skill. Her techniques, successes, and failures deserve a wider audience.

In Mexico the terms "public sector" and "private sector" are used with a special meaning. "Public sector" embraces more than fully governmental ownership and operation. It includes also a number of enterprises whose ownership is partly public and partly private but whose control is public. In this category belong the central bank and most of the other important public financial institutions, as well as some industrial, commercial, and agricultural enterprises. Further, funds from the public sector are often used in Mexico to assist essentially private firms, and representatives of public-sector entities may even be directors of such firms. For present purposes, an enterprise is presumed to belong to the private sector unless there is clear evidence of public dominance in its important policy decisions. Classified in this way, the banking system falls rather clearly into public and private groupings, and ambiguous cases are rare.

At the head of the group of public-sector entities stands the federal government of Mexico. Within the federal government, power is centered in the person of the president. The working out of the details of economic and other policies may be decentralized, but the federal executive is the final authority. Rarely does either the congress or the judiciary exert much independent influence or contravene the wishes of the president. Financial policies hence require at least the tacit endorsement of the executive and, when he wishes, they reflect also his specific philosophy and tactics.

In monetary and financial affairs, the most important federal entity is the Secretaría de Hacienda y Crédito Público, or ministry of finance. The man who heads this cabinet department is responsible for budgetary affairs and debt management. He also exercises effective control over many policies of the public-sector financial institutions, including the Banco de México, the nation's central bank.

Two commissions of the federal government, both under the general supervision of the finance minister, are closely related to the banking system. These are the Comisión Nacional de Valores (national securities commission) and the Comisión Nacional Bancaria (national banking commission).

The Comisión Nacional de Valores regulates the issuance of new private securities, authorizes registry in the securities exchanges, and may set coupon rates of interest. It also regulates the operation of private investment trusts (mutual funds). Since the Banco de México and the principal development bank, Nacional Financiera, continually intervene in the securities markets, the Comisión Nacional de Valores must work closely with these institutions. Its decisions often reflect their general policies and aims.

The Comisión Nacional Bancaria is the supervisory agency for technical aspects of bank operation. Mexico's banking laws provide for detailed regulation of many asset and liability categories, and the Comisión Nacional Bancaria must interpret, apply, and enforce these laws. It is also in a position to determine compliance with the Banco de México's edicts, and cooperates closely in implementing the Bank's intricate selective credit controls.

The business of banking is carried on by both public and private enterprises in Mexico.[1] In the public sector the banking entities are a group of state-controlled institutions known as "national credit institutions" or "national banks." The Banco de México is one of these. Together they loom quite large in the nation's total banking picture. At the end of 1962, the Banco de México had assets of 16.1 billion pesos, and the other national institutions 26.0 billion — a total of 42.1 billion. At the same time, all private banks combined had an asset total of 35.3 billion pesos.[2] A simple comparison of assets tends, however, to exaggerate somewhat the importance of the public institutions in everyday business transactions. Official government borrowing, particularly foreign borrowing, is often done through one of the national credit institutions, and funds allocated from the federal budget are often dispensed to developmental undertakings through those institutions. Such transactions swell the total assets and liabilities without necessarily indicating competition with private entities. Inside Mexico, financing of most sorts of activity and provision of routine banking services to the general public are predominantly private.

The Banco de México is the most powerful financial institution in Mexico, and it is also the chief operational architect of monetary policy. But both these statements must be qualified with an immediate recognition that there is no place in the Mexican conceptual scheme for an "independent" central bank. The Banco de México operates within the policy orientation set for it by the federal government. All important monetary actions of the Bank are subject to the veto of the finance minister, and the institution is expected regularly to place the financial needs of the public sector above whatever specifically monetary goals it may be pursuing. Nonetheless, the Banco de México does enjoy a status not shared by most other public-sector entities and does exert a significant independent influence on the course of economic policy. Its technical competence is respected by bankers in both the public sector and the private sector, and its management is regarded as skillful, impartial, and honest. This position of prestige and leadership is of comparatively recent origin, and is one measure of the success with which ancient and bitter differences between the government and the private banks have been ameliorated.

The duties and technical powers of the Banco de México are considerable. It is charged with the issuance of paper currency and coin, management of foreign-exchange reserves, stabilization of the external value of the peso (there is no exchange control), regulation of the internal money supply, and promotion of credit conditions conducive to economic growth. The Bank, in conjunction with Nacional Financiera, assists in handling the public debt and promotes a broader market for securities. The Bank also acts as commercial banker to the government, its agencies, and the national credit institutions. For carrying out these functions, the central bank has authority to engage in open-market operations in both public and private securities and to hold such securities as permanent investments; it may vary reserve requirements over a wide range and may specify not only the reserve ratio but also the composition of reserve assets; it may buy and sell gold and foreign exchange; it may rediscount or extend credit on many kinds of paper at rates both variable and differential; and it may set interest rates directly on a variety of private financial instruments. All institutions legally classified as "credit institutions" must become "associates" of the Banco de México and are subject to its regulation. As banks of all sorts meet the definition of "credit institution," this means that the scope of control by the central bank spreads much beyond commercial banking. Furthermore, where the Bank does not itself have direct power to act, desired results may often be obtained through the Comisión Nacional Bancaria or the Comisión Nacional de Valores.

Because the position of the Banco de México in public-private financial interrelationships is crucial, much of the discussion in later chapters centers on the development of the Bank. Its evolution epitomizes many of the strengths and weaknesses of the pragmatic philosophy that has shaped financial change. As the government has become more and more committed to economic growth as a goal, the central bank has become more and more the keystone of a banking system whose intended orientation is the financing of growth. As the definition of a policy for growth has become more complex, so the task of the Banco de México has become more intricate and demanding.

In 1961 there were nineteen other "national credit institutions" and a number of special funds, trusts, and other appendages to these or to the Banco de México. The national credit institutions are best thought of as a group of government-controlled investment banks, though they are quite diverse in character. In general, it is accurate to say that each of the national credit institutions was created to serve a special and limited purpose and is comparatively inactive outside its own province. Most of the individual institutions are small and depend heavily on allocations from the government budget for their loanable funds. A few, however, are large and exert a broad influence throughout the Mexican economy.

Among the large ones, the most important by far is Nacional Financiera. Since this entity is the subject of a separate paper in this volume, it will be given but summary treatment here. In brief, Nacional Financiera is a large development bank with power to promote and finance economic enterprises, assist them technically, and even operate them. It also has power to underwrite, market, and trade freely in securities of all kinds. Working with the government, Nacional Financiera has facilitated public-sector investment in transportation facilities, irrigation projects, electric power installations, and other overhead capital. Working with private firms or on its own, it has created or expanded industrial enterprises of many kinds. Working with the Banco de México, it has tried to encourage savings and create a broader market for securities, public and private. As agent for the federal government, Nacional Financiera has sought, obtained, and distributed very large credits from abroad. Without serious exaggeration, Nacional Financiera may be regarded as the main channel through which the system of national credit institutions affects industrial development and influences the internal money markets.

Also of importance is the Banco Nacional Hipotecario Urbano y de Obras Públicas (national urban mortgage and public works bank). This institution devotes itself primarily to financing state and municipal public works and developing low-cost housing. In another area, the Banco Nacional de Comercio Exterior (national bank for foreign commerce) deals mainly in short-term credits for the stimulation of exports, particularly agricultural exports. Through related institutions it has also collaborated importantly in government efforts to hold down the cost of living for the urban poor. Two agricultural banks assist the farmers. The Banco Nacional de Crédito Agrícola (national bank for agricultural credit) deals with agricultural credit societies and individual farmers, and the Banco Nacional de Crédito Ejidal (national bank for ejidal credit) is concerned with the financing of *ejidos,* semi-collective agricultural enterprises which have risen to prominence with the Mexican land reform. Several lesser banks serve particular crops or restricted geographic areas. An increasingly significant institution, the Patronato del Ahorro Nacional (trusteeship for national saving), has successfully marketed substantial quantities of national savings bonds to the non-bank public.

Private institutions classed as part of the banking system include commercial banks (banks of deposit and discount), savings banks, industrial finance companies (*financieras*), mortgage banks, fiduciary companies, capitalization banks, and savings and home loan banks. Mexican banking law is at some pains to keep kinds of banking separated along functional lines, though commercial banks normally have savings and trust departments.

Until after World War II, the commercial banks were Mexico's only significant class of private financial institution, and their commercial banking function tended heavily to overshadow their savings and trust activities. Since the war commercial banks have lost some of their dominance, but at the end of 1962 they still possessed some 56 per cent of the assets of all private banking institutions.

In second place and growing rapidly are the private *financieras.* These are institutions which accept time deposits, sell certificates of deposit, and market longer-term debt liabilities in order to supply medium-term to long-term credit and equity capital. The *financieras,* because they were created to be instruments for promoting industrial and related developments, have broad legal powers and are the most versatile of Mexican banks. Their versatility and their usefulness as outlets for the closely regulated funds of commercial banks have permitted the *financieras* to grow to major proportions. They are the first class of financial institutions other than commercial banks to attain significant size within the private sector. By the end of 1962 the private *financieras* held some 38 per cent of the total assets of private banks.

Mortgage banks are also of some importance, especially in the financing of residential construction. In 1962 these institutions had about 2 per cent of the assets of private banks, but beyond their assets proper they assist in real estate financing by acting as guarantors of a kind of mortgage certificate, the *cédula hipotecaria,* issued by individual borrowers and widely held in Mexico. *Cédulas* in circulation at the end of 1962 totaled roughly three times the assets of mortgage banks. Other types of banking institution are so small as to merit little mention; together they possessed about 3 per cent of private bank assets.[3]

As noted above, each type of private financial institution is limited in the range of operations which it can legally perform. No single institution can offer all the financial services which a client might need. Historically, this specialization was intended to promote the growth of institutions outside commercial banking and to prevent the commercial banks from supplying kinds of credit which would threaten their liquidity. This strategy failed. The imposed specialization, together with the limited demand for many kinds of banking, long inhibited the growth of all *but* commercial banks.

In recent years other banks have grown rapidly, but not altogether independently. Institutions found it advantageous to band together because they could thereby reduce competitive pressures, enhance profit opportunities, and cushion the impact of Banco de México regulation. Financial "groups" consisting usually of a major commercial bank, a strong *financiera,* and lesser insurance, banking, or similar firms have come to dominate private finance. These groups are often allied with a circle of commercial or industrial firms which absorbs a considerable part of the credit which the financial entities are able to provide.

Financial markets in Mexico have notable peculiarities. Despite great post-1940 expansion and diversification, they are primarily debt markets rather than markets for equity securities. Even within this limited scope, short-term transactions predominate. Individually arranged transfers of funds far outweigh public offerings of securities in aggregate importance, and it seems improbable that borrowers often have many alternative sources of credit. Indeed, it seems reasonable to speak of a "market" for funds only in Mexico City and two or three other large cities. Both public and private financial institutions have sought with some success to increase the importance of security sales as sources of funds and to popularize securities as an outlet for the personal savings of a broader sector of the public. But by the end of 1962, fixed-income debt obligations outstanding totaled no more than about 22.9 billion pesos (some 1.8 billion dollars at the exchange rate of 12.5 pesos per U.S. dollar). Of this amount, about 72 per cent consisted of debts contracted by public-sector entities; about three quarters of this public-sector debt was held by the financial system or within the public sector itself. Of the 28 per cent of total fixed-income debt that originated in the private sector, the great bulk was held by private enterprises or individuals.[4] The smallness of the 22.9 billion figure for fixed-income debt obligations accurately suggests that long-term lending is not yet a large source or use of funds in Mexico. Equity securities are outstanding in considerable quantities, but they are not widely distributed and are rarely traded in volume. Organized securities exchanges do a fair volume of business in Mexico City, and a small amount in Monterrey and Guadalajara. Almost all of this is in fixed-income securities, mainly debts of public-sector entities.

Even the modest amounts of fixed-income securities in circulation tend to exaggerate the extent to which money is lent for more than short periods. One of the most striking aspects of Mexico's money markets is the fact that almost every liability of the government, the national credit institutions, and most of the private banks has been given nearly perfect liquidity. Government bonds have been supported at par or near it for over two decades. Issues of the Nacional Financiera are likewise supported at par. Most private *financieras* support their securities, and mortgage banks will purchase (or make loans against) *cédulas hipotecarias* and *bonos hipotecarios* (mortgage bonds) on demand. All or a substantial portion of time and savings deposits can be had by the depositors when desired. All these practices, which began with efforts to make government paper attractive to investors, have so permeated the debt market that the whole structure resembles a "call money" market almost without regard to the technical maturities of the various instruments employed. This situation could not endure without tacit assurance that the Banco de México will support the market in the face of any sustained liquidation.

This assurance has been present, though the need actually to use central-bank credit for maintenance of liquidity has tended to diminish. The public sector, especially the Banco de México, has long looked with disfavor on guarantees of absolute liquidity by the private institutions, but has not felt free to demand the abandonment of such guarantees. New legislation promulgated in late 1962 seems to place significant restrictions on the degree to which some financial institutions, notably *financieras* and savings banks, can supply cash on demand to holders of their liabilities.[5]

Interest rates in Mexico seem surprisingly high when one considers the liquidity afforded most securities, the moderateness of inflation in recent years, and the size and diversity of the financial system. Rates are, in fact, high by comparison with levels in developed nations. But they do not compare unfavorably with rates paid by borrowers in other capital-poor countries in the process of rapid economic development.*

In the private sector, commercial bank loans at short term to business borrowers in mid-1962 cost some 10 per cent to 12 per cent. Intermediate-term loans from private *financieras* cost established borrowers 14 to 18 per cent. Small businesses often paid 20 to 30 per cent or more when funds could be had, and a true rate

---

* Comprehensive and reliable data on interest rates are not available for Mexico. A maze of legally fixed rates and supported securities puts limits on the usefulness of much of the published interest-rate material, and a variety of subterfuges produces a considerable difference between apparent rates and actual rates paid. The rates cited here (apart from several which are enforced legal maxima) are those most frequently mentioned by Mexican bankers and businessmen in interviews conducted during 1961 and 1962 or encountered in other informal sources. They apply to funds obtained within Mexico. In the case of money borrowed abroad through official institutions and re-lent within Mexico, interest rates are generally lower.

for many secured consumer loans was 36 per cent. Suppliers of funds who saved via savings accounts received only 4½ per cent, but 8 per cent could easily be had with *cédulas hipotecarias;* and 11, 12, or even more could be earned on private *financiera* liabilities. Most equities bought at market prices were yielding 6 to 10 per cent in the early 1960's.

The public sector presents a more mixed picture. Except for Nacional Financiera itself, the financial institutions in the public sector borrow comparatively limited amounts, and the interest rates they pay reflect support of their securities by the Banco de México and Nacional Financiera. State governments borrow very little and do so mainly from public-sector financial entities on preferential terms. The federal government has been consistently unrealistic in the terms offered on internally issued debt since the 1930's, and its 5 per cent bonds are not purchased voluntarily in appreciable quantities. One agency of the federal government, the Patronato del Ahorro Nacional, has successfully marketed quite large quantities of national savings bonds at a yield of over 7 per cent (plus a lottery feature). Nacional Financiera has tried to attract savers to its security issues through attractive terms as well as through guaranteed liquidity. Yields on new peso securities issues by Nacional Financiera in 1962 ranged as high as 10 per cent.[6]

Interest rates apparently rose between the middle 1950's and 1962, though neither the magnitude nor the consistency of the rise is precisely ascertainable. Money rates of interest drifted upward only moderately. But real interest rates climbed more rapidly because of the slowing of inflation. This period of rising interest rates was one in which external and internal shocks to the Mexican economy were mild and in which the Banco de México maintained fairly secure control over the money supply. Competition among financial institutions for loanable funds was intense, and strenuous efforts were made by both public and private institutions to induce people with savings to hold bank liabilities in lieu of other assets.

Recent vigorous competition for savings in an environment of moderate monetary restraint has highlighted a circumstance which has complicated Mexican development for a long time. This is the shortage of voluntary savings and investible public-sector revenues which persists despite exhortations to save, assured liquidity, high interest rates, and piecemeal fiscal reform. Rarely, it appears, have such funds sufficed to finance the volume of investment desired by public and private investing entities.

One consequence of the inadequate supply of investible resources has been a heavy emphasis by the government and its financial arms on systematic efforts to force funds to flow in certain directions. At least since World War II, a conceptual dichotomy between "productive" and "unproductive" uses of funds has been reflected in public policy. Financial institutions are subject to rigorous selective controls whose purpose is the diversion of funds toward "productive" uses and away from "unproductive" uses, as well as to general quantitative regulations on the creation of new credit.

A "productive" use of funds has, in general, been considered to be one which permitted direct expansion of the output of things consumed heavily by low-income and middle-income groups, or one which helped increase exports, or which furthered substitution of domestic products for imports. Thus, the provision of fixed and working capital for most agriculture, industry, or mining has been considered a "productive" use of funds. Financing of low-cost housing is "productive." Financing of elaborate facilities for the tourist trade is "productive." But the financing of larger inventories tends to be regarded as an "unproductive" use of funds and is discouraged. So are credit to consumers, lending for luxury housing, and financing of many service or distribution facilities. Providing money for public-sector investment is considered "productive" by definition.

Controls have been accompanied by a vigorous effort to encourage the growth and diversification of financial institutions, public and private. Through such growth and diversification, it is hoped, a higher rate of saving will be stimulated and a larger share of total saving will flow through the network of financial institutions. Despite these efforts, however, the Mexican public still holds an accumulation of financial assets which seems small by comparison with total economic activity. Estimates by the Banco de México of the "liquid assets" of private enterprises and individuals indicate that these totaled but 36.0 billion pesos at the end of 1962, a year in which the nation's gross national product amounted to 177.5 billion pesos. The liquid asset total has been growing rapidly in recent years both absolutely and by comparison with gross national product. For the five-year period from 1957 to 1962, liquid asset holdings of enterprises and individuals increased by some 76 per cent while the gross national product at current prices was rising about 55 per cent.[7]

In the accompanying table Mexico's gross national product, the level of prices, investment rate, and money supply are shown for 1939, 1940, and each calendar year from 1945 through 1962. These figures accurately suggest that change has been proceeding at a fast clip. For more than two decades economic growth has been continuous, though variable. It has been accompanied by rapid monetary expansion and considerable, but diminishing, inflation. Throughout this period of accelerated change, public banking and private banking have played crucial roles in producing and shaping the course of economic development.

SHELTON, TABLE 1

Gross national product (GNP), prices, rate of investment,
and money supply in Mexico, 1939–1962

Year	GNP in current pesos[a] (billions)	GNP at 1950 prices[a] (billions of pesos)	Price index[b] (1950 = 100)	Gross investment as per cent of GNP[c]	Money supply Dec. 31[d] (billions of pesos)	Annual change[e]		
						GNP in 1950 prices (per cent)	Price level (per cent)	Money supply (per cent)
1939	6.8	20.5	33.2	9.8	0.92	—	—	—
1940	7.3	20.7	35.3	10.9	1.11	1.0	6.3	20.7
1945	20.5	32.0	64.1	11.2	3.59	9.1[f]	12.7[f]	26.5[f]
1946	26.1	34.1	76.6	12.6	3.51	6.6	19.5	−2.2
1947	29.0	34.5	84.0	14.3	3.49	1.2	9.7	−0.6
1948	31.7	36.1	87.9	14.3	3.99	4.6	4.6	14.3
1949	35.2	37.6	93.5	14.3	4.46	4.2	6.4	11.8
1950	40.6	40.6	100.0	14.7	6.12	8.0	7.0	37.2
1951	52.3	43.6	120.0	14.6	6.80	7.4	20.0	11.1
1952	58.6	45.4	129.1	13.9	7.08	4.1	7.6	4.1
1953	58.4	45.6	128.1	13.4	7.65	0.4	−1.0	8.1
1954	71.5	50.4	141.9	13.7	8.70	10.5	10.8	13.7
1955	87.3	54.8	159.3	14.4	10.52	8.7	12.3	20.9
1956	99.3	58.2	170.6	14.1	11.69	6.2	7.1	11.1
1957	114.2	62.7	182.1	14.1	12.49	7.7	6.7	6.8
1958	127.2	66.2	192.1	13.6	13.39	5.6	5.5	7.2
1959	136.2	68.1	200.0	13.3	15.43	2.9	4.1	15.2
1960	154.1	73.5	209.7	13.7	16.89	7.9	4.8	9.5
1961	163.8	76.0	215.5	14.0	18.01	3.4	2.8	6.6
1962	177.5	79.7	222.7	n.a.	20.27	4.9	3.3	12.5

n.a. = not available.

[a] In 1963, the Banco de México published a revised series of gross national product statistics. This revision applies to 1950 and subsequent years, and the figures shown in the table above for these years are the revised figures. The effect of this is to make comparison of years before and after 1950 somewhat misleading if the total time span is short (say, a comparison of 1949 with 1951). For comparisons involving a longer lapse of time (say, as much as four years), the revision either has little effect or actually improves the comparability of the data.

[b] The price index used is the GNP implicit deflator. It was derived from the indicated figures for GNP at current and at 1950 prices.

[c] Investment in fixed capital only.

[d] Non-bank public's holdings of coin, currency, and peso demand deposits.

[e] Percentages are computed.

[f] Annual rate for the period 1940–1945.

Sources: Banco de México, *Informe anual*, 1940 to 1962; Raymond Vernon, *The Dilemma of Mexico's Development* (Cambridge, Mass.: Harvard University Press, 1963), p. 199; Nacional Financiera, *Informe anual correspondiente a 1961* (pub. 1962), p. 38.

Chapter 2

Background of the Modern System

IT is difficult to understand Mexico's unique mixture of public and private enterprise in banking, or the purposes it is intended to serve, without considering what happened to banks before, during, and immediately after the Revolution which began in 1910. Pre-Revolutionary development created an image of banking and a set of banking concepts which have been slow to disappear. The Revolution itself wrought changes in governmental philosophy and in the capabilities of private banks. These changes go far toward explaining the attention lavished by post-Revolutionary governments on banking policy and the hostility and suspicion with which this attention was frequently received.

Until the middle 1930's, the banking system of Mexico was almost entirely in private hands. Public authority limited itself mainly to superficial regulation and to sporadic supplementation of private banking in unusual circumstances. The private sector, for its part, was principally concerned with minding its banking business and avoiding governmental interference with profit opportunities.

Nevertheless, the question of the government's relation to modern forms of credit, savings, and financial institutions had begun to arise during the latter part of the nineteenth century. Mexico's first enduring commercial bank appeared in 1864, and by the 1880's several banks had come into existence and had introduced to urban areas a variety of credit instruments, including the bank note and the demand deposit.[1]

In 1884, the government asserted its right to charter commercial banks and to regulate their operations. The government's emphasis at that stage was on maintenance of liquidity and prevention of fraud. In this regulatory pattern, banks continued to issue their own bank notes, but only upon authorization by the federal government and under fairly rigorous legal constraints which linked the maximum allowable note issue to the capital and cash reserve of the issuer bank. Throughout the years before the Revolution, issuance of paper money remained a private function performed under special concession from government. Apart from general laws and regulations, however, the government's control over banking was not onerous, and was limited largely to banks of issue. A financial writer of the pre-Revolutionary era described the extent of regulated institutions and functions as follows: "The banking system of Mexico consists of a plural monopoly in the emission of bank notes; of free contracting in mortgage and medium-term credit operations, although federally chartered institutions are more secure and are subject to legal regulation; and, finally, of absolute freedom in all other credit operations which, while they may be carried on by federally chartered banks, may also be carried on by everyone else . . ."[2]

Private banks quickly established themselves as an important force in the economy. This success was traceable to several circumstances favorable to their growth in the era of Porfirio Díaz (1876–1910). First, there was a numerically tiny but economically potent segment of the population which had real need for the services of the banks. This group was engaged in production for export, in the import of goods from abroad, and in large-scale domestic commerce. Its capital, personnel, and orientation were heavily foreign, and the banking services desired were those of the type offered by commercial banks in other lands. Second, a latent demand for credit existed within the indigenous agricultural aristocracy. The landlords often had little interest in obtaining credit for expansion of production, but they did have the desire to spend beyond their current incomes and they had real property which could secure bank loans. Finally, the Díaz government itself was anxious to have investment from abroad; and it especially wanted investment in banking because banks were a source of both domestic and foreign funds for a government often in need of money.

The Mexican environment, however, was much more favorable to the establishment of commercial banks than to other institutions. There was a demand for short-term credit for the financing of commerce, especially exports and imports; there was a demand for long-term funds to be used by the agricultural elite or in the construction and sale of urban real estate; and there was a sporadic demand for credit on the part of the government. But on the side of supply, though foreign capital was available for the founding of banks, there was very little financial saving which would support the operation of any institution which acted as a true intermediary. Commercial banks, to the extent that they were able to gain public acceptance of their liabilities, could exist and grow through creating credit, but other banking institutions faced a much less favorable prospect.

In the 1880's and 1890's, the commercial banks — that is to say, the banks authorized to issue bank notes — grew rapidly in size, but other banking institutions did not. Two basic types of institutions outside commercial banking, mortgage banks (*bancos hipotecarios*) and banks for medium-term credit (*bancos refaccionarios*), were authorized under the law. But as late as 1897 these institutions had assets totaling only about 10 million pesos and 8 million pesos, respectively, as compared with 137 million for the commercial banks.[3]

In that year the principal banking legislation of the pre-Revolutionary period was promulgated. Its chief designer, José Yves Limantour, was the most famous and influential of Díaz' finance ministers. He was anxious that Mexico have a more diversified set of banks, and particularly wished the medium-term credit banks to develop as aids to agriculture, mining, and manufacturing. Limantour's 1897 law empowered the mortgage and medium-term credit banks to perform all of the major functions performed by commercial banks *except* that of note issue, and gave them much more freedom than commercial banks both in raising funds and in financing economic activity.

Despite favorable legal treatment, however, the institutions lacking the power to create money continued to lag far behind those with this power. Limantour, in his preface to a 1908 banking reform, observed that there were many banks of issue but too few mortgage banks and banks for medium-term credit. The vacuum, he said, was even greater with regard to establishments organized especially to make loans for more than short periods to agriculture, to industry, and to commerce. In these circumstances, it was not surprising that commercial banks circumvented the banking laws which since 1884 had attempted to bind them to short-term loans. As Limantour went on to add in 1908: ". . . in the lack of special entities . . . the banks of issue have been compelled to deviate somewhat from the goal which is appropriate for them in order to satisfy . . . certain requirements of the development of the national wealth which render the funds of the establishment illiquid . . . for a greater time than truly commercial operations." [4]

Thus, only commercial banks established themselves strongly in Mexico before the Revolution. The extent of their expansion was impressive. In 1909, most of the 667 million pesos in banking assets belonged to these banks.[5] The accumulation of resources in the banking system at this time was greater relative to the total of economic activity than Mexico would have again until the middle of World War II.

The banking system of Díaz' Mexico was transplanted from abroad. It was foreign in concept and largely foreign in ownership and management. This alien character extended to banking law as well as to the institutions themselves. Mexican laws were copied from the laws and practices of Europe and North America with little allowance for the gulf between the level of economic development in Mexico and that in the model countries. The banks, in effect, were part of the enclave of foreign capitalist enterprises which thrived in feudal Mexico under Díaz. This copying of foreign patterns may have been inevitable. There were, after all, no other models to follow, and the banks along with the rest of the enclave could be considered a leading force in the economic growth of Mexico. But the foreign origin and foreign orientation of the banks were certain to bring trouble when the Díaz era gave way to the highly nationalistic Revolution.

The Díaz banks were deeply enmeshed in the web of special exemptions, rights, and privileges which constituted the government's approach to stimulating economic growth and serving its own interests. Banks of issue were severely restricted in number, and a special dispensation from the government was necessary to obtain a banking charter. Only twenty-odd banking firms were in operation as late as 1910. Two large firms, the Banco Nacional de México and the Banco de Londres y México, were allowed to monopolize commercial banking in Mexico City and to establish branches elsewhere. Certain regional banks also had special legal status, tax concessions, and favorable reserve requirements. This semi-monopolistic character was bitterly resented by the Revolutionary leaders of later years. It came to be symbolized by the power to issue notes, the authority which most clearly divided the favored and powerful banks of emission from other financial entities or private lenders.[6]

The banks in the pre-Revolutionary world were private, profit-making institutions pure and simple. They belonged to the ideological world of nineteenth-century capitalism. The bankers were neither required nor expected to do more than live within hailing distance of the legal and extralegal code of conduct laid down for them by a friendly government with which they could do a mutually profitable business. No conscious social role was asked of banking, and none was volunteered.

The years from 1910 to 1913, though signaling the beginning of the Revolutionary period, brought comparatively little disorder or damage to the banks. With the fall of Francisco Madero's gov-

ernment to Victoriano Huerta in 1913, civil war erupted in earnest
and the economic and political position of the banks deteriorated
rapidly. During most of his short rule, Huerta controlled Mexico
City. His regime was supported by many of the conservatives who
had backed Díaz, including most of the influential bankers. Many
of Huerta's expenditures were financed with bank loans, and
whether or not the banks had any choice in extending this credit,
they were placed in the position of supporting a corrupt and reac-
tionary regime — and one, moreover, which lost the struggle. As
disorder and civil strife engulfed more and more of Mexico, loss
of life, destruction of property, and paralysis of economic activity
grew apace. For the banks this meant chaos. Banking offices were
looted and records destroyed; depositors withdrew funds in panic;
the banks' note issues expanded; debts became uncollectable; and
the real value of the assets underlying the paper in bank vaults
steadily eroded.

When Venustiano Carranza and his followers established themselves in Mexico City in 1915, they saw the banks as supporters of
Victoriano Huerta and opponents of the Revolution. Accordingly,
they almost immediately included the investigation and reform of
banking in their crowded agenda. All changes in legislation made
by Huerta were abrogated, Huerta securities were repudiated, and
the banks were examined to determine their conformity with pre-
1910 banking law. The examination resulted in the revocation of
the charters of more than half the banks. In 1916, all banking
laws were revoked, and no new legislation was forthcoming. This
deprived the banks of legal existence, and they were placed in
liquidation, a state which came to resemble suspended animation
since little progress could be made in realizing assets or clearing
liabilities. The remaining metal reserves of the banks were "borrowed" by the government in 1917 to meet pressing fiscal needs.
For a period of more than five years Mexico had no functioning
domestic banks.[7]

Meanwhile a new monetary philosophy had been growing out of
the actions of the Revolutionary armies. In their battle to win the

country, the Revolutionaries were forced to print large sums of paper currency which eventually proved unmanageable and was repudiated. Carranza, who controlled Mexico from 1915 to 1920, defended reliance on paper money in words highly significant to later policy formulation: "From the time that the Revolution was unified through the Plan of Guadalupe [in 1913], I considered it necessary to resort to the system of issues of paper money, which, notwithstanding the disadvantages which they might carry for the future, afforded nevertheless — as a revolutionary procedure — the advantage of being the *most just distribution of loans* among the inhabitants of the regions occupied by the revolutionary armies . . ." (italics added).[8]

Power to print paper currency was thus employed by the Revolutionary government with two important implied corollaries: (1) that the issue of paper money is a means of gaining control over real resources but carries with it a real cost to the public; and (2) that use of this device is justified when an important social purpose is involved. Events prevented immediate elaboration of these ideas. But the germ of a conceptual basis for using created means of payment to finance the on-going Revolution was present. Significantly for the future, early Revolutionary experience with money revealed both the advantages and faults of monetary expansion. Complete collapse of the paper currency of 1913–1917 produced widespread antipathy to paper money among the Mexican people. There was a limit beyond which paper (later bank credit) could not be effectively employed for seizing real resources whether a good social purpose or a bad one was involved, and the government was forcefully apprised of this fact.

Revolutionary opinion regarded delegation of the right to create paper money to private banks as unjustifiable because, in the words of a historian of Mexican banking, it permitted those institutions, "with no compensation to the state, to enjoy a monopoly in the issuance of notes in greater quantities than the sum of their metallic reserves."[9] To correct this, the government appropriated to itself the sole right to emit paper money. This authority was expressed

— and a vehicle provided for its implementation — in Article 28 of the constitution of 1917, which conferred the right to issue paper currency on a single bank to be established and controlled by the federal government (actually the bank was not created until 1925). Thus the private banks lost the power to create money which had been their mainstay during the Díaz era. Demand deposits remained as a potential substitute, but these would not for many years attain the status which bank notes had enjoyed in pre-Revolutionary Mexico.

A tentative reconstruction of the remnants of the banking system was begun in 1921 under President Alvaro Obregón. Banks judged to be solvent resumed operations in essentially the same form as before 1910, though without the power of note issue. The restored institutions were in no position to function normally. Survival was their main concern, and this required cautious attention to building liquid reserves, collecting old debts, clearing away note liabilities, and restoring deposit accounts to a current basis. Years would be required to remove enough of the debris left by the first decade of the Revolution to restore even minimal commercial banking services to the nation.

For the first years after their re-establishment, the banks operated without definite charters or a new set of banking laws. In early 1924, the government was ready to seek a new legal framework for the banking system. It convoked a national convention of banking leaders which set the stage for agreement on new legislation which appeared in 1924 and 1925.[10] Plutarco Elías Calles, who was elected president in 1924, wanted economic revival, and his finance minister, Alberto J. Pani, had ideas about banking which the private banks could accept. Pani and the bankers agreed upon what amounted to a reconstitution of the Limantour–Díaz system without those features most objectionable to the Revolutionists and with a central bank of sharply limited powers. The Banco de México, envisioned in the 1917 constitution, was finally created by the law of August 25, 1925, as manager of the nation's gold standard, as bank of issue, and as bank of rediscount for commercial paper.[11] Commercial banks were authorized to receive demand deposits and lend at short term, and specialized institutions were authorized to market time liabilities and lend at medium and long term. The underlying hope was that private banks would "stimulate . . . sources of national wealth without being converted into instruments of monopoly by particular industries or individuals." [12] Supplementing private facilities, the Banco de México was given power to perform the same operations as commercial banks. A special institution (the Banco Nacional de Crédito Agrícola) was set up in 1926 to speed the flow of credit to agriculture.

The size of the catastrophe that had been wrought on banking by the initial phase of the Revolution is indicated by a few statistical comparisons. Statistics alone do not convey the full import of the change (and in any case the statistics of this period must be regarded as approximations which convey only a general idea of magnitude), but they suggest what had happened. Whereas in 1909, prior to the Revolution, private banks had held assets of 667 million pesos, in 1925, after about four years of restored operation, all banks combined held assets of 581 million pesos, of which about 89 million belonged to the new Banco de México, leaving some 492 million for the private banks. Detailed accounts are not available for private banks alone, but short-term and long-term credit outstanding for all banks amounted in 1925 to only 123 million pesos. A much larger sum, 218 million pesos, was carried in an account labeled "various debtors," which included a high proportion of matured paper in default. On the liabilities side, 132 million pesos appeared as "old accounts," which must be imputed to private banks since the central bank had existed for only a few months. Sight liabilities, including those of the Banco de México, were only 161 million pesos — a sum equal to about 5 U.S. dollars per Mexican inhabitant at the then prevailing exchange rate of about 2 pesos per dollar.[13]

Even though the Calles–Pani approach of the middle 1920's was fairly orthodox, relations between the public and private sectors were not quite the same as before the Revolution. Government did not delegate full responsibility for economic growth to private entities, and, when necessary, was willing to take direct action. For banking institutions, this changed climate was most apparent in the working out of relationships between the private banks and the new central institution.

From the point of view of the private bankers, a less alarming institution than the fledgling Banco de México could scarcely have been imagined. Though it possessed the right of note issue which once had been theirs, the central bank seemed to pose no additional threat. As a central bank it was a rigidly constrained institution. Its means of affecting bank credit were few and were tied to gold and commercial paper. Private banks were neither required to join the system to be headed by the Banco de México nor to submit to its regulation. They could become "associated institutions" through buying series "B" stock of the central bank and agreeing to hold certain reserves with it; in return, they could rediscount commercial paper and receive secured credits from the Bank in limited quantities. But they saw little advantage in establishing a close relationship to the central bank and proceeded to ignore it almost entirely. Only two banks became associates of the Banco de México in the beginning, and this number had risen to only five banks in 1930.[14] As the Banco de México itself rather sadly noted in its 1928 annual report (p. 30):

> The first condition of . . . functioning is association with other credit institutions, and the situation of other credit institutions . . . with some incapacitated for operation and others very much reduced in their possibilities for action, has not permitted to date the formation . . . of a system of associated banks. Besides, it has not been possible . . . to count on all those credit institutions whose situation would permit . . . their association with the system of the Banco de México. Some of these institutions . . . have declined [to associate] . . . through . . . censurable hostility. Though it is legitimate to abstain from entering into a work whose accomplishment is doubtful, it denotes a lack of public spirit to maintain a hostile attitude toward an undertaking . . . which merits, in any case, the sympathy with which . . . a serious effort for national betterment should be received.

The private bankers were still rather more concerned with pursuing their own interests and avoiding the public sector than they were with "national betterment."

But in the changed ideological atmosphere the public sector was not limited to waiting for private action. The Banco de México vigorously used its power to act as an ordinary commercial bank. It built a large banking business in competition with the private banks, complaining all the while that this represented a "deviation" from the true purpose of a central bank. Among private banks, the weakness and caution of the early 1920's continued. Total assets of all banking institutions declined from 581 million pesos in 1925 to 535 million pesos in 1930, even though the assets of the Banco de México (included in the total) rose from 89 to 139 million pesos, and even though by 1930 the new Banco Nacional de Crédito Agrícola was also represented in the figures. On the other hand it should not be overlooked that the declining total conceals internal changes in the accounts which suggest that the private banks were slowly recovering and that the availability of credit in the economy was increasing. Short-term and long-term credit outstanding for all banks almost doubled between 1925 and 1930, while the bad-debt account fell to less than half its 1925 level. Sight liabilities of the banking system rose from 161 million pesos to 232 million, while the "old account" liabilities of the banks fell from 132 million to 20 million pesos.[15]

The Banco de México, in its role as a central bank, is usually regarded as impotent during its early years. But its ordinary banking operations were an important source of improvement in the supply of credit. Vigorous competition with the private banks could not have been expected to endear the central institution to them, and it did not. The private banks remained aloof and hostile until the crisis produced by the Great Depression forced them into closer association with the Banco de México.

Even before the onset of the depression, Mexico's internal monetary situation began to deteriorate. Government deficits reappeared in the latter 1920's and were met in part through coining silver. Inside the country, silver pesos depreciated relative to gold. Between 1926 and 1930 the country's foreign-trade surplus (including shipments of precious metals) fell from about 150 million U.S. dollars to about 51 million, and the foreign value of the peso started a moderate slide. From 1929 on, the situation grew rapidly worse. The limited gold reserves of the Banco de México fell sharply to about 7 million dollars in 1930. This was not entirely due to the worsening balance of payments, for unwise and perhaps corrupt loans had placed the Bank in a difficult position even before balance-of-payments pressure became severe.[16] Domestic hoarding increased, capital moved out of Mexico, and the position of the banking system grew increasingly precarious. Demand liabilities of banking institutions fell by about 35 per cent during the calendar year 1931. Depositors withdrew funds, reserves plummeted, and credits were sharply restricted as the banks attempted to defend their liquidity.[17] A few banking institutions actually failed, though most avoided collapse. The Banco de México lent what support it could, but there was little that it could do at the beginning of the crisis, and the private banks survived largely on their own.

Initial government reaction made the banking crisis worse. A new monetary law in 1931 demonetized gold and made silver pesos the only unlimited legal tender money. But at the same time, further coinage of silver was prohibited in an effort to convince the public that inflation was not in prospect and to help prevent a further fall of the peso in the foreign exchanges. With gold out of circulation, with demand deposits small and falling, and with Banco de México notes outstanding in insignificant quantities, restriction of the silver coinage generated an acute scarcity of money. Both the internal depression and the external pressure on the peso grew worse.[18]

On top of the suffocating silver restriction, the Banco de México was prohibited from expanding its banking business with the public, a change which further reduced the availability of credit. However, this limitation of the competition which the Banco de México could offer, coupled with provision of a preferential discount rate for associated banks, began to crack the resistance of private institutions to association with the central bank. The number of associated banks rose from five in 1930 to thirteen at the end of 1931.

Sweeping changes in both the approach to monetary policy and the internal structure of the banking system came early in 1932. Their result was to terminate the banking crisis and also to put an end to the independence of private banks from the Banco de México. Alberto J. Pani was again the architect of banking reform, and the structure which emerged was again orthodox enough to please the private bankers and flexible enough to deal with the most immediate problems of the financial system.

As a first step, a primitive but effective means of increasing the money supply was employed. The ban on expanding the silver coinage was revoked, and silver pesos began to be produced "at the full capacity of the mint." This increased the money supply directly and eased the strain on bank reserves, thus reducing pressure on the banks to restrict their own lending. Coining silver was a stop-gap measure, but it was a helpful one.[19]

More fundamental changes were made in a new organic law for the Banco de México and a new law for other credit institutions, both of which appeared in 1932.[20] All commercial banks and most important related institutions were required to become associates of the Banco de México. This meant the purchase of small amounts of stock in the Bank and also the holding of a reserve with it equal to 5 per cent of those deposits that were payable in less than thirty days. Thus, the Banco de México acquired a closer contact with managements of private banks, and for the first time access to central-bank credit came to be an important concern to the private bankers.

The other side of the reorganization gave major advantages to the private sector. Through a moderate liberalization of the Banco de México's authority to lend and rediscount, the credit of the Bank was made more easily available to its associates. The Banco de México was also authorized to lend a part of the money required for the establishment of new private banks, and it could purchase a small portion of their capital stock as a permanent investment.

Most importantly, however, the central bank was compelled to liquidate its private banking business. In carrying out this liquidation, the Banco de México ceased to be a competitor of the private institutions and became exclusively a central bank.

Both the severity of the financial crisis and the end of direct competition from the Banco de México helped ease the opposition of the private banks to the central bank. Little outcry was heard against enforced association with the Bank, and private banks shortly began to resort heavily to the credit of the Banco de México as well as to promote the use of Banco de México notes as a supplement to the silver coinage.

There were signs that the internal crisis was passing even before the reforms of 1932, but these undoubtedly acted to speed recovery. Between January and December 1932, the sight liabilities of the banking system rose from 150 million pesos to 187 million; Banco de México notes in circulation jumped from less than 2 million pesos to 42 million; and discounts at the Banco de México by other banks from less than 2 million pesos to 23 million. Two years later, at the end of 1934, the three categories stood at 260 million, 100 million, and 34 million pesos, respectively.[21]

Other government actions also assisted the Mexican private banks. Official pressure and legal changes in 1934 and 1935 practically eliminated branches of foreign banks as significant competitors of domestic banks. Economic revival and fiscal reform permitted the government to balance its budget and clear away much of the floating debt left by the crisis. Two new national credit institutions, the Banco Nacional Hipotecario Urbano y de Obras Públicas and Nacional Financiera, had begun operations by 1934. The Banco Nacional Hipotecario tried to assist the government in financing public works and was able to place moderate amounts of government bonds in cooperation with private banks. Nacional Financiera in its original form was intended mainly to assist the government and private financial institutions in disposing of illiquid holdings of real estate which they had acquired during the depression. Piecemeal changes in the banking laws also expanded the freedom of the banks to extend short-term credit for agricultural and industrial, as well as strictly commercial, purposes.

Public-sector actions had helped save the private banks during the worst of the depression, and government policies in 1933 and 1934 were successfully promoting the recovery of banking along with other sectors of the economy. There were few grounds for serious conflict between the public and private sectors; relations between the government and the banks were probably more harmonious than at any time since the Revolution.

But this harmony was destined to be short-lived. The government of President Abelardo L. Rodríguez (1932–1934) was concerned first with recovery but it was already beginning to think of Mexico's longer-range development, and it had shown itself willing to use public-sector banking institutions as primary means for accomplishing its purposes. If and when the government committed itself wholeheartedly to a development program it was certain to need large sums of money, and when this happened government needs were sure to contrast sharply with the tiny resources and orthodox policies of the private banks. Harmony could have been maintained only through government inaction or a revolution in private banking. Neither occurred.

With the accession of Lázaro Cárdenas to the presidency in 1934 a vigorous and eclectic public economic policy was assured. As soon as he felt politically secure, Cárdenas began to implement his conviction that long-term economic advance required above all else a prosperous agriculture and a vastly expanded supply of overhead capital. Land reform, technical and financial aid to agriculture, and heavy federal spending on public works became the basic ingredients of a formula for economic growth. The government soon was involved in agricultural improvement, highway construction, irrigation projects, electrification, school construction, and many other forms of public investment. New national credit institutions appeared, and older institutions were reoriented toward the financing of development. At first, financing of public-sector endeavors was relatively orthodox, but inevitably the desire for

economic expansion outran revenues available for public investment. Given the low levels of total income and the still tentative
character of recovery from a severe depression, borrowing held
more attraction for the public sector than did increased taxation.
But borrowing posed the problem of finding lenders. The world
depression continued, and foreign funds were unobtainable. Within
Mexico, potential sources of loan funds were almost equally scarce.
The public sector endeavored to sell securities to the banks and to
the public. But the liquid savings of the public were small, and the
debt-service record of the government was abysmal. Nor were
private banks immediately willing and able to supply the necessary
funds.

Though the private banks were recovering, they were still a
relatively minor force within the Mexican economy. At the end of
1936, total assets of private institutions amounted to only 404
million pesos. This was a sum substantially less than assets had
been in 1925, and far less than banks had held in the smaller
Mexican economy of pre-Revolutionary days. The entire resources
of private financial institutions amounted in 1936 to no more than
about 8 per cent of Mexico's gross national product, and the year-
to-year changes in their assets for most of the past decade had been
negative.[22] Even had every centavo received by the private institutions beyond the needs of current transactions gone for the purchase
of government debt, their maximum contribution would have been
small. It was, moreover, still true that commercial banks — the
only private banking institutions with appreciable resources — were
almost totally restricted by law and custom to short-term lending.

The financial capabilities of private institutions could have been
expanded through massive credits from the Banco de México.
Central-bank credit was in fact easily available to private banks
until the closing years of the 1930's, when significant restraint was
applied. But the use of this device would have been awkward for
at least two reasons. First, there was no assurance that the private
institutions would use any added funds for the acquisition of
public-sector securities. Second, the central bank would have had

to lend almost as much as the private institutions lent. For there was at this time no substantial multiplication of the amount of money in circulation when the Banco de México expanded its credit. Demand deposits constituted no more than 30 per cent to 40 per cent of the money supply in the middle 1930's, and their share was not tending to increase. A cash drain of large proportions would thus accompany any expansion of bank lending. This drain, plus the reserves held by commercial banks in their vaults and at the Banco de México, held secondary expansion to not more than perhaps 25 per cent of primary expansion of credit by the Banco de México.

There is little reason in any case to suppose that the Cárdenas government (1934–1940) wished to delay its investment plans until some way of borrowing from the private sector could be found. Cooperation which might some day grow to sizable proportions was certainly desired of the private banks. But, for the immediate future, the government was quite willing to rely on the Banco de México and other public credit institutions. The private banks were shouldered aside with an exhortation to think great thoughts and do great deeds, and the public sector plunged ahead using its own potent and tractable instruments for finance.

Within the Cárdenas scheme of thought, Mexico's foremost need was greater output, and this was held to depend on greater capital formation, most particularly in agriculture and basic public facilities. Responsibility for expanding the rate of capital formation was enthusiastically seized by government. Private capital spending was not excluded, but the driving force was clearly expected to be the public sector. Little importance was attached to maintaining any "reserved" field of enterprise for private efforts, to criteria of monetary orthodoxy inherited from the past, or to the price level. The dominant concern was unequivocally stated by Eduardo Suárez, finance minister under both Cárdenas and his successor, Manuel Avila Camacho (1940–1946). As late as 1941 when questions regarding inflation had begun to be heard, Suárez declared: "It must be remembered that, as long as investment does not reach a level at which it begins to be employed with diminished efficiency, it is not sensible to talk about inflation, and I believe that it is obvious to all of us that we are a long way from arriving at this point of saturation." [23]

The function expected of banks, including the central bank, was simply that of generating funds as needed for public-sector investment and for such private investment as was ventured. National credit institutions multiplied, and received wide powers to look for money, together with an orientation toward agriculture and other sectors favored by the government. The search for lenders to the public sector produced not a solution but an expedient. The Banco de México was turned after 1936 into a fountain of credit which financed a large government deficit,[24] provided most of the money lent by the national credit institutions, and gave some support to private banks.

While the Cárdenas policy was still in its formative stages, new difficulties appeared. Economic recovery slowed in 1937 with the onset of recession in the United States, and this further heightened private fear of the directions in which the public sector was moving. Cárdenas had never based his political appeal or his political program on stimulation of private enterprise. His pitch had been made to peasants and workers. Accelerated expropriations of land, broadened social legislation, and increased support of unionization had marked the early years of his presidency. None of this was calculated to reassure private business, and it did not. In 1937, as economic activity began to slacken, as rumors of heavy illegal borrowings at the Banco de México circulated, and as labor difficulties mounted, uneasiness grew steadily. Panic erupted in 1938 when the foreign petroleum companies were expropriated. Again depositors withdrew funds, hoarding spread, and the banking system faced a crisis. Foreign capitalists and Mexican capitalists alike sought to transfer their money to safety in other countries, and a severe run on the peso developed. The Banco de México was forced to abandon the exchange rate, though it was able to support the internal liquidity of most of the banks. Despite central-bank support, demand deposits in the banking system closed the year 1938 at the lowest levels since 1934. Total assets of private banking institutions also fell after having risen for several years.[25]

Between 1938 and 1940, heavy borrowing by the government at the Banco de México, together with moderate improvements in economic activity and the balance of payments, produced a sharp rise in the money supply and in bank assets. The money supply, which had fallen in 1938 with recession and banking panic, increased by almost 20 per cent in 1939 and by about 12 per cent in 1940. Assets of all financial institutions grew from 1,072 million pesos at the end of 1937 to 1,622 million pesos at the end of 1940 despite a temporary decline in 1938.[26]

Private banks fared much less well than financial institutions as a whole. Their assets, which amounted to 437 million pesos at the end of 1937, grew only to 601 million by 1940.[27] This slower rate of increase is explained by continuing uneasiness in the business community and by the beginning of mild Banco de México restraints on private credit. A critical private banker, Heliodoro Duenes, later stated an opinion which was popular for years in banking circles. In Duenes' view: "The Bank had no scruples in stopping the progress of the public [i.e., private business], restricting its assistance to the banks in operations which the law indicated as . . . its principal functions, while on the other hand violating its organic law and giving to the government all the money which was asked of it." [28] Though perhaps exaggerated, Duenes' statement is essentially correct. The Banco de México had begun to move toward a policy of restraining the private sector in order to accommodate the demands of the public sector.

Controls notwithstanding, a large potential for inflation was created in the 1930's. Overt price increases were small, but between 1937 and 1940, the rise in the money supply amounted to about 31 per cent while the real gross national product grew by no more than about 8 per cent. Nor did private credit expand during these years as much as the growth of central-bank credit permitted. A return of private confidence would almost surely bring further monetary expansion and substantial inflation.[29]

By the close of the 1930's, the government and the private banking sector were at ideological loggerheads, and there was little common ground for practical cooperation. Since 1932, the public authorities had made many changes in Mexican banking, but neither the rationale of these changes nor the direction in which they led had become apparent by 1940. Certainly no clear role for the private banks had been outlined. The independence of private institutions from the Banco de México had been terminated; they had become dependent on its assistance; and its control over them had been strengthened. But only a passing effort had been made to integrate the private institutions with public programs to stimulate growth, and this effort had produced few results. Cooperation of the private sector was desired, but the Cárdenas goal of growth and the instruments employed to attain it implied no dependence on the private banks. In their turn, these banks wished to go their own way unmolested by public-sector ambitions, which they feared, and unrestricted by central-bank regulation, which they resented.

Chapter 3

Emergence of the Modern System

THE Cárdenas era saw a transformation in the relation of public initiative to national economic growth and the beginnings of a new national concept of the relation of banks to development. But the working out of the new views had just begun. By the beginning of World War II, the Cárdenas innovations had created little more than a number of public credit institutions and a precedent for using the central bank to finance public-sector deficits. After 1940, public and private banking institutions gradually began to be aligned in a stable structure capable of effective functioning within a climate which soon began to stress price and exchange-rate stability along with growth. This structure evolved during and after the war into a coherent banking system conducive to rapid economic advance and to a workable interlacing of public and private banking enterprises.

It would be mistaken to suppose that the emergency-oriented policies of the 1930's reflected the whole substance of Mexican financial thought. Despite the generally tolerant Cárdenas view of credit expansion, cautious undertones could be detected.

As early as 1935, the distinction between "productive" and "unproductive" uses of funds had begun to suggest itself to the public authorities. In that year a minor amendment to the banking laws declared: "As the funds available in the money market have continued to increase . . . it has been the constant preoccupation of the government to channel these funds in such a way as to assure their application to productive purposes and developmental purposes, removing them, consequently, from inactivity or from speculative operations, both of which are sterile and prejudicial to economic life." [1] Little was done in the 1930's to enforce the use of funds for "productive" purposes, but the distinction became a cornerstone of later policy.

The Cárdenas adventures with the credit of the Banco de México were not the work of a politically impotent government grasping at straws, nor were they the work of an economically naïve government unaware of what it was doing. They were stopgap means of equipping Mexico with an indispensable minimum of basic capital facilities and rejuvenating her agriculture. There was the clear hope that a foundation could be laid for movement beyond the existing situation. The Banco de México used what monetary controls it possessed to place mild restraints on credit expansion by the private banks. Nacional Financiera began to trade in securities as a means of strengthening the market and also began in 1937 its first serious efforts to borrow from the public. In 1938, the Banco de México started consistent support of government bonds in the hope that these could be made more attractive to private savers and financial institutions. Even the extensive borrowings of the public sector from the Banco de México were treated as extraordinary occurrences and were given a cloak of financial respectability. Much of the borrowing was for the account of national credit institutions rather than the government itself; and, when the government borrowed, its larger loans were treated for several years as "special credits" or "overdrafts" rather than longer-term debts. Though the legal prohibition against large-scale direct borrowing by the government at the Banco de México was temporarily ignored, it was not repealed. A further evolution of policy was plainly desired.

To move beyond the measures of the 1930's required reconciliation of a complex bundle of economic realities. First, the public sector was not inclined to eliminate its deficit with the rest of the economy. Even though the federal government might balance its ordinary budget, income was not likely to be sufficient also to pay the costs of the ambitious investment program required for development. Nor was the government prepared to incur the political or the economic risks inherent in substantially increasing its revenues or curtailing expenditures. Second, government debt was unsalable to the public in any appreciable amounts without duress — unsalable, that is, on terms the government was willing to accept. Third, voluntary private saving, even if it had flowed into government debt, would have been inadequate to finance the public-sector deficit plus any reasonable volume of private investment. Fourth, government investment and related public-sector activities could provide only a part of the capital essential for stimulating economic development. The bulk of the economy was private, and private entrepreneurs would be called upon to provide a large share of the capital formation needed for an acceptable rate of growth. They, too, would need financing. Since government political and economic convictions ruled out a vigorous fiscal policy for the foreseeable future, the burden of accommodating these circumstances fell on monetary and credit policy.

Before a serious effort could be made to reconcile these diverse and difficult conditions, the external situation confronting Mexico was suddenly transformed. When war erupted in Europe in 1939, a re-examination of the dominant ideas and policies of the depression decade became essential in Mexico. The economic policies of the 1930's and the concept of the requisites of growth which had guided them had promoted a substantial internal recovery, but their longer-term efficacy had not been proved. Mexico's economy remained semi-colonial in structure, and neither agricultural reform nor public works alone could alter this fact very much. As Finance Minister Eduardo Suárez stated in early 1941: "We must confess that basic Mexican production is deficient in relation to our needs. Through the import of a great number of primary materials and essential articles of a manufactured or semi-manufactured nature we have been able to satisfy our needs; but . . . an economy which supports itself [through foreign trade] . . . to such a substantial extent has no firm base; it is unstable and in fact needs to be reoriented and to proceed in new directions." [2] In the context of the early 1940's, moving in "new directions" meant a much increased effort to make manufacturing industry a mainstay of Mexican economic development.

Once Mexico turned toward industry, new questions appeared. So long as economic advance was thought to require no more than increased capital formation in agriculture and in basic installations, the private sector could be left almost out of account. Public agencies were quite willing to assume responsibility for agricultural development and to implement this through land reform, technical assistance, and agricultural credit. Likewise, basic public works were in the hands of public-sector entities, and no great private effort could be expected in these activities. But if economic growth required rapid formation of industrial capital, the situation was different. Except in unusual cases such as that of petroleum, where political as well as economic considerations were important, the government was not prepared to take full responsibility for industrial growth. Not simply the support but also the active initiative of the private sector must be brought to bear on the problem of industrialization.

Nor was the stimulation of private initiative the only problem. Funds had to be made available to finance the undertakings of private entrepreneurs. The Mexican money and capital markets of the early 1940's were scarcely more capable of financing private development than they were adequate for public-sector needs. Accommodation of the public sector during the late 1930's, a time of extremely low private investment, had required free resort to the credit of the Banco de México. Was this institution now to become the source of money for private investment, and, if so, with what result? Even had the answer to the first question been an unreserved "yes," the effectiveness of such a procedure would have been doubtful. Earlier, severe inflation arising out of the expansion of central-bank credit had been avoided mainly because of the stagnation of private activity. The untrammeled growth of this credit for financing private-sector investment would surely produce acute inflation and defeat its purpose unless public capital spending were concurrently slashed. There was little prospect of such a cut.

In 1941, sweeping legislative changes laid the basis for adjustment of the banking system to Mexico's newly broadened concept of the problem of economic growth. Major revisions were made in the legal status and powers of the Banco de México, Nacional Financiera, and the important private financial institutions.

The Banco de México received new authority to vary reserve requirements, to alter discount policy, and to buy, sell, and hold securities, both public and private. After these changes, the central bank could exercise broad control over private commercial banks and could assure the success of any security issue of the public or private sector if it chose to do so.[3] As a powerful companion institution to the central bank, Nacional Financiera was reorganized and strengthened. It became a full-fledged development bank designed to give the public sector additional means for promoting industry directly, tapping the savings of the public and the credit of banks, and supporting the securities markets without direct resort to the credit of the Banco de México.

The new banking laws brought private banks as well into the financing of industrial and related developments. All kinds of private financial institutions were affected, but the changes that turned out to be most important in the long run were those in the commercial banks and the *financieras*.

The ancient legal tie of commercial banks to short-term lending was breached in 1941. A conceptual distinction between commercial banks and other institutions remained, for the new legislation recognized the distinctive character of the commercial banks as creators of credit; but now they could acquire stocks, bonds, mortgages, and other long-term instruments up to 20 per cent of their investible funds, and they could use another 20 per cent for medium-term credits up to one year. In effect, it was recognized that commercial banks had always been faced with demands for credit of a medium-term and long-term nature. They generally had attempted to meet these demands through subterfuges such as renewable short-term credits, and they had been roundly criticized for doing so. Now the banks were more easily able to lend as customers' demands required, and it was hoped that a considerable proportion of these customers would seek funds for industrial investments.[4]

Commercial banks were also given a potent new running mate. Up to this time, private financial institutions outside commercial banking had never attained any real measure of success. To fill this gap, an existing group of intermediaries, the private *financieras,* was converted into a tool for industrial promotion and finance. Authority was given the *financieras* to issue securities for sale to the public, to guarantee security issues for others, to promote the organization or reorganization of business enterprises, to become open or silent partners in firms, to hold all kinds of stocks, bonds, and other credit instruments, to accept time deposits, to grant loans of almost all kinds, to underwrite and trade in securities, and "in general, to carry out those operations necessary for fulfilling the duties of financing production and placing capital." [5] *Financieras* were excluded from commercial banking and from fields specifically reserved for other credit institutions, but their grant of authority was broad enough to make them the most versatile private financial entities in Mexico.

A parallel structure in the public and private sectors was thus created. For financing public-sector expenditures which could not be covered by revenues, funds would be raised from the public sale of government and Nacional Financiera securities and (as a residual source) from the Banco de México. For financing those private investments which required funds not supplied directly by investors, there would be private *financieras* backed by the commercial banks. The two systems were cross-linked, in that private institutions could devote funds to the securities of public-sector entities; Nacional Financiera could promote and assist private undertakings, and the Banco de México could protect the liquidity of all.

The deepening of the world conflict in 1941 and 1942 in some respects eased and in others complicated the problems of stimulating and financing Mexican growth. Mexico was inundated with funds from abroad as the trade balance improved, as Mexicans repatriated their money, and as foreigners sought a refuge from wartime destruction and controls.[6] At the same time, the burgeoning export markets, shortages of imported items, and rapidly rising domestic incomes provided a stimulus to private Mexican business stronger than had ever existed before. These circumstances provided incentives for investment, and thus served the goal of growth. But the internal money supply more than tripled from 1940 to 1945 (see Table 1, p. 126). This rise, coupled with the shortages of imported goods and the inability of domestic producers to expand output as rapidly as demand, threatened Mexico with an inflationary rout instead of stable expansion.

A hasty acceleration occurred in the evolution of monetary and banking policy. To the objective of growth, the control of inflation was now added as an urgent, though subsidiary, goal. The public sector pressed forward with its basic investment in such things as dams and roads and its aids to agriculture while now giving increased support to industry, mainly via Nacional Financiera. Savings and the snowballing funds of the private banks were solicited more actively than ever before to reduce the need for borrowing at the central bank. But the demand for investible funds far outran the supply originating in savings and public-sector revenues. Hence, the Banco de México was expected to perform two roles. On one side, it was supposed to ensure the availability of sufficient funds to meet the deficit of the public sector and to finance essential private investment. On the other, it was supposed to limit the quantitative expansion of the money supply to a rate which did not produce intolerable inflation. All this had to take place in an economy with a meager flow of financial saving and a public psychology highly resistant to holding securities.

The government's fiscal policy provided little support to monetary measures. Rapidly rising revenues reduced the federal deficit during the early years of World War II, and a small surplus in the current expenditures budget was achieved in 1944. This did not, however, indicate a greater participation of federal revenue in the gross national product. The net budgetary income of the federal government declined from about 6.8 per cent of gross national product in 1940 to about 5.8 per cent in 1945. For the public sector as a whole, funded internal debt rose from 458.9 million pesos in 1940 to 1,593.5 million pesos in 1945 (this figure also includes short-term debt of the federal government itself).[7]

To serve the partially contradictory goals of growth and inflation control, the Banco de México began to evolve a compromise which is still the basis of its policy. Three essential components form the system:

First, there is the remarkable assurance of liquidity mentioned in my first chapter. The government debt and the securities of the national credit institutions are assured a market through support either by the Banco de México or by the issuing institution. At the same time the liabilities of private credit institutions are made attractive to investors through supported liquidity tacitly underwritten by the Banco de México. No important bank will fail; no security issue of a major bank will depreciate seriously in price.[8]

Second, the asset holdings of private financial institutions are regulated selectively in an attempt to move credit and savings into favored investments — that is, into public-sector debt and the debts of private enterprises undertaking "productive" investments. The financial priority scale is as follows: The federal government's needs come first, the needs of other public-sector entities come second, "productive" private uses of funds come third, and other uses of funds last. Once a federal program is politically approved there is no question of the availability of funds on whatever terms the government decides are appropriate, though federal revenues and the state of the money markets may be factors in the initial political decision. Where other public-sector entities are involved, an undertaking is also generally assured of financing once it is begun, but approval of new ventures depends more heavily upon the opinion of the Banco de México regarding their effects on the money supply and the price level. The private sector, especially its uses of funds considered "speculative" or "unproductive," bears the brunt of control.

Third, an attempt is made to limit inflationary pressures through quantitative control of the money supply. Control has generally taken the forms of conventional reserve requirements, obligatory holding of certain kinds of securities, and transfers of assets between the portfolios of the Banco de México and the private banks. True open-market operations are impossible and rediscount policy is rarely decisive.

During the war period, when the rudiments of the Banco de México's control system were developed, inflationary pressures were overwhelmingly strong. There was little chance that even rigorous controls would create a scarcity of credit serious enough to impair investment or growth. The Bank began by raising reserve requirements moderately and restricting access to its rediscount facilities. As the war progressed and inflationary pressure mounted, limitations on rediscounts which did not finance an appreciable amount of "production" were tightened. Negotiations with Mexico City banks culminated in two agreements to restrict lending beyond certain levels, but these did not work well. More important, reserve requirements were repeatedly boosted. By the end of the war, reserve requirements for commercial banks in the Federal District had been raised to 50 per cent, all of which was to be held as a deposit with the Banco de México; and requirements for banks elsewhere were almost as high. In total, the central bank's actions sterilized a substantial part of the money-creating power which the private banks were steadily acquiring.[9]

But, throughout this same period, the Banco de México was

compelled to pump more and more of its own credit into the economy as it provided funds to the government, government-controlled enterprises, and some of the national credit institutions. At the end of 1945 the accounts of the Banco de México showed about 956 million pesos in identifiable holdings of public-sector debt — a sum roughly 30 per cent greater than the entire assets of the bank in 1940.[10] Sterilization of the price-level effects of the inflow of funds from abroad would have been difficult at best, but the need to accommodate a large public-sector deficit made it impossible. Prices almost doubled from 1939 to 1945.

All in all, the period of World War II saw a notable change in the underlying relationships between the public and private sectors in banking. Mexico became aware of the acute need for industry and commercial agriculture and other pursuits in which private enterprise was likely to be dominant. As this happened, the goals of the public sector and those of private bankers began to move toward each other. The public sector, without abandoning its commitment to growth or lessening its aid to those sectors where private activity was insufficient, made room in its philosophy for a vastly expanded private effort. And the promotion of these private activities demanded little more of the banks than a re-direction of their own familiar and profitable banking business. Private bankers readily grasped the idea that rapid economic growth contributed to their prosperity, and they gradually accepted the premise that broad-ranging investment by the public sector was an indispensable support to growth. In effect, the public sector started to drift "right" in admitting the need for private investment and acting accordingly, while the private sector began to inch "left" by admitting the value of a conscious developmental effort in which a major role was assigned to the public sector. Cults religiously dedicated to the absolute dominance of the public sector or of private enterprise remained in banking, as elsewhere, but they came to be much less influential than supporters of a mixed effort. The divisions between the public and private sectors began a significant shift from the realm of ideology to the arena of practical problems and tactical maneuvers.

Much of the reduction in acrimony and conflict is traceable to the growth which the war brought to the private banks. Between 1940 and 1945, private institutions regained a prominence and a prosperity which they had not enjoyed since before the Revolution. Despite regulations which limited credit creation, the assets of private banking institutions (still largely commercial banks) jumped from 601 million pesos in 1940 to 3,766 million pesos in 1945. This rise was much greater than that which occurred in general economic activity. Whereas in 1940 the assets of private banks were a little over 8 per cent of gross national product, in 1945 they were 18 per cent. Before the war, the private banks were much overshadowed in size by the Banco de México, but by the end of 1945 their assets exceeded those of the central bank, and their loans and investments were greater than those of the central bank by about a third.[11]

Though the private banks gained in quantitative importance relative to the Banco de México, this did not represent a diminution of public-sector participation in banking. It is true that, by 1945, the central bank itself held only about 30 per cent of the combined loans and investments of all banking institutions (excluding inter-bank lending), but other public-sector credit institutions now held another 22 per cent — a public total of 52 per cent.[12] Precisely comparable figures for prewar years are not available; it appears, however, that the shares of public and private sectors in the financing of economic activity did not change greatly. The wartime inflow of funds and the need for internal monetary restraint allowed the central bank to begin a disengagement from financing public-sector expenditures directly and to reduce the share of private business spending which it financed indirectly through rediscounts. As the central bank withdrew, its place was filled by other national credit institutions, notably Nacional Financiera.

The gradual withdrawal of the Banco de México from direct

financing of economic activity has been a continuing postwar trend. By the end of 1960, its portfolio comprised only about 13 per cent of the total loans and investments of all banks. Other national credit institutions held 42 per cent of the total. There has been no persistent tendency for the combined loans and investments of public-sector banks to grow or shrink relative to those of private banks. However, when some allowance is made for the share of the public-sector portfolio which has grown out of official borrowing abroad, a field in which the national institutions cannot reasonably be said to compete with private banks, it appears that the share of private institutions in financing undertakings with funds obtained within Mexico has increased since 1945.[13]

Replacement of the central bank, which creates its own funds, by the other national credit institutions, which do not, may have eased somewhat the problem of inflation control, but it also implied something else. Competition for sources of loanable funds was bound to be intensified. The national credit institutions and the private banks unavoidably became rivals in seeking the savings of the public at large, funds of private commercial banks, and funds which the Banco de México was willing to supply directly. Even in the easy-money atmosphere of the war this led to continual charges that private banks were being squeezed so that public banks (and the government) could be accommodated. With an intensity which has varied with the degree of monetary restraint exercised and the rate at which the public sector was requisitioning funds, these complaints have continued to the present day.[14] Such charges have been valid, of course, as both private and public sectors are aware. But the discrimination has been far from fatal, and in a general atmosphere of expansion it generated no ill feeling pronounced enough to block widespread public-private cooperation. Agile and imaginative private institutions quickly developed defense mechanisms which enabled them to strengthen their competitive positions and make central-bank regulation less onerous. Public-sector spokesmen periodically denounced attempts at evasion but there was no harsh action aimed at closing "loopholes."

To compete effectively with national institutions for funds and to capitalize on profit opportunities offered by wartime and postwar expansion, the private institutions rather quickly began to create financial groups instead of proliferating independent institutions. Common management of several institutions was not a new phenomenon in Mexico, but financial groups greatly increased their strength and prominence during and after World War II.

The developments envisioned by the 1941 reorganization of the banking system had included a major role for private institutions. Private investment, especially industrial investment, was much desired, and a means for active promotion and financing of industrial enterprises was provided in the rejuvenated private *financieras*. But *financieras* had no source of funds except what they could attract from the public through security issues and time deposits. Commercial banks had large sums available for lending, but were still constrained by legal restrictions on their lending and on the interest rates they could charge. Even more limiting were Banco de México reserve requirements and a ceiling on interest rates payable to time depositors. A wedding of *financieras* and commercial banks under common management was clearly in order, and special emphasis in the combined operation was bound to be placed on its most flexible member, the *financiera*.

Beyond the commercial-bank-and-*financiera* nexus, groups came also to include insurance companies, capitalization banks, mortgage banks, or other institutions needed to round out the range of financial services offered, the variety of liabilities held out to the investing public, and the geographic area covered. With a nucleus of financial institutions, extension of control to include industrial and commercial undertakings was easy. For those undertakings, adherence was advantageous because it assured funds for working capital and expansion. For the financial institutions, a circle of favored business borrowers meant profitable outlets for investible funds and, more importantly, a measure of supervision over the use of their money. After the war, when selective credit controls required the channeling of a large share of bank funds to "productive" purposes, a financial institution belonging to a group could often comply with the regulations largely through lending within its circle of associated enterprises.

Groups emerged in several ways. Strong commercial banks created *financieras* or acquired and strengthened existing ones. In a few cases, the *financiera* was the central institution which created or promoted a commercial bank and perhaps other entities to form a complete group. In at least one outstanding case, the initiative for formation of the group came from established commercial and industrial firms; they formed a *financiera* which, in turn, assisted the development of the firms themselves and built a network of allied financial institutions. In the financial groups, members may be owned by a central firm, but the association may also be much less formal, even to the point of only cooperation among "friendly" institutions for competitive advantage. Interlocking directorates are a common device for assuring uniformity of policy.

Though the growth of financial groups in postwar Mexico implies some amount of monopoly control, it does not necessarily follow that monopoly has been aggravated by this development. Indeed, competition within the financial community may have actually increased. Before World War II, Mexico had only two strong banking firms in the private sector. In the postwar period, the country has developed some ten or twelve financial groups of significant (though far from equal) size. A good part of the resources of these groups is devoted to uses within the circle of affiliated firms and favored borrowers which surrounds the financiers; but significant amounts of money are also lent outside the group. And the large financial powers compete for savings with one another, with lesser private institutions, and with public-sector entities.

Details of the composition and functioning of the financial alliances are not widely publicized, but the groups are not to be considered *sub rosa* or furtive associations, and the identity of their major components is readily ascertainable. Very little, however, has been written about them or their effect on the financial or general economic development of Mexico. One author has estimated that at the end of 1952 the four major financial groups (each headed by a commercial bank) controlled about 70 per cent of the resources of Mexican private financial institutions.[15] This figure is put in somewhat different perspective, however, when it is realized that even the largest private group did not remotely approach the power of the Banco de México–Nacional Financiera "group," which is in many respects directly competitive with the private institutions.

To the public sector, the growth of powerful private financial groups was no particular threat since it introduced no new means of contravening public policy. In competing for funds, government institutions are always at an advantage because they have the support of the central bank. General quantitative control of credit is not greatly affected by internal reshuffling of funds within financial groups. Probably the only major area of conflict comes in the degree to which combinations of financial institutions and non-financial enterprises can facilitate the systematic evasion of selective credit controls. Any firm with enough funds to meet its capital needs may use them instead for expenditures which lack official sanction and then borrow, if this seems profitable, to finance its "productive" investments. Where groups exist, the cooperation of other firms, especially financial institutions, makes the evasion simpler. Internal shifts of funds among allied financial institutions may also tend to concentrate resources in those institutions least subject to detailed regulation, a fact which unquestionably accounts for some of the rapid growth of *financieras*. On the other hand, financial institutions seem in some cases to have put funds into "productive" investments within the group (even to the extent of creating new enterprises or whole new industries) which they might have refused to consider had they not had some voice in the use to be made of the money. The ability to spread the risk of new undertakings among several financial entities without loss of profit for the group as a whole may encourage innovation in view of the relatively small size and limited risk-bearing capabilities of many suppliers of funds. In any case, whatever disturbance of public policy may have accompanied financial combination does not seem to have been severe, and no serious effort has been made to dissolve the groups. It is true that the rise of the groups may have facilitated collusion among companies in price-fixing and market-sharing arrangements. But this is a subject about which Mexico's government, except in certain special situations, expresses little active concern.

When World War II ended, there was no drastic change in Mexican economic policy or the character of the growth goals of the public sector. The heavy emphasis on public investment and increased agricultural productivity was continued, and the stress on industrialization was intensified. However, the goal of inflation control emerged more clearly and assumed a new practical feasibility.

The first overt signs of a decline in inflationary pressures appeared in 1945 when the inflow of funds which had so influenced monetary conditions reversed itself. Imports rose at an accelerated rate, and money which had sought a temporary haven in Mexico shortly began to pour out in torrents. At the end of 1945, the central bank's holdings of gold, silver, and foreign exchange stood at 1,800 million pesos. By the end of 1947, this account had dropped to 778 million pesos and the nation was approaching its first postwar devaluation.[16] Thus, the largest source of expansionary pressure on the money supply during wartime, the balance of payments, now came to exert a strong deflationary influence. Public-sector borrowing, the second major source of monetary expansion in earlier years, was also a less inflationary factor in 1946 and 1947. The federal government itself developed a surplus in its current budget in 1946, and its 1947 deficit was small. Other public-sector entities continued to borrow, but their needs were relatively smaller than in the war years, and reliance on Banco de México credit to meet those needs was not heavy. Thus, for the first time since 1936, the central bank was not subject to heavy expansionary pressure from either the balance of payments or the borrowing of the public sector.

Left to construct its own monetary policy, the Banco de México followed a mildly deflationary course. As funds flowed out of the country, placing a strain on the reserves of the private commercial banks, the central bank eased reserve requirements and rapidly expanded its loans and investments. The Bank did not, however, quite offset the outflow of funds; it permitted the money supply to contract slightly in 1946 and 1947. Output was rising and the money supply was falling, but inflation continued. Capital and consumption spending mounted rapidly as long-absent goods reappeared in Mexican markets. Funds which had accumulated and been held semi-idle during the war now financed increased expenditures, so that a sharp rise in the velocity of circulation of the money supply far more than offset the small decline in its quantity.[17] A glance back at Table 1 shows that prices rose nearly 20 per cent in 1946 and nearly 10 per cent in 1947. By the end of 1947 the immediate postwar inflationary pressures had spent their force. But Mexican prices in 1947 had already reached a level more than two and a half times that of 1939.

At first, the mildly deflationary policy of the Banco de México did not interfere seriously with investment since it did not fully offset the potential for financial expansion which had been created during the war. Total investment rose from only 9.3 per cent of gross national product in 1943 to 14.3 per cent in 1947. This increase in the rate of capital formation was traceable more to the improved availability of capital goods and materials than to financial factors, but the termination of the increase in 1947 probably was related to the fact that monetary policy was beginning to take hold. There was a limit to the extent to which velocity of circulation could rise as a substitute for the accustomed monetary expansion. After 1947, no further increase of any consequence occurred in the rate of capital formation.

Had the Banco de México continued its policy of 1945–1947, the postwar inflation would probably have been relatively mild and brief. But the drain of foreign exchange was becoming intolerable, and the rate of internal growth was dropping sharply. A crisis began to develop in late 1947 and continued into 1948. With it, the Banco de México began again to churn frantically in an effort to reconcile the aims of continued growth, avoidance of domestic banking panic, limitation of the inevitable fall in the external value of the peso, control of inflation, and service of a now rising public-sector deficit. The Bank expanded its credit to stimulate growth and finance the public sector; it aided those banks most hurt by the external drain; it accelerated the development of selective controls to limit the credit expansion needed to serve essential investment; and it allowed the peso to fall in the foreign exchanges. The latter action sent the exchange rate from 4.85 per U.S. dollar, which had prevailed since early in the war, to a new level of 8.65 in 1949.

The first effects of the turnabout in central-bank policy were moderate. Though the assets of the Banco de México rose by almost 35 per cent between the end of 1947 and the end of 1949, the money supply, the price level, and the rate of growth all responded less vigorously than might have been expected.[18] A new turn of events was not, however, long delayed. In 1950, Mexico's monetary structure was subjected to an inflationary blast more severe than any since the worst months of World War II. Economic recovery in the United States, the Korean conflict, and the mounting effects of internal monetary expansion and devaluation produced a feverish boom. During 1950 the money supply rose by an alarming 37 per cent, real gross product grew by 8 per cent, and prices climbed by 7 per cent. In 1951, monetary expansion slowed to 11 per cent, and the rise in real gross product was 7.4 per cent, but prices shot up by 20 per cent. By the next year, the boom was ending. Both the money supply and real gross product rose in 1952 by only about 4 per cent, and the rate of price increase dropped under 8 per cent. (All percentages are from Table 1, p. 126.) Mexico was on the verge of a recession, and the following year, 1953, saw a near-stoppage of the growth of output and the first price-level decline in many years.

The various dilemmas posed by the complex growth goal which

Mexico was by now pursuing were thrown into strong relief by the sharp upswing of 1948 to 1952. Public-sector investment was again expanding rapidly, and it was coming to be a larger share of total investment than it had been immediately after the war. In order to support this level of investment, the public sector's funded debt jumped by 81 per cent, from 2,410 million pesos to 4,372 million pesos.[19] Private investment was also rising. Both types of investment had official sanction, and both required funds. Yet savings and the investible revenues of the public sector could not supply money in adequate amounts, given the low national propensity to save and the government's reluctance to raise public-sector income sharply.[20] There was also a sincere desire to control inflation, but this would have required rigorous control of the money supply. The balance-of-payments pressures of 1950–1951 would alone have made it doubtful that controls could be fully effective. Given the need to support the public sector and the productive investments of the private sector, fully effective control was impossible.

For the monetary authorities this meant that a way had to be found to finance public-sector investment and approved private investment without wholly abandoning the objective of price stability. The pattern followed was similar to that of earlier periods but included technical refinements and entailed less heavy dependence on the credit of the Banco de México. The national credit institutions were encouraged to expand very rapidly, relying on some funds from the government, on borrowings from the private banks and the public, on foreign credits, and, as necessary, on money from the central bank. Vigorous efforts were made by Nacional Financiera, the Patronato del Ahorro Nacional, and a few other national entities to place securities with the non-bank public and to encourage greater saving. The Banco de México continued to support the market for public-sector securities and some private issues, but until 1952 did not find it necessary to absorb large quantities of paper. By this time, the inflationary surge was over and recession was in the offing. All in all, internal expansion of central-bank credit was a relatively minor source of inflationary pressure by comparison with the balance of payments.[21]

The methods employed to moderate monetary expansion represented a considerable refinement of earlier control techniques. The commercial banks no longer were required to hold such exaggerated cash reserves with the Banco de México. Instead, a security reserve system was developed which, in effect, came close to substituting for open-market operations. Beginning with the accelerated growth of Banco de México credit in 1947 and 1948, commercial banks were required to hold certain kinds of securities in addition to their cash reserves. These assets might be bought by the banks in the open market, but they frequently were purchased from the portfolio of the Banco de México itself. However they were acquired, the effect was to substitute lending by the commercial banks for lending by the central bank, since the paper in question was of a sort which otherwise would have gravitated to the Banco de México. Thus, the central bank was able to limit the amount of its own credit outstanding through exchanging securities and other paper for the excess reserves of the commercial banks.

With the heightening of inflationary pressures in 1949, the device was supplemented with a legacy from World War II. During the war, the Banco de México had negotiated two agreements with the banks of the Federal District specifying that these banks would not lend beyond certain levels — based on the amount of credit outstanding as of certain dates — and would hold any excess funds as idle deposits with the Banco de México or in cash. In 1949, a variation of this device was used to serve the purposes of general credit restraint and to direct the private banks' credit into channels where it might replace Banco de México money. Two reserve requirements were established for Mexico's commercial banks, one applying to deposits held on September 30, 1949, and the other a marginal reserve requirement applying to increases in deposits beyond the amount held on that date. Since this kind of reserve system continued for some years, and since the security reserve requirements incorporated in it have become a well-established part of regulation of private financial institutions, an example of the requirements is interesting.

In 1950, reserve requirements for commercial banks located in the Federal District were as follows. First, they had to maintain a reserve of 50 per cent of the amount of demand deposits and certain time liabilities (not including savings deposits) which had existed as of September 30, 1949, and which were denominated in pesos. (There were different rules for liabilities denominated in foreign currencies and for savings deposits.) Within this 50 per cent requirement, a 10 per cent deficiency was permitted on condition that the funds were invested in bonds of the federal government, certificates of participation of Nacional Financiera, or bonds of the Banco Nacional Hipotecario Urbano y de Obras Públicas. Another deficiency of 10 per cent was permitted on condition that the funds were invested in bonds of private *financieras* or other securities designated by the Banco de México and acquired from this institution. That is, the basic reserve requirement could be satisfied by a conventional reserve of 30 per cent and the other 20 per cent in approved securities. In the case of demand and time liabilities exceeding the amount held on September 30, 1949, the reserve requirement was technically 100 per cent, but deficiencies up to 70 per cent were permitted on condition that the funds were used for specified purposes. Two deficiencies of 10 per cent each were permitted on the same terms given above; a 15 per cent deficiency was permitted on condition the funds were used for production loans to agriculture and industry, and loans for the import of primary materials and equipment; 15 per cent was allowed for intermediate credits to agriculture or industry; 10 per cent for each of three classes of securities of greater than two years' maturity selected by the minister of finance; and 15 per cent for production credits of less than one year granted through agricultural credit societies. Obviously a bank could not take the maximum percentages allowed in all these categories, since this would bring the total above the 70 per cent maximum deficiency allowed.[22]

This system also applied, though not with identical terms, to banks located outside the Federal District. In effect, these complex requirements established for every commercial bank in the nation a substantial obligatory deposit at the Banco de México (30 per cent for peso demand and time liabilities of Federal District banks) and supplemented this with security reserve requirements which were much more stringent 'for deposits received after September 30, 1949, than for the amount in existence on that date.

Though the details of reserve requirements have varied many times in subsequent years, the basic concept of combining conventional reserve requirements and special securities holdings has continued to characterize Banco de México regulation of commercial banks. Securities holdings of insurance companies, capitalization banks, and, more recently, private *financieras,* have also been regulated in such a way as to assure acquisition of considerable quantities of paper of the federal government and the national credit institutions.

For the central bank, the security reserve arrangement provides far more flexibility in combining credit control and developmental finance than could a single reserve requirement. For the private banks, it is a complex and often confusing system which deprives them of much freedom in the use of funds and encourages subterfuges for evasion of requirements, but it is probably more palatable than the much higher deposit reserve requirement which would almost certainly be the alternative.

In more recent years, the Banco de México has moved seriously into the regulation of liability accounts as well as asset holdings of the private institutions. Especially since 1958, the Bank has attempted to discourage the holding of liabilities denominated in foreign currencies (dollars) by the private institutions, and has set quantitative limits on the annual rate of growth of issues of *cédulas hipotecarias* by mortgage banks and on the acquisition of short-term liabilities by private *financieras.*

The boom of 1950 and 1952 was followed by a recession whose trough was passed in 1953. With the recession, monetary restraint eased and public investment expanded in an effort to restore the upward movement of real economic activity. In early 1954 the peso was once more devalued sharply, this time from 8.65 pesos per U.S. dollar to 12.50 pesos per dollar. No protracted period of crisis preceded the 1954 devaluation, and the foreign-exchange reserves of the Banco de México were still substantial when it occurred. Devaluation in this case was evidently a preventive action motivated by fear of a worsening of the 1953–54 recession in the United States, by expectation of a coming run on the peso, by a desire to stimulate exports, and by a wish to give domestic producers more effective protection against imports. The rapid inflation which had occurred since 1948 had substantially eliminated the advantage afforded by the previous devaluation, and the 1954 action seemed an advisable step.

Advisable or not, the new devaluation had a profound impact on the thinking of many Mexicans. Earlier falls in the value of the peso had been obviously linked to the crises of the 1930's and the dislocations produced by World War II. But the 1954 move, coming without such obvious causes, brought shock and dismay. Confidence in the economic policies of the government was rudely shaken, as was faith in any permanent stability of the peso at any time. Much of the economically literate population has lived in continuous expectation of new devaluations through all the years since 1954. The 1954 devaluation came just before Easter; and Mexico City bankers claimed as late as 1962 that there continued to be a mild but perceptible shift from pesos to dollars in the several weeks before Easter.

The trauma produced by the devaluation has made the Mexican government highly sensitive to even a hint of further depreciation. Attachment to the exchange rate has reached proportions which bear little relation to its purely economic significance. Avoidance of devaluation has joined growth and price stability as an independent, though related, objective of economic policy.

A short burst of inflation and a rapid rise in economic activity occurred between 1954 and 1956. This acceleration of Mexican growth was stimulated by the devaluation, by the after-effects of

the anti-recessionary measures of 1952–53, by burgeoning public
and private investment, and by the sharp gains in economic activity
in the United States. This period was the last of the post-1940
series of feverish expansions. By 1957, the upward thrust had
weakened. From that year through 1962 Mexico was free of severe
expansionary or contractionary pressures. Increases in output and
rises in the price level continued, but the pace of both seemed to
have slowed markedly. Though a respite from inflation was wel-
come, concern began to appear over Mexico's ability to continue
to expand her real gross national product at a pace appreciably
faster than population growth.

The Cuban revolution in 1959 and the steadily worsening relations between that nation and the United States added political unrest to the concern over the vitality of the Mexican economy.
Despite the fact that 1960 was a good year, confidence was not
restored. In 1961, the rate of expansion seemed to sag again, and
there was open uneasiness in the private sector over both the performance of the economy and the intentions of the public sector
with respect to future economic policy.

Official statistics available at the time apparently confirmed a
slowdown of significant proportions. Only once between 1957 and
1961 (according to those statistics) did the annual rise in real
gross national product exceed 5 per cent, and it twice fell so low
as almost to eliminate improvement in per capita production.

As a matter of fact, data published by the Banco de México in
1963 indicate that fears of stagnation were somewhat exaggerated.
A revised gross national product series (see Table 1, p. 126) shows
that the expansion of output between 1956 and 1962 amounted to
about 37 per cent in real terms, a figure but moderately smaller than
the growth of some 43 per cent in real gross national product
registered between 1950 and 1956. Inflation slowed markedly from
the first of these two periods to the second; the price rise between
1950 and 1956 was about 71 per cent, while that between 1956
and 1962 amounted to some 31 per cent. Prices were still rising

appreciably by the close of the second period, however. The average increase for 1961–1962 was roughly 3 per cent per year.

Whatever revised statistics may show to have been the true state of economic affairs in Mexico during the late 1950's and early 1960's, the feeling of a slowdown in the pace of progress was real. Combined with a dimming of economic optimism was a feeling that the now-aging Revolution was floundering ideologically and politically. In the private sector there was the fear that a new and sharp leftward turn might be in the making, and this fear was buttressed by much talk and some action in the public sector which looked toward further restrictions on private business.

Reaction in the public sector to the presumed slowdown in economic growth was actually, in Mexican terms, rather orthodox and conventional. The government of President Adolfo López Mateos sought to revitalize the old slogans of the Revolution and moved further along lines of economic policy that had become traditional. Land reform was accelerated and widely publicized; public investment was increased; most of the remaining private electric power interests were nationalized; foreign investment was treated less well; expanded efforts were made to supply the urban poor with cheap food and clothing; fiscal reform and centralized economic planning were endorsed and were advanced moderately; the reins of monetary control were relaxed in 1959 and again in 1962. But these are long-familiar kinds of response to less-than-satisfactory growth in Mexico. In general, the government spoke and acted with a cautious eye to political and economic compromise.

The failure of private investment to provide a strong impetus to economic growth has been a matter of particular concern in recent years. Partisans of political or economic philosophies to the left of the Mexican center tend to blame private investors for their failure to expand "productive" investments rapidly. Advocates of rightist positions are distressed that the government has not placed itself firmly on the side of private enterprise. They condemn controls, taxes, needless government economic endeavors, and consequent lack of private confidence as culprits in the weakness of investment. That private investment has not been notably strong since 1957 is not questioned even by the government itself. Official pronouncements indicate and official figures support the contention that only rapid expansions in public investment prevented a more pronounced slowing of economic activity in the late 1950's and early 1960's.

For the two years, 1955 and 1956, a period of rapid expansion, total fixed investment in Mexico was about 65 per cent private and 35 per cent public. In 1959–1960, the ratio was 60 per cent private and 40 per cent public. Data for 1961 indicate a proportion of 54 per cent private investment and 46 per cent public investment, and though private investment seems to have rallied in 1962, it is doubtful that much of its former relative position was recovered.[23]

Financial policy during the years from 1956 through 1962 followed generally familiar lines. The most important difference in the monetary environment was the absence of the severe instability which had earlier plagued Mexico's balance of payments. Relative stability in the external accounts permitted firmer control over the internal monetary situation than during any other period of comparable length in modern Mexican history. Banco de México policy was generally restrictive, and it successfully limited the rate of price increase to moderate proportions, though no serious effort was made wholly to stop inflation. There were limits to the restrictiveness of policy; sharp increases in the money supply during 1959 and again during 1962 were permitted, apparently for the purpose of stimulating private investment and the rate of growth.

Both quantitative and selective controls over commercial bank credit were employed by the Banco de México to prevent too rapid a rate of monetary expansion and to channel available credit into "productive" uses of funds. Vigorous efforts were likewise made by the Banco de México and Nacional Financiera to broaden the securities market and make the holding of bank liabilities attractive to savers.

As in earlier periods, the public sector required substantially more investible funds than its revenues produced. The funded debt of public-sector entities rose in total by about 125 per cent from 1956 to 1962, a rate of increase slightly more rapid than that of private debt. In absolute terms, the rise in public-sector funded debt was 9.2 billion pesos. This sum far outweighed the increase of 3.4 billion pesos in private funded debt outstanding which took place in the same period.[24]

Strenuous efforts by the government, the Banco de México, Nacional Financiera, and other public financial entities were required to place such a volume of new public-sector securities without a highly inflationary rate of credit expansion. Added pressure was put on banks, insurance companies, and other institutional lenders to hold public-sector paper and to restrict their lending for "unproductive" private undertakings. Controls were placed on the rate at which some private financial institutions could issue kinds of securities or accept kinds of deposits which competed directly with public-sector securities as outlets for investible funds. Some public-sector paper, notably securities of Nacional Financiera, was made more attractive through increased yields as well as assured liquidity.

Altogether, credit was tighter in Mexico between 1957 and 1962 than it had been for many years, and this was reflected in rising interest rates. Though the precise extent of the rise is not ascertainable, money rates of interest apparently drifted upward moderately. As we saw in Chapter 1, real rates of interest increased sharply under the combined influence of rising money rates and a declining rate of inflation. The effect of tight credit was concentrated on private-sector borrowing, particularly that thought to be for "unproductive" purposes. The control structure was continually manipulated to assure adequate financing at preferential interest rates to public-sector borrowers and to those private borrowers favored by official policy. Credit shortages and high interest rates may have been responsible for a part of the weakness of private investment during the same period, though there is no way of isolating their effect from the myriad other influences at work.

For the investigator surveying Mexican financial experience over the last few decades and the complex interplay of forces in the public and the private sectors, the safest conclusions are none at all. It might be well to say that this is a most interesting case and let things go at that. But the temptation to take an interpretive look at the emergent relations between private banking and the public sector is irresistible. Since banking policy has been so much an instrument for economic change and since the financial system of the early 1960's is a relatively mature one, such an attempt may not be wholly amiss.

Chapter 4

Banking Policy and Economic Growth

CHANGE has been the aspiration and the accomplishment of Mexico's rulers for more than a century. By fits and starts the cultural fabric of an ancient, complex, and primitive society has been rewoven into a design more like the economically developed parts of the Western world. The process of institutionalizing and accommodating the forces of change has been erratic, but a profound transformation seems now well-advanced. It is to this transformation that Mexico refers when she speaks of the "Revolution."

The Revolution is supposed to express the will of the Mexican people and to find its practical driving force in the government. As a producer of the Revolution, government is conceived ideally as both the servant and the master of the individual citizen. According to Mexican doctrine, the government is not to repress and coerce personal aspirations and behavior into monolithic conformity. Neither is it supposed passively to represent and serve the wishes of the people as they now think and live. Government should be the agent of, and instructor in, Revolutionary change. From close contact with all strata of society the public authority is presumed to sense the required direction of change and to foster movement in that direction.

Effective playing out of this scheme of things requires an easily perceived consensus among those groups that are in communication with the government. The wider the spectrum of points of view passed along to the power center (via the official political party) the more "democratic" the system becomes. But the more inclusive the network of *de facto* communication grows, the less likely it is that a mandate for a clearly defined program will emerge from the working of the system. Like most broadly based movements, the "Revolution" must concern itself more with maintaining momentum along familiar paths than with trail-blazing.

Mexican ideology admits no rigid boundary between kinds of economic activity considered the preserves of public and private enterprise. The public sector is expected to innovate, to guide, to regulate, and to participate in economic processes as necessary, though it is not expected to overwhelm private undertakings. Where the process of socio-economic transformation is not affected or is well-served by private enterprise, the government is not bound to take any action at all. But where it appears that the unregulated progress of events will contravene the advance of the Revolution, the government is ideologically free to take whatever action is necessary to speed the pace of desired change. There is, of course, no easy way to determine when changes contravene the advance of the Revolution and when they further it. Hence this scheme of interrelationships poses a continual problem of distinguishing between oppressive and liberating intervention.

It is to the credit of Mexico's better Revolutionary governments that their guiding ambitions have been relatively simple and have responded to the most obvious deficiencies of Mexican society in affording status, dignity, security, and opportunity to the mass of citizens. Apparent long-range objectives may be summarized as the creation of a domestically united and internationally proud Mexico within which stable prosperity offers to every Mexican the opportunity to realize his potentialities. These goals imply a striving for status, national and individual; they are heavily interlarded with the feeling commonly called nationalism; and they require sustained economic growth for their attainment.

The dual Mexican emphasis on the individual and the collectivity has been seen as comprising an operational whole. The unity of aspirations was stated by Ramón Beteta as early as 1930:

With the Revolution, our great effort, we have discovered our-
selves: in analyzing the Revolution, we have understood our hetero-
geneity, our lack of unity; in studying its causes, we have found in
the basis of our society a system of injustice and oppression; in investi-
gating its results, we have found a movement toward integration, a
desire for mutual understanding, and a means for the improvement
of the economic status of our humbler classes. The diverse directions
. . . the labor movement . . . the nationalization of natural resources . . . our petroleum and mining laws . . . the paintings which
cover the walls of our public buildings . . . our songs . . . In all of
these . . . we see the realization of our great hope: that Mexico may
become a great nation.[1]

Broad goals are given specific embodiment in particular undertakings, and this union is heavily stressed. While dedicating a
long-wanted railroad in northern Mexico, President Adolfo López
Mateos declared in 1961:

. . . the Chihuahua-Pacific Railroad has a transcendental significance. It is not only a means of communication and of national
integration; not only a factor which must stimulate the economy of a
vast region of the nation. It is something more; it is a symbol of what
our people is capable of accomplishing through its effort, its desire to
improve, and its encompassing patriotism.
This work has been achieved through the determination of Mexicans, through the technical competence of Mexicans, through the
faith of Mexicans, and it therefore has an exemplary significance for
this generation: the Mexican is capable of the conquest of nature
for the benefit of the Mexican; he is capable of placing technology
in the service of his people.[2]

As both quotations suggest, economic improvement is regarded
as an indispensable component of cultural revolution, and economic
policy has occupied a position of pre-eminence in over-all government policy. The economic goal has been growth, and growth has
been conceived in the relatively uncomplicated terms of greater
output per Mexican in an environment consistent with the broadly
liberal aims of the Revolution.

Government intervention in Mexico's economy has been widespread and frequently effective. For the most part, however, it

has been pragmatic rather than doctrinaire, since the Revolution contains little in the way of a unique economic doctrine. When examined after the fact, actions aimed at provisional objectives and implemented with the tools most conveniently at hand have often shown surprising consistency. But seldom can a plausible case be made that these represented, at the time, deliberate steps in a soundly conceived and carefully articulated program for Mexican development.

Further, public policy in Mexico has usually been free of attempts to force the processes of change into conformity with a pre-congealed notion of the correct path for historical evolution. Policy-makers have retained a considerable ability to modify concrete programs with changing public attitudes and the vagaries of objective reality. At the same time, the lack of an unambiguous ideological mandate has tended to produce compromise, caution, and a willingness to rationalize faulty but viable programs.

During most of the period since 1910, government policy has spearheaded the socio-economic transformation of Mexico. But one would be wrong to think of Mexico's economy as dominated by the public sector. The economy rests fundamentally on private enterprise. There are some nationalized industries and others in which government participation is extensive, but these do not make up the bulk of economic activity. Moreover, government policy itself is hammered out amidst clamorous representations by strong private-interest groups, all vociferously "Revolutionary," but each having its own ideas regarding the means for furthering the Revolution. No government of Mexico has yet seen itself as the sole engine of economic progress, though each has sought to lead in the creation of an environment within which it and those private groups that sympathize with it could work in tandem toward shared goals.

These general considerations provide a better basis for understanding present-day Mexican banking. Operating within them, Mexico has moved far toward creating a set of banking institutions and financial practices capable of a positive contribution to attainment of her national goals. Innovation by the public sector has created a powerful central bank, a widespread network of government financial institutions, and a set of control techniques able to direct credit toward those undertakings thought most important to economic growth. Financial institutions in the private sector have found it possible to adapt to regulation and public competition and, at the same time, to grow and prosper. The gulf which once separated the Revolutionary governments from private enterprise is today easily bridged in the course of everyday transactions. The lofty aims of the Revolution and the more mundane goals of private bankers have been rather successfully merged into an operating creed which holds that "a good Revolution requires good business," and "good business requires a good Revolution."

It is true that embers of ideological conflict still glow beneath the surface in banking as elsewhere. Small but vocal minorities in Mexico bitterly oppose the compromise which harmony between public and private sectors suggests. At one extreme is a group which feels that the Revolution ended when Cárdenas went out of office in 1940 and which seeks a sharp leftward swing toward a true "proletarian" revolution. At the opposite political pole, a radical right seems to want either anarchy or a return to the social philosophy of Porfirio Díaz.

But the ideological embers are not continually fanned by overt public-private clashes. Both public and private sectors seem increasingly tolerant of the banking concepts and structural relationships which developed largely in the late 1930's and early 1940's and which in the years since then have attained an increasing technical sophistication. Dissatisfaction with banking legislation and monetary controls exists, but it does not generate deep animosity, nor does it strike at the rationale of the present system.

Private bankers would, in general, be prone to agree with Rolando Vega who, upon inauguration as president of the Asociación de Banqueros de México in 1961, declared:

Mexican banking . . . faces a task to which it should direct its full effort, that of increasing its resources . . . in order to continue

cooperating in the economic development of the nation through adequate channeling of these resources to the different economic activities, which will permit acceleration of growth, neutralization of population pressure, and broadening of internal and external markets . . .

We reaffirm our faith in the principles of free enterprise, and we
are confident that the directive and complementary action of the State
will be structured within bounds which recognize that the fundamental
task, in banking and credit, belongs to us. [We are likewise confident
that] the State will come to our aid occasionally and temporarily in
order that the rhythm of our march toward progress may not be
disturbed.[3]

This statement, even if one tries to read between the lines, implies
an acceptance — mildly wary though it may be — of the present
state of affairs in banking. It presumes a basic coincidence between
the growth goals of the public sector and the desire of the private
banks for profitable operation. There is likewise a recognition that
both advantages and dangers inhere in the complex interdependence
of public and private enterprise which now exists.

On the other side, a distillation of the expressed and implied
content of statements by public-sector leaders of the 1950's and
early 1960's would produce a set of operational relationships much
like what seems to have been in Vega's mind. Few important
figures in the public sector express a desire for radical change in
banking. Though important technical modifications in banking
legislation were made at the end of 1962, these brought no basic
change in either the concept or the structure of the system.[4]

Thus there has been achieved in Mexican financial affairs a
compromise which seems to offer something to everyone. The outcries of many former critics have been quieted and — barring a
striking political upset — no telling demand for a major new turn
of events is likely to be heard in the next few years. Since the
middle 1950's, a semi-equilibrium state of banking interrelationships has prevailed and has proved itself capable of weathering
moderately severe vicissitudes of confidence and economic conditions. In these circumstances, it is interesting to look again at the
web of ideas linking Mexico's desire for economic growth, her

collateral economic goals, and her financial system. It is also interesting to speculate on the degree to which financial development has actually performed the tasks assigned to it in the drive for general growth.

The importance of banking policy to Mexico's attempt to revolutionize her economic life stems from strong convictions on the part of policy-makers that a rapid rate of capital formation is the key to growth and that the financial system is at least one principal key to capital formation. Money, banks, credit, and related institutions have received so much attention from Mexico's government largely because of this imputed relationship.

In the Mexican view, under-utilized natural resources, superabundant labor, a potentially large domestic market, a growing entrepreneurial class, access to advanced technology, and a social and economic structure increasingly receptive to change, combine to form in Mexico an environment in which investment is highly fruitful. The total volume of investment which can be undertaken is, however, seen as limited by the availability of funds for financing it. These funds (neglecting inflows from abroad) depend on surpluses generated by investing entities, voluntary financial savings by the public, and new credit created within the banking system. The first two of these have been, in general, inadequate; therefore, recurring reliance has been put on new credit created within the banking system. This has been a source of inflation, and since World War II few people have been willing to espouse deliberate inflation as a device for capital creation. (Whether or not inflation works as a means of capital formation when employed continuously is, of course, another question.) Official policy has opposed inflation with increasing vigor. Mexico's reasons for opposing inflation are worth noting, for they are significant politically and economically.

It is widely believed in Mexico that rapidly rising prices shift the distribution of income in such a way as to hurt those economic groups whose welfare is the special political and ideological concern of the Revolution. A famous study of Mexico's economic growth published in the early 1950's seemed to show a marked rise in the share of income received by upper income groups, especially recipients of profits, during the highly inflationary 1940's. Subsequent studies have tended, in general, to characterize the 1940's and early 1950's in the same way.[5] As a result, Mexican leaders tend to assume that a severe inflation will lower the relative position of the nation's many poor people and may even reduce their absolute level of living. The impact of inflation is most severe on the urban poor, since they depend more on purchased means of subsistence than do their rural counterparts. Urban proletarians, though still outnumbered by the rural, are a concentrated and explosive group. Control of inflation and other efforts to keep down the cost of simple consumption items comprise an important part of the price of their support for any government. Commentaries on economic policy by leading *políticos* have thus come in the past two decades to include an almost ritual obeisance to price stability on grounds of its effects on the "economically weak" classes.

Inflation is opposed, too, on the more strictly economic ground that it discourages saving and distorts the pattern of investment. As was pointed out earlier, stocks and other variable-income securities have never been widely popular in Mexico. Most public and private efforts to promote a wider market for securities have involved paper denominated in fixed amounts of pesos, to yield a fixed income. The lessened attractiveness of such assets in an inflation is well known. Inflation is thought to drive would-be savers to consume more or to speculate in inventories, real estate, and foreign exchange. Speculation in real estate or inventories is dubbed "unproductive" in Mexican theory, while speculation in foreign exchange drains the reserves of the Banco de México and raises the specter of devaluation and more inflation. Public-sector saving, too, is likely to be impeded by rising prices. Many kinds of tax revenues tend to lag behind the price level, and it is difficult politically to increase taxes, or raise the prices of publicly provided goods and services, when popular outcries against the cost of living are loud.

Since 1954, avoidance of devaluation has risen to the status of a near-independent goal though it is closely related to the anti-inflationary aim. By comparison with many other currencies, Mexico's peso has not fared badly. It dropped from roughly 2 per U.S. dollar in 1925 to 12.5 per dollar in 1954 and has remained stable since then. But the exchange rate has become a symbol of the success of government economic policy, and its extra-economic significance is great. Opposition to exchange-rate depreciation adds much force to the general case against inflation as a device for accelerating growth.

With these things in mind, let us look again at the country's recent financial evolution, starting with the Cárdenas era.

Mexico, to keep her Revolution going past the mid-1930's, needed rapid expansion of an ever broadening range of economic activities. Basic to this expansion was a high rate of capital formation. To create capital, initiative had to be seized and means of finance — real and monetary — had to be found. Public-sector energy under Cárdenas and vigor in both public and private sectors thereafter provided the initiative but not the resources. Savings and public-sector revenues were inadequate, hence heavy reliance was placed on credit creation. But credit creation — often aggravated by external circumstances — led to inflation and real or potential exchange crises. These, unless constrained, would undermine political stability, especially if the public sector continued, as in the 1930's, to ignore private industry, commerce, and their allies, the private banks. A compromise plan of action which sought to promote growth while restraining the depreciation of the peso and meeting pressing private needs had to be devised. Such a compromise was found in what has become the present network of institutions and regulations.

Conceived in the early 1940's and perfected over two decades of experience and tinkering, the intricate financial structure of modern Mexico is a striking politico-economic accomplishment. Its vocal espousal of "sound money and productive investment" appeals strongly to the fundamental orthodoxy of popular Mexican views of money and economic activity in general. At the same time, the system has maintained a continual tolerance for credit expansion (albeit a restrained expansion) and a considerable internal flexibility in apportioning funds. These have made the system viable in a rapidly changing Mexico committed to growth but short of voluntary saving and reluctant to expand public-sector revenues rapidly.

Mexico's ingenious maze of institutions and controls, in their early years, may very well have increased the rate of capital formation by creating a situation in which new money from a variety of sources could be made to force additional real saving from the economy. Since the early 1950's, the effect of monetary controls has more likely been to substitute public investment for private investment and "productive" investment for "unproductive" investment. The national propensity to save may have been increased by economic growth and the structural changes which have occurred within Mexican society. Attempts to multiply and diversify financial institutions and instruments may also have worked in this direction. But, whatever has happened to rates of voluntary saving, one could not say with confidence that financial policies in the 1950's and early 1960's have increased the aggregate rate of capital formation — hence economic growth — as compared with what would otherwise have happened, *all other things being equal.* A more probable conclusion is that the rate of inflation likely to accompany a politically tolerable rate of capital formation and economic growth has been reduced.

However, it cannot be concluded that other things would have been the same without the financial developments of the past few decades. In retrospect, those developments seem a notable and essential leap forward in the drive for economic expansion.

Mexico had seen a promising start toward economic development collapse in the tragedy of the military phases of the Revolution. Successor governments barely managed in the 1920's and early 1930's to maintain a semblance of order and a minimum of economic subsistence. The Cárdenas-led surge of national desire and energy promised future development. But after an initial period of almost unopposed authority, followers of the Cárdenas line would surely have faced mounting political (and possibly military) pressure from moderate and rightist groups. For the Cárdenas program was mainly *ad hoc* and was badly out of balance. It contained no room for most of the elements of the Mexican private sector which have in fact become mainstays of subsequent economic development. Over a long-run period, accommodation with these groups had to be accomplished unless the government proposed severe political repression and wholesale nationalization of economic activity — actions which would have produced widespread confusion and bitterness or worse.

Nowhere was the hiatus between the developmental zeal of Cárdenas and the caution of the dissenters thrown into sharper relief than in the management of financial affairs. So long as the policies of the late 1930's were followed with open enthusiasm, no philosophic or practical rapport between private business and bankers and the government was possible. Had no rapport been attained, and had this forced a continuation of the emergency monetary policies, financial collapse would have been a probable result as the pressures of World War II aggravated an already dangerous situation.

The compromise pattern of institutions and regulations which emerged has never provided full control over credit expansion or changes in the price level; it was powerless to prevent sharp devaluations of the peso; it may even, at times, have reduced private capital formation instead of increasing it. An observer looking at the record of financial policy in Mexico might also reasonably argue that a very long time was required for the attainment of tolerable rates of growth and tolerable rates of inflation combined with each other — even if one accepts the performance of the late 1950's and early 1960's as "tolerable" on both counts.

Despite these faults, one must also be impressed by what has been accomplished in Mexico. The record shows that Mexico's public sector was able to mount and sustain a drive for national economic development despite a low propensity to save, inadequate governmental revenues, and a pitifully weak set of private financial institutions. It was possible to cope with the crises of World War II and after without stern political repression, a cessation of growth, or surrender to uncontrolled inflation. Increasingly, means were found for financing the public sector without outraging the sensibilities of the private sector, and grounds were created for collaboration of public and private entities within psychologically important rules of financial orthodoxy. In all these ways, financial development has made tangible contributions to long-term economic growth and to political stability.

For the future, the picture is less easily sketched. Though it seems probable that the concepts guiding Mexico's financial policy-makers are entrenched firmly enough to endure for a time, it is not so clear that they deserve to maintain this hold on thinking. The basic political and economic compromises have now been effected; the essential monetary controls have been developed; and the fundamental institutional structures have been put in place. In concept and technique, Mexico's financial policy and the institutional structure which it guides seem rather well-adapted to solving the problems they were built to solve. But these were the problems of the 1930's and the 1940's, problems of getting development going and keeping it going with a minimum of undesirable side-effects in an atmosphere of internal and external crisis. Neither the bundle of problems nor the atmosphere of the 1960's and 1970's seems likely to be the same as that which the rationale of the Mexican financial complex envisions. This is not to say that the present system will not continue to work. It almost certainly will. In a much-changed Mexico, however, the elaborate controls may do more harm than good, and a far from perfect underlying theory of the relation of finance to growth may lead policy in wrong directions.

Mexico is no longer just beginning her journey along the road to economic progress; she has moved far enough to enjoy the luxuries of confidence in the future and critical re-evaluation of the past. In the financial field, a confident look ahead might produce a realization that private-sector institutions are now large and diversified and will become more so. Pursuit of their own best interests is likely to lead them to do most of the things which controls have, in the past, been designed to force upon them. A critical backward look might throw a different light on the reasons why public-sector financial institutions and an elaborate set of controls over the private-sector institutions were thought necessary.

Three important judgments, not always explicitly recognized, underlie the Mexican approach to guiding financial development. One is the assumption that total demand for loanable funds will always exceed the supply arising from non-inflationary sources at interest rates which are politically acceptable. A second is the belief that the efforts of the private sector to make profits are likely to lead to uses of funds which contribute little to economic growth. The third is a presumption that the public sector, taken as a whole, will always have a large deficit with the rest of the economy and that this deficit must be financed on terms more favorable to the public sector than voluntary lenders would accept. All of these positions had a measure of usefulness in the past; all are now partially or wholly obsolete.

Of the three positions, the first is the most nearly justifiable. Total demand for funds in Mexico is of such proportions that very high interest rates would result if supply were wholly limited to savings (public and private) and an amount of credit creation corresponding to expected real economic growth. No such stringent limitation has actually been enforced in recent times, but the period since 1957 has seen relatively severe credit restraint, and interest rates have risen sharply. This kind of supply-and-demand situation may well argue for stringent regulation of the total quantity of money for purposes of inflation control, but it does not necessarily argue for complex selective controls to favor some borrowers over others. In fact, were it not for the presumption of a continual public-sector deficit, Mexican policy-makers themselves probably would not maintain that high interest rates constitute such a serious problem as to make rigorous selective controls desirable policy.

The still-powerful suspicion of private profit as an adequate stimulus to productive investment and the consequent fear of allowing too large a share of available financing to flow in the directions desired by the private sector are largely anachronisms. Whatever economic validity there was in the distinction between "productive" and "unproductive" uses of funds rested mainly on the temptations to speculation afforded by wartime and postwar inflation or on the outright unavailability of essential goods in emergency periods. These times have passed, and the distinction should have passed with them. In part, of course, the "productive" versus "unproductive" dichotomy has been ideological and hence not related directly to economic gain or loss. But even its ideological virtues may, perhaps, better be judged when it is recognized that they may have a price in terms of lost growth.

Of vital importance to understanding the logic of past financial policy is a recognition of the role played by public-sector fiscal affairs. To a much greater extent than has ever been frankly admitted, the rationale of Mexico's guidance of institutional development and devising of monetary controls rests on the continual need to finance a large public-sector deficit. In essence, the banking system has continually been forced to produce funds for public-sector entities within constraints which tended, insofar as possible, to minimize both political unrest and inflation. This has been done skillfully and with imagination, but it may often have meant that private investment had to be reduced so that public-sector investment could be undertaken. Mexico's greatest need for the future seems more likely to be an expanded rate of total capital formation than a further substitution of public for private investment.

The fact that the public sector (including the nationalized industries and other entities) has not generated sufficient revenues to finance its current expenses plus large investment outlays is neither surprising nor "unsound" in any invidious sense. This state of affairs may, nonetheless, inhibit growth. Public-sector decisions to invest in a low-saving economy which wishes — like Mexico's — to maintain price stability do not, in themselves, increase the rate of capital formation. The public sector cannot be accommodated without either displacing private investment or generating inflation. In Mexico, despite the best that financial policy could do, the public-sector deficits seem to have accomplished both.

NACIONAL FINANCIERA

Entrepreneurship in a Mixed Economy

by
Calvin P. Blair

Chapter **I**

The Nature of Nacional Financiera

EVERY society, in the course of its evolution, is likely to develop a variety of institutional forms designed to promote, control, or direct the forces making for economic change. In many cases these forms are merely traditional patterns of behavior; but sometimes they are concrete organizational units. In modern nations one often finds an agency charged in some general way with promoting development and with achieving some acceptable compromise of roles between the public and private sectors.

In Mexico, the institution which stands out as the central promotional agency is Nacional Financiera, S.A. (national financing institution).* A product of the Mexican growth experience since 1934, Nacional Financiera, commonly called NAFIN, is a complex institution which combines subtle elements of public and private influence in formulae which have led to an essentially nondoctrinaire approach to questions of economic development, state intervention, social control, and protection of the public interest.

To an analyst looking for a clear demarcation between the public and private sectors, Nacional Financiera offers some bewilderment. It is technically a public institution, and *de facto* is responsive to the Mexican chief executive; yet it leaves much promotional

---

* The term *financiera* has no good literal translation. Many *financieras* exist in Mexico—both in the private and public sectors—with the principal objective of financing industrial development. This special kind of finance company performs the function of an investment bank. It also guarantees bonds, lends money at short and long term, and deals in securities.

initiative to the private sector, even while making heavy commitments of public funds. To proponents of private enterprise who might prefer a public development agency that "does everything it can to help private business," and no more, the institution seems annoying in its role as stockholder, policy-maker, and competitor in a broad range of activities. To proponents of state-owned enterprise — or indeed to a partisan of merely a well-defined public sector — Nacional Financiera likewise presents some peculiar features. It takes on private capitalists as its partners, frequently rescues a mismanaged private venture, and regularly lends money to private and public firms in the same industry.

In its eclectic approach to Mexican economic development, Nacional Financiera has come to occupy an important position. As of mid-1961, it was creditor, investor, or guarantor for 533 business enterprises of all kinds; it held stocks in 60 industrial firms; and it was majority stockholder in 13 firms producing steel, textiles, motion pictures, plywood, paper, fertilizers, electrical energy, sugar, lumber, and refrigerated meats.[1] At the end of 1961, as shown in Table 1, Nacional Financiera's loans were nearly half as large as those of all private credit institutions, and they accounted for more than one third of total lending by Mexico's public credit institutions. Long-term loans by NAFIN were considerably greater than those of the private lending agencies taken together. Judged by the amount of its loans, the size of its capital and reserves, or its holdings of securities, NAFIN was obviously a financial giant by Mexican standards.

At any given point in time, Nacional Financiera's loans and investments are, of course, modest in comparison to any measure that purports to show the size of Mexico's industry. For example, total capital invested in manufacturing, as reported in the Mexican 1955 industrial census, was more than thirty times as great as NAFIN's loans and investments in manufacturing enterprises. Nevertheless, NAFIN's holdings in some industries (e.g., fertilizer, iron and steel, sugar refining) were of considerable importance.[2]

To a student of economic development interested in the relative

BLAIR, TABLE 1

Selected indicators of Nacional Financiera's relative
position among Mexican credit institutions, 1961

(balances in millions of pesos as of December 31)

Item	All private credit institutions[a]	All public credit institutions[b]	Nacional Financiera
Capital and reserves	2,952	4,448	806
Loans outstanding	16,516	22,367	8,114
Long-term[c]	4,706	12,085	[d]
Bond holdings[e]	5,776	3,327	838
Stock holdings[f]	1,848	2,051	1,159[f]

[a] Includes all commercial and savings banks, savings and loan associations, private *financieras*, mortgage banks, capitalization banks, and trust companies. Does not include insurance or bonding companies.

[b] Includes, among other institutions, the Banco de México and Nacional Financiera itself. The sums shown include preliminary estimates for the Banco Nacional de Crédito Ejidal (national bank for ejidal credit).

[c] Long-term loans, as shown here, include only those loans of more than 360 days maturity which are outstanding to business firms and individuals. Long-term loans to banks and to the federal government are not identified in the published data. *Total* loans to those two sectors amounted to 1,717 million pesos by all private credit institutions and 817 million pesos by all public credit institutions as of December 31, 1961; these amounts are included in "loans outstanding" as shown above.

[d] Not available. Nacional Financiera, however, rarely makes loans of less than one year maturity.

[e] Bond holdings shown here are confined to Mexican issues, public and private. They are valued at par or stated value.

[f] Stock holdings shown separately for Nacional Financiera are not comparable to those shown for all private and all public credit institutions, because of a difference in the basis of evaluation and because of the inclusion in NAFIN's holdings of some items not included in the data for other credit institutions (trust department operations, securities purchased under agreement to resell, and securities held as guarantee).

Sources: Banco de México, *Informe anual* for 1960 (pub. 1961), table 17, pp. 80–81, and table 33, pp. 110–111; and Nacional Financiera, *Informe anual* for 1961 (pub. 1962), table 9, p. 49; appendix table 9, p. 114; and appendix table 13, p. 122.

roles of the public and private sectors, Nacional Financiera presents a fascinating case study with a diversity of forms of interplay between the two sectors. What kind of social animal is Nacional Financiera? How did it come to be what it is? What entrepreneurial roles, subtle and obvious, has it played in the economic development of Mexico? And what is likely to be its behavior in the future? These and other questions have prompted the present inquiry.

No attempt is made here to treat exhaustively every role which Nacional Financiera has played. Its efforts to develop a national securities market, for example, will be treated only briefly; and its role as fiduciary for the federal government will be treated hardly at all. Our emphasis is on the entrepreneurial function.

THE FORM AND SUBSTANCE OF POWER

Nacional Financiera combines elements of investment, savings, and central banking with a multitude of other duties. Its own organic law asserts that its primary role is to act as intermediary between, on the one hand, national and foreign investors and, on the other, enterprises in need of capital.[3] Its objectives, as spelled out in the law, include regulating the securities market, promoting business enterprises, aiding financial institutions, acting as fiduciary for the federal government and as adviser and agent for the sale of public securities, and counseling the Comisión Nacional Bancaria (national banking commission). In its promotion activities, NAFIN is charged to direct its help to enterprises which use unexploited natural resources; which advance technology or substantially increase output in important industries; or which contribute to improvement in the balance of payments by earning foreign exchange or substituting for imports.

To carry out its objectives NAFIN is authorized to deal in securities and commercial paper, obtain concessions for exploiting natural resources, purchase a financial interest in corporations and partnerships, control and administer businesses, issue its own securities and guarantee others, lend money, act as trustee of properties, accept deposits, and engage in other operations necessary to its functions. It is exclusive agent for all long-term federal bond issues and for negotiating foreign credits — public or private — requiring a Mexican government guarantee. NAFIN is a member of Mexico's three stock exchanges and has a representative on the regulatory Comisión Nacional de Valores (national securities commission). Three NAFIN officers and directors sit as the Comisión Especial de Financiamientos Exteriores (special commission on foreign financing), a body whose favorable ruling is required by all public-sector agencies for any foreign credits exceeding one year in term and 1,250,000 pesos in amount.

Nacional Financiera is a joint-venture enterprise with public and private capital and with directors from both sectors. The public sector is dominant. In the first place, NAFIN's organic law requires the NAFIN capital stock held by the federal government (Series "A") always to be in a majority. In the second place, the "general public," which subscribes the rest of the stock (Series "B"), includes any person, natural or corporate, public or private; it can and does embrace official institutions such as the nation's central bank, the Banco de México. In theory, shares in the hands of the "general public" could reach 49 per cent of capital stock. In fact, however, they barely amounted to 9 per cent as of mid-1961.[4] And only a small fraction of this was held by investors in the private sector.

NAFIN's stock is not especially attractive from the point of view of the private calculus of returns; the 6 or 8 per cent paid in recent years is small in comparison to yields on alternative investments. However, many private financial institutions are required by law to be stockholders in NAFIN; and in any event the private sector, for reasons of strategy and the exercise of some voice in policy, might wish to retain a stockholder position. Membership on NAFIN's board of directors is important to the private sector.

Of the seven board members, the federal government is legally entitled to three, who control the agency by voting the Series "A" shares. These three are usually cabinet members; as of 1963 they were the Secretario de Hacienda y Crédito Público (finance minister), the Secretario de Industria y Comercio (minister of industry and commerce), and the Secretario del Patrimonio Nacional (minister of national properties). Series "B" shareholders have the legal right to elect the other four members. As of 1963 two of these were from the public sector, one being the president and general manager of the Banco de México, the other an adviser to the finance minister and an ex-official of several public ministries and institutions. The remaining two members of the board came directly from the private sector, one being chairman of the board of the nation's largest commercial bank, the other an ex-president of the Confederación de Cámaras Industriales (CONCAMIN), a national confederation of industrial trade associations.

So much for form; now for substance. NAFIN's administrative structure itself is a clue to the forces at work, and the behavior of the institution reveals quite clearly that representation is more than mere formality. NAFIN is subject to the leadership of the chief executive and his cabinet, is constrained by its ties to the central bank, and is responsive to a significant degree to both initiative and opposition from the private sector.

Within limits, Nacional Financiera is a body of competent *técnicos* making microeconomic decisions on the basis of criteria familiar to any lending institution in the private sector: market potential, debt-service capacity, managerial talent, past performance. The operating credit department has the authority to grant individual loans as big as half a million pesos without formal approval even from NAFIN's board of directors.

NAFIN has helped to organize business firms and maintained a significant voice in many of those in which it has equity investments. It has developed a complex of interlocking directorates and stockholdings much after the fashion of Mexico's major private financial groups. With its ties through cabinet officials to the president of Mexico, however, its power to influence economic activity is undoubtedly greater than that of any financial group in the private sector. NAFIN's president and general manager sits on the board of directors of the central bank, the country's largest steel company, the telephone company, the nationalized petroleum company, and key corporations in textiles, cellulose and paper, coke and coal, light and power, electrical apparatus, automotive assembly, and railroad car manufacture — most of them enterprises in which state participation is important. Other NAFIN personnel are on the boards of dozens of companies in the public and private sectors. Their presence may offer the enterprises an influence with NAFIN and hence preferential access to credits, but it is also a channel through which NAFIN's *técnicos* make their own ideas felt.

The jobs of the principal officers of NAFIN — in contrast to those of its board of directors — are quasi-political only, a fact attested to by the continuity of management across two or more presidential terms. True, no major officer could hold his post against the will of the President of the Republic; true, top managerial ranks will likely include someone who is the chief executive's eyes and ears at NAFIN's operating level; true, too, NAFIN policy and practice are subject to criticism from other agencies and ministries depending from the presidency. But by and large NAFIN's *técnicos* are a respected voice in the councils of government — or better said, respected voices, for there are major differences of opinion honestly held and openly expressed within the ranks of NAFIN's top officers with regard to policy issues.

In a more subtle fashion, Nacional Financiera's influence has been diffused throughout the Mexican economy. Over the years the institution has been the training ground for numbers of bright and active men whose technical and political expertise has moved them into important government positions. Two finance ministers came up through the ranks of NAFIN, and the public service career of each led to an ambassadorial post. Former NAFIN functionaries occupy positions of counsel and influence in the national securities commission, the Secretaría de la Presidencia (the president's coordinating ministry), and other agencies in which economic policy is made.

If Nacional Financiera's influence is diffuse and important, its power is strictly circumscribed. NAFIN's decisions, despite the increasing role of nonpolitical, technically competent personnel, must always be consistent with economic policy as evolved by the president and his advisers. Since 1946 the chairman of NAFIN's board of directors has always been the finance minister; and he is the principal channel whereby the chief executive exerts influence over NAFIN's activities. The finance minister, together with the two other cabinet ministers and Banco de México president who are members of NAFIN's board, assure any "government position" a majority representation in NAFIN's major decisions. The government position is neither simple nor monolithic, but it certainly has been responsible for the grand directions which NAFIN policy has taken — and often for many specific short-run measures as well.

The objectives of Mexican economic policy most important for NAFIN's behavior since 1940 have been: (1) to foster industrialization, (2) to promote import replacement, (3) to develop the infrastructure, (4) to develop native entrepreneurial talent, (5) to reassure the Mexican private sector, (6) to reduce the role of direct foreign investment in industry and the role of foreigners in general in business enterprise, and (7) to avoid inflation.

These elements of government policy have largely determined NAFIN's choice of industrial investments, prompted its heavy lending to state enterprises in transportation and energy fields, limited the extent to which it associates with foreigners in new ventures, reduced its ability to move aggressively into many industries (even when it feels that private initiative is flagging), and forced its increasing reliance on foreign loan capital for its operations.

NAFIN has a very special relation to the central bank. In recent years, as we have seen, the president and general manager (*director general*) of each institution has been a member of the board of directors of the other; and, in addition, a representative of the private sector has sat as interlocking director on the boards of both. The relation is not only structural but functional, and it is at once a source of strength and weakness for Nacional Financiera. NAFIN's success in borrowing and the acceptability of its own securities rest in part on the implicit support of the Bank. In time of need, the Bank can see that NAFIN gets funds by lending directly to it, purchasing some of its holdings of government bonds, or requiring private and public financial institutions to invest part of their reserves in NAFIN securities. But the close working relationship with the central bank also means that NAFIN is used as an agent of monetary policy. On occasion NAFIN's sales of securities have been designed primarily to absorb excess funds and check inflation rather than to raise capital for development financing.

The interplay between NAFIN and the private sector is a fascinating game, part bluff, part economic power, and part political pressure.

In the realm of economic power, NAFIN may have a slight edge. Its ability to grant or withhold credit, its ability to raise capital in amounts not common in the Mexican private sector, its control of the largest and most modern plants in a few industries, its position as supplier of intermediate goods to many private manufacturers, and its direct interlocking with certain federal ministries — all these are foundations of some power and the source of some worry on the part of the private sector.

The power, however, is much constrained; and influence and pressure have not traveled exclusively in one direction. The private sector exercises some influence on NAFIN directly through its representatives on NAFIN's board and indirectly via a number of channels: through majority ownership in ventures with NAFIN participation, through the press, and through political pressure. NAFIN officials and Mexican presidents (to some extent including even Lázaro Cárdenas in the 1930's) have had genuine desires to develop the private sector. If indeed no administration has found a magic formula for defining the public-private relationship, all of those since 1940 have shown a certain tender concern for private enterprise. Moreover, no chief executive eager to win business over to his political system would let NAFIN exercise autonomy damaging to his purposes. NAFIN's behavior is thus subject to an important political restraint.

PROFITS AND GROWTH

Despite its nature as a public institution, Nacional Financiera has posted a profit record which would do credit to some of the best-managed of private enterprises. Over the first twenty-seven years of its life, from mid-1934 to mid-1961, its profits aggregated more than 851 million pesos, and it earned some net income in every year.[5] It collects net interest on re-lending operations, commissions on endorsements of loans, dividend income from industrial securities, and fees on trust fund and brokerage operations. These types of income give NAFIN a record of profits quite high in proportion to its own paid-in capital, though not unusual for successful brokerage business on a large scale.

At first NAFIN was somewhat embarrassed over its financial success, and it issued frequent disclaimers of the profit motive as central in any way to its operations.[6] Quickly, however, it developed a fondness for its net earnings: they were indispensable to NAFIN's growth, and a growing NAFIN could stimulate growth in the Mexican economy. "Profits for growth" became one of Nacional Financiera's standard rationales. For example, its president and general manager declared in a major policy speech in 1961: "Like the other banks created by the state in Mexico, Nacional Financiera is a service institution, and in a service institution, profits are a means and not an end. Had the institution not earned considerable profits; if, having earned them, it had not reinvested them, it would not have been possible for it to have assumed the outstanding role it now occupies in the Mexican banking system." [7]

NAFIN's behavior bears out the contention that it sought profits in order to grow. In its first twenty-seven years the dividends it paid amounted to less than 17 per cent of its net earnings. The administrations of Presidents Miguel Alemán, Adolfo Ruiz Cortines, and Adolfo López Mateos successively increased NAFIN's authorized capital; and NAFIN repeatedly capitalized its reserves. Since the federal government is NAFIN's majority stockholder, decisions to allocate profits to reserves for subsequent capitalization may be considered part of a continuing fiscal and development policy clearly meant to maintain NAFIN as one of the country's major financial institutions.

Nonetheless, NAFIN's capital and reserves have provided a relatively small part of its funds. What NAFIN has called its "own resources" (*recursos propios*) include: (1) capital and reserves; (2) direct credits to the institution from abroad; (3) funds raised from issues of NAFIN's own non-equity securities — the *títulos financieros* (a form of bond) and the *certificados de participación* (a security which technically gives participation in the variable income from a common fund, but which *de facto* has been treated as a bond); and (4) other items, including credits from other banks and a variety of demand and time liabilities of NAFIN. As seen in Table 2, capital and reserves, despite their rapid growth in absolute amount, have declined in relative importance. Meanwhile, since 1942, when NAFIN obtained its first credits from abroad, foreign loans have come to play a dominant role in the institution's "own resources."

The total funds made available by or through Nacional Financiera greatly exceed its "own resources." NAFIN manages a number of trust funds and, in addition, lends its guarantee (*aval* or *endoso*) to large sums borrowed from other financial institutions by Mexican firms and agencies, both public and private. As of mid-1962, the total of funds channeled into economic activity by NAFIN from all sources stood at 19.4 billion pesos, of which NAFIN's capital and reserves accounted for less than 5 per cent.[8]

Judged by the origin of its funds, NAFIN clearly has lived up to the role of financial intermediary proposed in its organic law. Moreover, by using borrowed funds and by guaranteeing foreign loans and domestic bond issues, it has greatly increased the scope of its operations, the number and variety of enterprises in which it has had some promotional role, and its own profit-making potential.

The record of this interesting agent of a pragmatic and interventionist state is worthy of some close scrutiny; and that record in historical perspective now demands our attention.

BLAIR, TABLE 2

Nacional Financiera's own resources,[a] grouped by
origins, selected years, 1941–1961

(balances as of December 31)

Year	Total	NAFIN's non-equity securities			Capital and reserves	Other items[c]
		Foreign loans to NAFIN[b]	Títulos finan-cieros	Certificados de partici-pación		
		Expressed in millions of pesos				
1941	53	0	2	7	11	33
1943	435	40	5	143	17	231
1946	869	220	44	226	37	344
1949	1,580	774	81	317	128	280
1952	2,638	1,033	236	879	188	301
1955	3,773	1,446	306	1,282	274	466
1958	4,726	2,020	709	1,124[d]	482	391
1961	11,406	6,576	1,869	1,438	806	717
		Expressed in percentages of total				
1941	100.0	0.0	3.8	13.2	20.8	62.2
1943	100.0	9.2	1.1	32.9	3.9	53.1
1946	100.0	25.3	5.1	26.0	4.2	39.6
1949	100.0	49.0	5.1	20.1	8.1	17.7
1952	100.0	39.2	8.9	33.3	7.1	11.4
1955	100.0	38.3	8.1	34.0	7.3	12.4
1958	100.0	42.7	15.0	23.8[d]	10.2	8.3
1961	100.0	57.7	16.4	12.6	7.1	6.3

Note: Because of rounding, detail will not necessarily add to totals.

[a] *Recursos propios*, as distinguished from other resources, which are trust funds committed to NAFIN plus amounts borrowed by other firms and agencies under NAFIN's guarantee.

[b] Converted to pesos at prevailing exchange rates.

[c] Includes credits from other banks, and a variety of deposits and other demand and time liabilities of NAFIN.

[d] Includes 14 million pesos worth of outstanding *certificados de copropiedad industrial* (a security similar to the *certificado de participación*).

Sources: Nacional Financiera, *Informe anual* for 1955 (pub. 1956), p. 51, and various later issues; also data furnished by NAFIN's accounting department. The figures for 1958 and 1961 were computed by the author from data given in the sources. For all years, separation of "capital and reserves" from "other items" was made by the author.

Chapter 2

The Record of Nacional Financiera

THE tenor of Nacional Financiera's activities has been to reflect at once prevailing economic conditions and the purposes of Mexican presidents. World events and domestic crises have often forced a course of action, and chief executives have used NAFIN as an instrument for accommodating pressures in Mexican society and achieving at least some goals which could be identified as carrying out the Mexican Revolution.

There have been five administrations during NAFIN's lifetime, but NAFIN's history may be divided into three periods. The first is an experimental period, 1934–1940, corresponding to the regime of Lázaro Cárdenas, during which time NAFIN tried out in incipient form every role it was later to play and one or two which it was to discard. The second, 1941–1947, is a period of uninhibited industrial promotion deriving largely out of the stimuli provided by World War II and corresponding roughly to the administration of Manuel Avila Camacho. After 1947, an entrenched and successful NAFIN served three administrations as agent for developing the infrastructure and promoting import substitution — with nuances of the characters and the times of Miguel Alemán, Adolfo Ruiz Cortines, and Adolfo López Mateos, to be sure, but with a continuity and a sameness that warrant treating the post-1947 years as one period of NAFIN history. As with any arbitrary division of time, policies and activities shade from one phase into the next;

and NAFIN seems usually to have foreseen by the end of one period the role which would characterize its behavior thereafter.

A QUEST FOR CHARACTER, 1934–1940

Nacional Financiera was conceived in 1933, a product of crisis and a creature of a government determined to create a viable financial system. The Mexican Revolution and the Great Depression had left credit institutions — both national entities and the branches of foreign banks — holding unusual amounts of mortgage paper forfeited for nonpayment of loans. For reasons of technique and of Mexican law, the banks could not hold real estate in such amounts, and means were sought frantically to restore liquidity to the system.

In August of 1933, Cárdenas' predecessor, Abelardo Rodríguez, issued a decree establishing "a financial society with the character of a public institution," [1] to which the banks could turn over real properties and mortgages which they were unable or unwilling to retain. The society would be capitalized at 100 million pesos, a bold sum for the day. The government would subscribe half of the capital stock, paying with cash or real estate. The society would administer, subdivide, colonize, and sell real properties; collect mortgage loans; and organize credit unions and other enterprises which might be needed to liquidate the properties and credits.

It is not at all clear just how the society was expected to restore liquidity. Credit institutions were to exchange real estate properties and mortgages for capital stock, not for cash. Success would depend upon the speed with which the new institution could move real estate and real estate paper into an already poor market. A banking system liquidity problem thus became a real estate development problem, with the new society as administrator, developer, and sales agent.

Whatever the merits of the scheme, it died aborning. Eight months elapsed, and a new decree by President Rodríguez on April 24, 1934, established the Nacional Financiera, S.A.[2] Capital was specified at 50 million pesos, with the federal government's contribution to be 25 million, one third of it in cash or prime credits and the rest in real properties.

The new decree retained as central objective the restoration of liquidity to the banking system, but Nacional Financiera was to be more than a mere rescue operation for real estate assets. It was specifically recognized as the fourth in a new system of public institutions meeting Mexican needs, following on the heels of the Banco de México, the Banco Nacional de Crédito Agrícola (national bank for agricultural credit), and the Banco Nacional Hipotecario Urbano y de Obras Públicas (national urban mortgage and public works bank). Considerable foresight seems to have gone into the 1934 decree creating NAFIN; it conceived a complex role for the institution in the future development of Mexico. The legal bases were set for most of the operations which the institution would ever engage in, including industrial promotion and the establishment of a securities market.

NAFIN did nothing for six months.[3] Then it occupied itself almost exclusively with the chores of administering rural properties and loans during 1935, at the end of which year the function of managing real estate credit was transferred to the Banco Nacional de Crédito Agrícola. Despite relief from the real estate function, NAFIN continued to concentrate on real estate loans, serving more as a mortgage bank than as a general finance company. It was not until 1937 that the value of other investments exceeded that of mortgages in its total assets. With the creation of its trust department in 1938, NAFIN re-acquired certain real estate management duties: selling or administering properties and auditing and collecting real estate development credits. By this time, however, the real estate function was no longer dominant. Four years of experience had allowed the evolution of other activities.

At the time of NAFIN's creation, the securities market in Mexico was feeble. In 1934 the country's only stock exchange, the Bolsa de Valores in Mexico City, recorded a mere 4 million pesos in total transactions; and the central bank, later to become a major trader, engaged in none at all.[4] Over-the-counter markets existed, with commercial banks serving as brokers between banking customers and issuing agencies; their volume is not known, but it must have been small. Nacional Financiera, urged by the 1934 decree to take the first steps toward creating a "true securities market," engaged to some extent over the following six years in every kind of transaction that it was authorized to pursue.

Taking its function seriously, NAFIN bought and sold 2 million pesos worth of securities in 1935 and rapidly increased its annual transactions to a level of 44 million in 1937. In 1940, in an effort to stabilize a market ruffled by world events and the uncertainties of an election year, it made purchases and sales totaling nearly 73 million pesos.

During the 1934–1940 period under Cárdenas, NAFIN intervened to a limited extent in the organized exchange. It bought and sold the stocks of a bank, a steel mill, a paper company, a major brewery, and a tobacco manufacturer — about the only shares being traded on the exchange. It further supported the market for private securities by guaranteeing the sale of bonds issued by a cement company and by subscribing for bonds of two breweries. But it concentrated its efforts on supporting government bond issues by making direct purchases, underwriting sales, and lending against bonds as collateral.

In 1937, NAFIN contributed a new security to the Mexican markets with the issue of half a million pesos worth of *títulos financieros*. Because of its desire to encourage widespread ownership, NAFIN refused the offers of credit institutions to buy the entire amount. Considerable difficulty was encountered in the sale, and it took NAFIN three years to dispose of the issue.

By the time 1940 rolled around, NAFIN, with its varied experience and its own outstanding issues, was clearly the most influential institution dealing in the Mexican securities market.

In 1936, NAFIN and the Banco de México had become officially tied through mutual holdings of each other's stock, and a close working relation soon developed between the two. The Bank extended a number of credits to finance NAFIN's activities. The latter, in turn, acted on occasion as an agent of central-bank policy. When, for example, the peso came under severe selling pressure in 1938, NAFIN helped to hold its decline in bounds by operating in gold and foreign exchange.

During its early years, NAFIN experimented with its promotional role. Its first significant industrial finance — in 1936 — included the purchase of mortgage bonds issued by a cement company and loans to a maker of bakelite products and to a public firm manufacturing and importing paper.[5] It also underwrote an issue of bonds to finance a public hospital for children. In 1937, NAFIN joined a consortium to sell the bonds of two breweries; and it extended credits to private enterprises in trucking, office machines, agricultural and industrial machinery, plywood, and furniture. In this year, too, NAFIN first performed the entrepreneurial function of organizing corporations, forming the Banco Nacional de Comercio Exterior, S.A. (national bank for foreign commerce), and an import-export affiliate designed to carry on commercial operations forbidden to the bank. NAFIN subscribed to stock in both firms.[6] Over the next two years NAFIN expanded its industrial loans to include credits to producers of alcohol and sugar, guaranteed the sale of cement company bonds, bought up the stock of six electrical energy generating companies on behalf of the federal government, and participated in the reorganization and administration of the electric companies.

By 1940, NAFIN was making a special point of its role of industrial promotion and lamenting with an air of experience that "there have not been enough . . . opportunities to stimulate the formation of new businesses . . . The viable cases have been served by the Financiera." [7]

The 1934–1940 period of NAFIN history has been characterized as one of "indefiniteness of functions and paucity of activity." [8] In historical retrospect the characterization is undoubtedly apt. It is certainly true that Cárdenas, whose major policies were concentrated on agrarian reform, did not make great use of Nacional Financiera; and the official summary account of his presidential years barely mentions its name.[9] As seen in the light of its times, however, NAFIN was a bold concept and a significant — if not very active — institution. During its first six years it had become the most important operator in the securities market, made industrial loans, underwritten issues of private and public bonds, acted as agent for the federal government, channeled funds to public welfare projects, performed as an entrepreneur in organizing a bank and a commercial company, profited from the use of borrowed funds, and issued its own securities.

By the end of the period, NAFIN was a reasonably robust institution with 18 million pesos in total assets, 47 employees, and a sense of destiny. It had "tried everything" and found its character: industrial promotion. Its new character was embodied in the organic law — the *Ley Orgánica* — of December 1940.[10]

The organic law did not, as a matter of fact, endow NAFIN with any power which it had not already possessed. But the deliberate emphasis given to the promotional function amounted to a significant change in degree, if not in kind: "The institution is being reorganized especially with the object of channeling national and foreign capital to enterprises which create new sources of wealth and new centers of employment . . ." [11]

Nacional Financiera, it was foreseen, might have to engage in a great variety of concrete operations "for the benefit of the public and private economy." Hence, it would be given much freedom of action, being prohibited categorically only from engaging in activities which might harm the public or damage the prestige of the institution itself. The role which the administration of the new president, Manuel Avila Camacho, conceived for NAFIN was clearly stated: "The federal government feels that Nacional Financiera, S.A., can become, in short, one of the most powerful and efficient instruments for the promotion of progress in the national economy and for the general well-being . . ." [12]

From this point forward, NAFIN was to become not merely an

entrepreneurial agent, creator and promoter of industrial enterprises, but a self-conscious entrepreneur.

SELF-CONSCIOUS ENTREPRENEURSHIP, 1941–1947

It is tempting to attribute NAFIN's new emphasis and much of its success in the 1941–1947 period to a drastic change in political outlook which came with the advent of Avila Camacho in 1940. The new president was a man of more bourgeois values than his predecessor, Cárdenas, and of sufficient religious sentiment to declare publicly that he was "a believer." His middle-class business views and his profession of faith may have been reassuring to the private sector. Perhaps, as a result, NAFIN could become a "powerful instrument for progress" without scaring off private enterprise. The same kind and degree of public activity under an agrarian and revolutionary administration might have deterred private investment or provoked a reaction which could have hamstrung NAFIN's operations. As it was, private enterprise proceeded both to invest on its own and to join NAFIN in many ventures.

But it is easy to overemphasize the importance of presidential pronouncements. The relative contributions of administrative attitudes and economic opportunity to "business confidence" is an interesting question. Cárdenas, agrarian that he was, had not opposed industrialization. The strength of his personal leadership and the effects of his public expenditures on communications, education, and health had helped to weld Mexico into a meaningful economic whole, safer and more attractive for private investments. Moreover, Avila Camacho, a mild man with "pro-business" feelings, used NAFIN to extend the public sector into many industries without undoing a single reform of the Cárdenas era.

Whatever the obvious or subtle political influences, Nacional Financiera found itself in an environment crying out for the development of its promotional function. It did not take men of extraordinary genius to recognize by mid-1941 that war likely would become world-scale. A world war would mean high and continuing levels of demand for Mexico's major agricultural and mineral exports. It would also mean that imports of manufactures would be subject to any priorities imposed by foreign governments in allocation programs. Export surpluses, reduced transfers of earnings, and inflows of capital in response to fears and taxes in foreign lands would soon combine to produce high levels of foreign exchange. For the first time in decades, Mexico would enjoy a surfeit of capital funds. Here was a combination of circumstances justifying a major industrialization effort.

With the opportunities so palpable, why didn't private initiative surge to the fore? Why did Nacional Financiera play such an important role in industrializing Mexico?

Part of the answer is that private enterprise did flourish, even to the point of initiating most of the projects in which NAFIN made major investments. However, private capital had no special compunctions about seeking public help. NAFIN, for its part, was more concerned with activity than with property right; and practically every promotion was a joint venture in some degree. It is not certain whether NAFIN's major investments could have been made by private Mexican capital. In theory, there were no insurmountable obstacles, but most of the projects required a great deal of official representation abroad, borrowing money and negotiating with the United States government for necessary material and equipment. It is not likely that private entrepreneurs could have gotten this outside help without significant government backing. And from 1942 forward, NAFIN's intervention in foreign capital markets on behalf of credit-seeking private firms was perhaps as important as its own investments were in promoting industrial development.

Remnants of recovery programs and preparations for war made the prevailing world-wide economic climate one of government participation. Countries of great power and influence were in no position to point accusing fingers at an interventionist Mexican state. Wartime demand for materials, and the desire on the part of the United States and its allies to enlist cooperation, changed many attitudes, even the old hostilities growing out of the petroleum expropriation of 1938. Mexico and the United States in 1942 negotiated a trade agreement and an agreement for servicing the Mexican external debt.

The stage was well set for NAFIN to play the roles which it had announced for itself. Though it was diverted on occasion into acting as an agent of central-bank policy — supporting government bond prices or absorbing funds through anti-inflationary sales of its securities — its persistent focus was on industrial promotion. It really did begin to act as a major financial intermediary, channeling domestic and foreign funds to productive investments. Over the 1941–1947 period, NAFIN issued 318 millions worth of securities in pesos and another 15 million dollars worth in U.S. currency. In the same interval, it helped to obtain some 93 million dollars in foreign loans, most of which went into highways and railroads.[13]

As a symbol of its new role, NAFIN established in 1941 a department of promotion and began to make systematic studies of industrial development projects. With a predilection for manufacturing, it promoted enterprises in practically every sector of the Mexican economy over the course of the next seven years. The roster of firms aided by loan, guarantee, or purchase of stocks and bonds reads like a "who's who" of Mexican business; and NAFIN made many investments which continue to the present as its major assets.

During the war years, one promotion rapidly followed another. By the end of 1945 (the first year for which detailed and organized data are available) NAFIN held outstanding credits or security investments in Mexican industry totaling nearly 300 million pesos. (See Table 3.) It had bought stocks or bonds in at least 49 corporations. Its largest purchases had been in iron and steel, electrical appliances, sugar, paper, and fertilizers; but it also held securities in firms producing electricity, coal, laboratory glassware, electrolytic copper, cement, and many other products. NAFIN was a stockholder in 35 corporations and majority owner of five. For

BLAIR, TABLE 3

Nacional Financiera's loans and investments in industrial
enterprises,[a] 1945, 1947, and 1952

(balances as of December 31)

Industry	In millions of pesos			In percentages of total		
	1945	1947	1952	1945	1947	1952
Total	297.2	501.3	1,559.4	100.0	100.0	100.0
Food (excl. sugar and beverages)	3.4	5.9	39.2	1.1	1.2	2.5
Sugar	18.4	90.8	118.0	6.2	18.1	7.6
Beer and wine	—	14.4	33.0	—	2.9	2.1
Textiles and products	15.9	32.0	41.9	5.3	6.4	2.7
Forest products	1.8	1.3	—	0.6	0.3	—
Furniture	—	1.2	0.9	—	0.2	0.1
Paper and products	11.0	33.1	39.2	3.7	6.6	2.5
Chemicals (excl. fertilizers)	—	4.6	27.6	—	0.9	1.8
Fertilizers	10.0	10.5	50.6	3.4	2.1	3.2
Petroleum	62.9	29.1	21.6	21.2	5.8	1.4
Coal	4.7	0.6	25.7	1.6	0.1	1.6
Glass	0.3	2.1	0.1	0.1	0.4	—
Cement	9.8	13.2	24.5	3.4	2.6	1.6
Construction and materials (excl. cement)	26.9	15.0	58.7	9.1	3.0	3.8
Iron and steel	71.2	79.8	143.6	24.0	15.9	9.2
Copper and tin	2.5	5.5	8.0	0.8	1.1	0.5
Metal products	3.9	4.7	12.2	1.3	0.9	0.8
Electrical equipment	23.0	3.8	17.0	7.7	0.8	1.1
Electricity	4.7	26.5	295.3	1.5	5.3	18.9
Transportation and communication	16.8	111.2	548.1	5.5	22.2	35.1
Mining	0.7	3.0	21.0	0.2	0.6	1.3
Hotels	—	4.3	7.3	—	0.9	0.5
Motion pictures	8.3	6.9	4.2	2.8	1.3	0.3
Others	1.0	1.8	21.7	0.4	0.4	1.4

Note: Because of rounding, detail will not necessarily add to totals. Dash means less than 0.05.
[a] NAFIN's definition of "industrial" enterprises here includes some service industries (e.g., hotels) and construction. Further information about the coverage of NAFIN investment statistics during this period will be found in the footnote on our p. 223.
Source: Nacional Financiera, Décimasexta asamblea general ordinaria de accionistas (annual report for 1949, pub. 1950), p. 73, and Informe anual for 1954 (pub. 1955), p. 65.

the 18 leading corporate enterprises which it had helped to promote, its security holdings accounted for nearly half of a total capitalization of 256 million pesos.[14]

NAFIN's principal credits, as distinct from security purchases, had gone to finance equipment for the national railways, a refinery for PEMEX (the government oil corporation), hydraulic works and generating plants for the Comisión Federal de Electricidad (federal electricity commission), highway construction, cellulose fiber and cement manufacture, and a national movie industry. Smaller loans had helped to finance asbestos cement, pharmaceutical vials, metal door and window frames, school construction, coal mining, agricultural improvements, national bus lines, and a water supply for the city of Acapulco.

Though NAFIN's procedure seems to have been *ad hoc,* many of its promotions were clearly interrelated. Thus coal mining was an adjunct of steel manufacture; cement was necessary to highway, school, and dam construction; bus lines went with extensions of the highway grid; and petroleum refining was auxiliary to increased rail and highway transport and the thermal generation of electricity. Many other promotions, though not clearly linked, fit the general ethos of development prevalent at the time. Most of them represented responses to specific problems which became manifest as development proceeded. A few examples will suffice to illustrate the mixture of motives and conditions which prompted Nacional Financiera to action.

Symbolic of its major efforts was its promotion of Altos Hornos de México, S.A., an integrated steel works at Monclova in the northern state of Coahuila. As in numerous other cases, private enterprise initiated the project. The plant was planned to alleviate wartime shortages of rolled steel products then available only as imports. Private financial resources proved inadequate for an enterprise of the size and scope of Altos Hornos. NAFIN stepped in, borrowed 6 million dollars from the Export-Import Bank of Washington, subscribed to securities, and extended credits to finance the new firm. Organized in 1942, Altos Hornos had difficulties at first in getting necessary machinery and equipment because of wartime priorities in the United States. However, by late 1944, its blast furnace, plate mill, and pipe mill were all operating; and it had completed studies for a projected coking plant to be added to the steel complex. At the end of 1945, NAFIN held all of the bonds, more than three fourths of the preferred stock, and over one fourth of the common stock of the firm — security investments totaling 61.5 million pesos. Two years later, NAFIN became majority stockholder and began to make of Altos Hornos a showcase of public intervention in the industrial sphere.

Other wartime shortages aroused NAFIN's promotional interest. Cement offers an illustration. At the outbreak of World War II, NAFIN had a financial interest in only one firm, which had sold its entire bond issue to the agency in 1937. Pressures of demand during the war years prompted NAFIN to finance the expansion of the industry. The list of cement firms in which NAFIN held securities grew to six in 1945 and to ten in 1946.[15] In most cases NAFIN bought bonds, preferred stocks, or a small minority of common shares; but in one of the firms it became the majority stockholder. As a result of both public and private promotional efforts, the number of cement plants in Mexico increased from eight in 1940 to nineteen by 1948.

Not all of NAFIN's attacks on specific problems were simple questions of import replacement or of wartime necessity. Some of them represented a longer-run view of raising productivity or of breaking old bottlenecks which antedated the war. Such, for example, were promotions in the fertilizer and food-processing industries.

Mexican agriculture had been a notoriously poor user of commercial fertilizers. Though production had begun as early as 1915,[16] total output in 1943 was estimated at only 33,000 metric tons.[17] Because of the production of "formulas" with imported components, the 1943 figure probably included most of the 20,700 tons imported in that year.[18] On the basis of a study which it had begun in 1942, NAFIN concluded that the fertilizer industry needed a new enterprise with "vast economic resources." In 1943 it created Guanos y Fertilizantes de México, S.A., capitalized at 10 million pesos and wholly owned by NAFIN. The firm's major purpose was to exploit guano deposits on the islands off the coast of Baja California, but it announced an intention to supply the market with all types of modern fertilizers. Production began in 1944 with a trickle of formula mixes of guano and imported chemicals. Early customers were exclusively government institutions associated with agriculture, but a deliberate campaign was undertaken to educate farmers to the use of chemical fertilizers, especially as cultivated acreage expanded under the impact of irrigation. The firm was not conceived of initially as import-replacing; its output was never significant during the war years proper, and its early effect was largely to create new markets for fertilizers rather than to displace imports. As raw material supplies grew with postwar expansion of petroleum refining and natural gas production, the firm added facilities for making ammonia, sulfuric acid, and superphosphates. NAFIN, in a departure from its usual joint-venture position, remained as sole owner.

Wartime concern with food-processing industries seems to have had two motives. There was a general desire to increase the internal supply of foodstuffs and an interest in diminishing periodic losses suffered by producers of perishables when lack of rapid transport or the vagaries of the market left them with surpluses. NAFIN served both ends by financing plants located in producing areas. By 1945, NAFIN had some 21.8 million pesos outstanding in credits and security investments in food-processing firms, including majority ownership of a dehydrating plant and holdings of stocks or bonds in three sugar mills, a tomato-canning plant, and a flour mill. From this base, NAFIN expanded during the postwar years to promote or finance dozens of additional firms producing sugar, meat, milk, frozen fish, canned fruits and vegetables, and other foods.

A final example of mixed motives may be cited in the case of the Banco Cinematográfico. Founded in 1941, the motion picture

bank was the first of several NAFIN investments in a national
movie industry. Import replacement was one clear motive; it was
hoped that Mexican movies would replace some U.S. pictures. But
NAFIN rationalized its investments partly on the ground that external distribution of Mexican films would provide foreign-
exchange earnings.[19]

When World War II ended, Mexicans were producing industrial
goods in quantity and quality which would have been thought impossible some five or ten years earlier. Cement, steel, coal, fertilizers, forest products, electrical energy, and plywood were being
turned out by enterprises organized or reorganized under auspices
of Nacional Financiera. With help from NAFIN, other firms soon
would be manufacturing canned foods, copper, enameled steel,
pulp and paper, rayon, glass, caustic soda, and other chemicals.
Out of the success of its wartime promotions, NAFIN developed a
philosophy of industrialism and structural change:

> The progress of the Mexican economy should not be based on the
> export of a relatively small number of articles, essentially mineral and
> agricultural raw materials . . . but rather should rest on a change in
> its structure, translated into the export not only of raw materials but
> also of certain manufactured products or of raw materials with some
> degree of processing, and in which imports consist preferably of capital
> goods.[20]

NAFIN's arguments for development momentarily followed
orthodox "comparative advantage" lines, and it was even asserted
that tariff protection which permanently maintained high-cost industries would tend to impoverish the country.[21] It was certainly
true that NAFIN's major investments had been reasonably well-
directed into industries suited to the state of Mexican resources,
particularly in the environment of wartime shortages. But the general optimism about industrial possibilities was based more on the
de facto success of past promotions than on theoretical analysis,
and the use of the orthodox comparative-advantage argument was
indeed momentary. At the war's end, prospects for further indus-

trial development looked good. Monetary reserves were high, capital equipment would soon be available from the industrial countries, an early return of export markets was expected, internal markets were growing rapidly, and improvements were foreseeable in rail and highway transport. But a cloud darkened the scene. Advanced industrial countries would likely try to recapture their old export markets, subjecting Mexican industry to severe international competition. Mexico began to adopt restrictive import policies. She refused to join in the General Agreement on Tariffs and Trade, and in 1950 she ended her trade agreement with the United States so that she might feel free to use trade restrictions to promote industrial development. Import replacement, which had been something of a wartime necessity, became a guiding principle of postwar policy.

Still, NAFIN found itself, as before, attacking *ad hoc* a series of specific problems. One of these was the long-standing deficit in sugar supply in a country obviously capable of self-sufficiency. NAFIN helped to establish five major sugar mills in the states of Sinaloa, Tamaulipas, Veracruz, Jalisco, and Tabasco. By 1948, Mexico was a net exporter of sugar. A second specific reaction grew out of the great epidemic of hoof-and-mouth disease. Mexican exports of live cattle to the United States, valued at more than 18 million dollars in 1946, suddenly fell to zero under force of embargo. The private and public sectors both responded quickly. As part of an effort to replace some of the lost market with canned beef, twelve new plants were shortly organized, six of them with technical or financial help from NAFIN.

The success of NAFIN as promoter gave rise to apprehensions in the private sector. NAFIN's investments were large and diversified, its ownership position was sometimes dominant, and its financial resources and government support put it in position to do what few entrepreneurs of national origin had ever done. Moreover, NAFIN saw fit to assume a moral posture critical of private financing with little equity capital and much debt. At the end of

1945 the agency actually proposed to the federal government that all firms seeking NAFIN's financial assistance be required to meet two conditions: that credit represented by bonds not exceed net worth, and that preferred stock not exceed the amount of common stock.[22] To NAFIN, advocating a "democratization" of investment through wider ownership of voting shares, these requirements seemed "generous" and "related to the realities of the environment." The realities, however, were precisely those of which NAFIN complained. Private industrial entrepreneurs had no intention of raising capital through equity issues. Equity issues could not realistically be sold by broadside offerings to the general public; the only way they could be sold, if at all, was through the sharing of control with other large equity holders. Accordingly, entrepreneurs continued to get their funds from the sale of debt instruments to their affiliated financial institutions, to the Mexican public, to foreign lenders, or to NAFIN itself. NAFIN did not have the power to insist upon its criteria.[23]

However circumscribed its powers, NAFIN appeared to certain segments of the private sector as a strong competitor and unfriendly critic; they complained about its size, strength, or profitability. NAFIN in turn issued an occasional statement of reassurance: "While intervening in the promotion and finance of industrial enterprises, Nacional Financiera has based its policy on the principle of not interfering in activities which belong to private initiative, limiting itself to those cases in which the magnitude of resources and the uncertainty of immediate results made the investment of private capital unattractive . . ."[24]

A private sector unimpressed with such pronouncements soon got other reassurances. The election of 1946 brought to office Miguel Alemán, a president who made a point of being overtly friendly to business enterprise. In 1947 Nacional Financiera's organic law of 1940 was amended.[25] The amending law included formal statements designed to assuage private apprehensions. When Alemán submitted the proposed legislation to Congress, he wrote, in part, that "it is appropriate to delimit Nacional Financiera's field of operations, so that it not invade activities which ought to belong to private banking or to other public institutions." [26]

Article 5 of the law itself contained the explicit assurance that NAFIN would make every effort to obtain private cooperation in any promotions which it might undertake and, before offering finance, would see that private promoters put up as much capital as could reasonably be expected under the circumstances.[27]

The new law, however, was not merely an attempt to placate private enterprise. At the same time that it issued reassurance, it broadened NAFIN's powers. It increased NAFIN's authorized capital, confirmed NAFIN as the only institution to handle issues of public securities, designated NAFIN as sole agent for medium-term and long-term foreign credits requiring government guarantee, and required all public agencies and enterprises to obtain NAFIN's approval before borrowing abroad. Channeling foreign loans through NAFIN was a conscious form of intervention in the resource allocation process on the part of a government increasingly concerned with Mexico's total capital needs and debt-service capacity. Many public and private enterprises required foreign capital, and investment priorities could be established in part through NAFIN's reviews and rulings. Though short-term credit would not be involved, the bulk of foreign borrowing would come under official scrutiny.

The law in no wise made a clear delineation between the public and private sectors. Though it insisted that the kinds of industries promoted and the kinds of investments made by NAFIN should exploit new resources, improve technology, or better the balance of payments, this did not prove a serious limitation on NAFIN's activities. Almost any new venture could be rationalized in terms of one or more of those criteria. Nevertheless, the reassurance to private enterprise was not meaningless. Whatever NAFIN might do, it would be hard put to justify a mere swallowing up of existing firms. NAFIN, which even before this time had rarely ever proceeded oblivious to private interests, now for the first time in its history was "required by law" to seek cooperation. That requirement might indeed have little legal force; but it had real meaning as a sign of solicitude on the part of an administration seeking the esteem of the private sector.

By the end of 1947, NAFIN had expanded its credits and security investments in industry to more than 500 million pesos, as Table 3 showed. It had increased to 89 the number of corporations in which it held stocks and bonds. One third of the 89 corporations were located in the Federal District and the neighboring state of México; the rest were distributed geographically over seventeen other states. NAFIN had invested in practically all of the larger industrial enterprises of recent vintage in Mexico.[28]

However, because of large credits granted to the national railways, transportation actually occupied first place in NAFIN's total financing of industry. A policy of increased emphasis on the infrastructure had clearly begun by 1947, and it continued over the subsequent fifteen years.

AFTER 1947: INFRASTRUCTURE AND HEAVY INDUSTRY

A combination of economic and political motives helps to explain NAFIN's postwar activities. Rapid industrial expansion had "caught up" to Mexico's overhead capital facilities. Transport and communication were becoming limiting factors to the efficient use of industrial capacity and to the creation of further investment opportunities. Electricity was acutely needed for manufacturing, for residential consumption in crowded urban centers, and for the fulfillment of the old revolutionary promise of raising rural living standards; and these demands gave investments in electric power a high priority in development policy. The principles of "agrarian reform" had shifted from mere land redistribution to a general program of improving productivity, and this called for increased outlays not only on rural electrification but also on irrigation. The time was clearly ripe for heavier investments in the infrastructure.

It is to the advantage of Mexican political regimes that such investments may be labeled "revolutionary" and thus in keeping with a trend of social change which all administrations are pledged to follow. It was a further advantage in the postwar period that most of them corresponded closely to the traditional domain of the state as conceived by conservative elements of the private sector. By concentrating much of its attention on the infrastructure, NAFIN performed the rather neat trick of simultaneously meeting major needs of the Mexican economy, "carrying out the Revolution," and — temporarily, at least — failing to arouse the fears of private enterprise.

The emphasis on the infrastructure was sudden at first and persistent thereafter.

Table 3, which was presented on page 214, suggests the rapidity of the shift. At the end of 1945, NAFIN's credits and investments in electrical energy, transportation, and communication totaled just 7 per cent of the 297 million pesos outstanding to all industrial enterprises. By the end of Alemán's first year in office, 1947, they had grown to more than a fourth of a 500-million-peso total. And when Ruiz Cortines took over the presidency at the end of 1952, they accounted for over half of the total, which by then had risen to about 1.6 billion pesos.*

The persistence of the attention to infrastructure is shown in Table 4. From 1953 to 1961, total financial resources channeled by NAFIN into economic activity of all types grew more than threefold. The share going to the infrastructure never fell far below one half, and it stood at 61 per cent in mid-1961.

NAFIN's aid to the infrastructure has gone principally into railways and electrical energy. Credits outstanding to the railways

---

* Published data make no reference to NAFIN's financing of irrigation prior to 1953, nor do they show credits and investments in all types of enterprises (industrial and otherwise) prior to 1952. Data for the rather arbitrary list called "industrial enterprises" are available from 1945. The reliable series are all balances as of year's end. (See our Table 3, earlier in this chapter.) Series on credits made available or used during the year have been published for the years 1948–1959, but they are not homogeneous series, and the data are defective. NAFIN personnel privately warn against their use, and their publication was discontinued in the agency's *Informe anual* for 1960 (pub. 1961). Readers who wish to see them will find them in the *Informe anual* for 1959 (pub. 1960), table 14, p. 110, and the analogous table in earlier annual reports, beginning with the one for 1949.

alone have stood near one billion pesos in recent years.[29] NAFIN has lent large sums to the government's Comisión Federal de Electricidad (CFE) and to the major private electrical utilities before they were nationalized in 1960. Small credits and occasional bond purchases have aided several individual electric companies. By

BLAIR, TABLE 4

Total financial resources channeled by Nacional Financiera to all economic activities, grouped by origins and recipients, 1953, 1958, and 1961

(balances as of December 31 in first two years and as of June 30 in 1961)

Origins and recipients	In millions of pesos			In percentages of total		
	1953	1958	1961	1953	1958	1961
ORIGINS OF RESOURCES						
Total	4,742	8,949	15,361	100.0	100.0	100.0
Foreign loans to NAFIN	1,097	2,020	5,318	23.1	22.6	34.6
NAFIN's non-equity securities	1,400	1,833	2,910	29.5	20.5	18.9
Capital and reserves	206	482	812	4.4	5.4	5.4
Guarantees and endorsements by NAFIN	993	3,550	5,164	20.9	39.7	33.6
Trust funds	583	720	1,062	12.3	8.0	6.9
Other	464	344	95	9.8	3.8	0.6
RECIPIENTS OF FINANCING[a]						
Total	4,742	8,949	15,361	100.0	100.0	100.0
Infrastructure	2,240	4,349	9,414	47.2	48.6	61.3
Electricity	817	1,698	4,198	17.2	19.0	27.3
Transportation and communication	1,015	2,364	2,632	21.4	26.4	17.2
Irrigation and other works	408	286	2,583	8.6	3.2	16.8
Basic industry	586	1,252	1,872	12.4	14.0	12.2
Petroleum and coal	298	548	1,014	6.3	6.1	6.6
Iron and steel	259	654	795	5.5	7.3	5.2
Cement and other construction materials	29	49	63	0.6	0.6	0.4
Other manufacturing	707	2,315	2,740	14.9	25.9	17.8
Food and beverages	309	430	490	6.5	4.8	3.2
Textiles and clothing	123	179	143	2.6	2.0	0.9
Paper and products	44	325	378	0.9	3.6	2.5
Chemicals and fertilizers	106	324	435	2.3	3.6	2.8
Transport equipment	7	641	780	0.1	7.2	5.1
Other	118	416	515	2.5	4.7	3.3
Other activities[b]	1,210	1,033	1,335	25.5	11.5	8.7

Note: Because of rounding, detail will not necessarily add to totals. Data for 1961 are shown as of June 30 instead of December 31; the later figures have been published, but a reclassification of the data by NAFIN makes then noncomparable to the 1953 and 1958 figures shown here.

[a] Total financing, including all loans, investments, and guarantees.

[b] "Other activities" include all of those not listed separately (e.g., finance, trade, the service industries, and general government).

Sources: Nacional Financiera, *Informe anual* for 1958 (pub. 1959), pp. 44–45; and Nacional Financiera, *Informe de actividades 1961* (report to stockholders for fiscal year, July 1, 1960, to June 30, 1961), pp. 5, 9.

mid-1961, total financing of the electric power industry by or through NAFIN exceeded 4 billion pesos. The agency had helped the federal government to build or to buy out very nearly all of Mexico's public utility generating capacity.

Though other infrastructure investments were viewed favorably by the private sector, the purchase of the two large foreign-owned power companies in 1960 heightened tensions and uncertainties in some quarters. It came at a time when apprehensive Mexican business groups had already called upon President López Mateos to clarify NAFIN's policies. The purchase was certainly consistent with long-standing government policy in the electric power industry, and strong economic and political reasons existed for it; but it was interpreted by some as a symbol of "unfriendliness" on the part of an administration openly acknowledging a "leftist" orientation. The government felt compelled to publish in the major newspapers reassurances of its "subsidiary" role in the economy.

Besides emphasizing the infrastructure, NAFIN continued its role of industrial promotion. Heavy industry in particular drew its attention. In the post-1947 period, its major promotions included manufacturers of cellulose, rayon, newsprint, paper, coke, coal tar chemicals, railroad cars, diesel trucks, passenger automobiles, fertilizers, insecticides, heavy chemicals, textile machinery, and steel pipe. In addition, the agency continued much of its earlier financing of petroleum, coal, steel, and cement.

NAFIN's interest in heavy industry reflected a complex of overlapping motives. The motives were not always consistent with one another, and there was no formula for priorities or relative weights. In the deliberating process within NAFIN, qualitative assignments of priorities were made in response to technical judgments and to economic and political pressures.

Import replacement continued to be a major over-all objective. But even the promotion of an obvious import-replacing industry sometimes required the stimulus of a special event. Cellulose and paper production, for example, received a major boost from the Korean War. Exporting countries limited their sales, and prices rose rapidly. NAFIN responded by helping to finance the expansion of cellulose and paper capacity in existing plants and the establishment of two new cellulose plants, a paper mill, and the country's first newsprint producer. Despite joint efforts by NAFIN and private capital, import replacement in this general field was far from complete.[30] The demand has grown faster than production over the last several years.

NAFIN's selection of industries at times represented a continuing policy of financing projects in which the size of initial capital requirements seemed to discourage the Mexican private sector. Other major motives seemed to be a desire to increase the direct participation of the public sector in those industries which NAFIN considered "basic," [31] and to strengthen the power position of NAFIN itself.

Often NAFIN seemed to be guided by an appreciation of what are now called "linkage effects," in which one industry calls into being others which will furnish it with inputs or fabricate its output. In the post-1947 years NAFIN was often drawn toward promotions in which new enterprises could be integrated with existing ones. Some of these projects have been in the private sector, but the largest and most impressive have been in industrial complexes where the public sector has majority ownership.

At Monclova, Coahuila, NAFIN promoted the rapid expansion of Altos Hornos de México, S.A. To the steel works it added first a plant producing coke and coal tar chemicals (Compañía Mexicana de Coque y Derivados, S.A. de C.V.) and then an ammonium nitrate fertilizer plant using by-product coke-oven gases (Fertilizantes de Monclova, S.A.). Later on, Altos Hornos was permitted to acquire control of three existing firms in the steel industry, thereby diversifying its product line and expanding its assured market for steel. This integration pattern is the familiar one observable in major steel-producing centers elsewhere in the world. NAFIN's behavior in this instance is akin to that of any private enterprise which has taken advantage of external producing economies by concentrating auxiliary facilities around basic plant, and of market economies by broadening its line and ensuring its outlets. At Ciudad Sahagún, Hidalgo, NAFIN helped to promote an industrial complex consisting of a railroad car construction company (Compañía Constructora Nacional de Carros de Ferrocarril, S.A.); a bus, truck, and passenger automobile plant (Diesel Nacional, S.A.); and a manufacturing firm designed originally to make textile machinery, sewing machines, and special steel and gray iron castings (Siderúrgica Nacional, S.A., formerly Toyoda de México, S.A.). NAFIN's managerial and financial relationships with the three firms have been diverse.

Basically, of course, the NAFIN criterion was that of import replacement. But choices of location and ownership at Ciudad Sahagún reflect an interesting interplay of social and economic forces. The area is an old mining center, almost exhausted. The government's decision to stimulate industry there was a part of a concern for solving chronic unemployment in regions outside the Federal District and forestalling some of the relentless migration to the capital. In addition, the production of vehicles was conceived as auxiliary to federal transportation programs — partly as a means of easing an acute shortage of rail cars through domestic production and partly as a substitution for imported trucks, buses, and passenger cars. In the case of both rail cars and automotive vehicles of Ciudad Sahagún, the government made the significant choice of public ownership.

Railroad car construction in the Mexican setting is probably a "natural monopoly" — an industry in which a single firm can satisfy total market demand at lower unit cost than could two or more firms. Moreover, domestic demand comes almost exclusively from a single buyer, the government-owned railway system. It is a plausible hypothesis that private entrepreneurs would not care to develop a firm whose regulating agent and sole customer would be the federal government. There certainly are many profitable alternative investments in industries without this pattern of government influence. It is also plausible to assume that the Mexican government preferred public-sector ownership as an acceptable solution to the monopoly problem. Nevertheless, although the private sector did not promote the Ciudad Sahagún railroad car venture, it did make some investments in it. Some of the preferred shares are owned by two of Mexico's investment companies. One of them is a financial affiliate of a private steel company which furnishes materials to the railroad car manufacturer. As of 1961, a major officer of each of the two investment companies sat on the board of directors of the railroad car corporation. Here we have one variant of the many forms of compromise of public-sector and private-sector interests which NAFIN's promotions have embraced.

The public ownership choice for automobiles at Ciudad Sahagún involved some different considerations. Ownership of Diesel Nacional enabled the federal government to regulate private producers through direct price and quality competition and to use its power as buyer of component parts to generate some integration of the national automotive industry. Like most public-sector firms which compete directly with private enterprise in Mexico (e.g., in steel, chemicals, fertilizers) this one gave some representation to the private sector on its board of directors. However, as of 1961, seven of the eight board members represented public agencies, including NAFIN.

The third plant of the Ciudad Sahagún complex also reflected a tangle of motives. Toyoda de México was originally promoted by NAFIN as a joint venture of public Mexican and private Japanese capital. The company was established primarily to manufacture textile machinery under Japanese patents, with production of sewing machines as a secondary line. But inadequate market surveys, insufficient tariff protection, production of old-style models which met with sales resistance, and a host of problems arising in part out of difficulties which Japanese managers had in adjusting to the Mexican milieu, made Toyoda limp along at a fraction of capacity. It lost money heavily. Nacional Financiera, in a rescue operation designed to reduce the losses of Japanese investors, to maintain employment, and to preserve something of the value of its own loans and holdings of preferred stock in the venture, bought complete control and reorganized the firm as Siderúrgica Nacional, S.A. The old board of directors with its majority of Japanese capitalists was replaced by a new and smaller board, all but one of whom represented the public sector. NAFIN made new investments in productive facilities and changed the pattern of output to integrate it with the needs of the automotive and railroad car firms of the industrial complex.

NAFIN's post-1947 emphases have led it inevitably to devote the bulk of its financial aid in recent years to the public sector.[32] In part, concentration on public firms has been a by-product of the decision to invest heavily in the infrastructure, where railroads, electric power companies, and irrigation works are properties of the state. But the pattern extends beyond the infrastructure. At the end of 1959, for example, 50 per cent of the 2.1 billion pesos which Nacional Financiera had outstanding as credits and security investments in manufacturing enterprises was in ten firms (and two subsidiaries) owned directly by NAFIN as majority stockholder. Another 20 per cent was invested in three firms owned by the federal government proper: Petróleos Mexicanos (PEMEX), Constructora Nacional de Carros de Ferrocarril, and Diesel Nacional.[33] Some 70 per cent of NAFIN's investment in manufacturing was thus accounted for without including firms in which public-sector ownership was less than a majority. Since some of NAFIN's own majority positions have resulted from "rescue" operations, the pattern of manufacturing investments may occasionally reflect the past failure of joint ventures rather than a predilection for public enterprises.

However, other indicators also reflect NAFIN's concentration on public rather than private development. Practically all of the 78.5 million pesos which NAFIN had invested in mining at the end of 1959 was in three public-sector firms producing sulfur, coal, and iron ore. Of nearly 1.5 billion dollars in long-term foreign loans obtained with NAFIN's help in the interval 1942–1960, more than four fifths can be identified as going to the public sector.[34] Finally, it may be noted that most of the mortgage bonds issued in Mexico with NAFIN's guarantee have been those of public-sector firms, notably producers of railroad cars, petroleum, textiles, and iron and steel.

Though a minority share of NAFIN's financial aid in recent years has gone to private enterprise, the absolute amount has been large, its distribution relatively widespread, and its forms diverse. The list of firms aided by NAFIN's loans, security purchases, or guarantees extends to several hundred. It includes a number of business enterprises with directors who are outspoken critics of government intervention and, in a few cases, leaders of the feeble though active political opposition party, the Partido de Acción Nacional (PAN). Nevertheless, attitudes of the private sector toward Nacional Financiera remain understandably ambivalent. On the one hand, NAFIN is a reliable source of cheap credit, is genuinely interested in promoting the success of business enterprise, and is often indulgent of the mistakes of private entrepreneurs. On the other hand, it has a vested interest in ventures competitive with many private firms. NAFIN has become a complex agent which must be dealt with at many a turn.

Chapter 3

The Character of Nacional Financiera's Entrepreneurial Role

As a result of its promotional activities, Nacional Financiera occupies practically every possible position as creditor or owner. It is majority stockholder, minority stockholder, bondholder, creditor, and guarantor of securities and loans. In some cases, it occupies several of these positions with respect to an individual firm.

Its dominant role, measured by both number and amount of investments, is that of creditor. NAFIN most often makes direct loans, typically secured by promissory notes or mortgages; but it also becomes a creditor by buying bonds. One study of the forms of financing extended by NAFIN to industrial enterprises in the period 1953–1958 shows that direct loans accounted for anywhere from 35 to 50 per cent of amounts outstanding at year's end, security investments accounted for 12 to 17 per cent, guarantees of credits extended by other lending institutions accounted for 25 to 40 per cent, guarantees of mortgage bonds accounted for 2 to 6 per cent, and loans out of trust funds accounted for 4 to 7 per cent.[1]

The predilection for the roles of creditor and guarantor (rather than owner) has a relatively simple explanation. NAFIN, as creditor or guarantor, can earn income with low risk, attract foreign funds from institutions which are duly impressed by the security and regularity of NAFIN's creditor income, and forestall some criticism from the Mexican private sector. NAFIN has acquired ownership shares under one or another of the following circumstances: when it has created a new firm at the behest of the federal government proper; when it has felt that an already debt-heavy enterprise warranted fresh contributions of capital; when it has been willing to accept stock in payment of its loans; when it has wanted to rescue a faltering venture by buying out private owners; or when it has wished to integrate some firm into a structure already under its control.

As we have seen in Chapter 1, Nacional Financiera was majority owner of thirteen enterprises as of mid-1961.[2] NAFIN also controls indirectly several corporations which are subsidiaries of those which it owns outright. In some cases it shares control with the federal government proper.

Through common directors and officers, Nacional Financiera interlocks with private and public enterprises in the fields of finance, manufacturing, mining, petroleum, and public utilities. In most of these instances, NAFIN's participation represents a means for protecting a significant creditor or minority-ownership position, or a means for voicing the official interest of the federal government. However, membership on a board of directors often means for NAFIN personnel, as for men in the private sector, a significant supplement to personal income in the form of honoraria derived from the profits of the firm.[3]

Nacional Financiera has clearly been something more than just another source of finance capital. It has advised, promoted, invested in, and directed business enterprises often enough to be identified as a genuine entrepreneurial agent. In the Mexican environment, with its scarcity of investment capital and of managerial talent for large-scale industry, and its traditional concentration of private capital in commerce and real estate, NAFIN has undoubtedly offered elements of entrepreneurship which the Mexican private sector had been unprepared to offer. Though foreigners may have been willing on occasion to provide those elements, the desire for development without foreign "domination" has led Mexico to adopt a number of laws and practices designed to substitute national for foreign entrepreneurial talent, even if the talent had to be furnished by governmental agencies. For a large segment of the populace, NAFIN has been an acceptable agent of the public sector, consistent with Mexican tradition in industry and commerce and a practical answer to a number of development needs. Moreover, entrepreneurial functions were clearly included among the objectives of the institution in the presidential decree which created Nacional Financiera in 1934,[4] and they were preserved in the organic law which was adopted in 1940 after a six-year experimental period.[5]

Nevertheless, animosities arising in the private sector, together with NAFIN's consciousness of its public service function, have prompted official statements that have been rather coy on the theme of entrepreneurship. On occasion, a rather strained attempt has been made to disclaim any entrepreneurial role at all.[6]

Major criticism has come from private-sector quarters whose interests are often competitive with those of Nacional Financiera. The criticism has been based in part on the fact that the institution behaves "too much like a private enterprise." It earns profits, holds onto its best stocks, expands into subsidiary activities. It has shown no particular desire to recover its investments through the sale of its portfolio nor any particular concern to "get the government out of business." Although its stated policy has been to sell out its security investments when it can, few have in fact been sold. Poor ones find no buyers, and NAFIN keeps its good ones to finance increases in its own capital, to serve as common funds to guarantee its own non-equity issues, and to carry the burden of bad investments. NAFIN has also been motivated in part by a fear that the sale of its stockholdings would increase the economic power of already powerful groups, since there is no mechanism to assure that the stocks would be widely bought or widely held. Nor has NAFIN cared to hand over going concerns to those who have not performed the entrepreneurial function. In the words of NAFIN's president and general manager, "It would not make sense for Nacional Financiera to divest itself of its industrial stocks to a small group of investors who would thereby be relieved of the responsibility to promote new enterprises (which, essentially, is the business of private initiative)." [7]

Income statements have not been made public for more than a few of the corporations in which NAFIN is majority owner; therefore one cannot review the profit-and-loss record for each firm. Enough information is available, however, to indicate clearly that some of them have been profitable indeed (e.g., in iron and steel, textiles) while others have been heavy losers (e.g., in motion pictures, sugar milling). There is little doubt that NAFIN itself would like to operate each of its thirteen corporate properties at a profit. There is little doubt, either, that it can hardly expect to do so, given the ordinary vagaries of management and the many constraints on NAFIN's behavior.

In the course of directing its own enterprises, Nacional Financiera has sometimes voiced the desire to run them in some manner as "yardstick firms," whose quality control, market research, and technical improvements would set the pace for private competitors. Thus, for example, the steel firm Altos Hornos and the textile firm Ayotla Textil, in their quest for optimum plant size, in their product diversification, and in their adoption of technological improvements, are held up as norms to the private sector. Their competition has evoked complaints of unfairness, since the firms have special access to public financing and to favorable administrative rulings.

If the competition is at all unfair, it is far from unbridled. In fact, the principal steel companies, both public and private, operate under a system of "accords" and of official prices fixed so that vested interests will not be prejudiced by too much competition. If the private sector is at all handicapped, it is certainly not helpless. When Ayotla in 1961 projected a plant expansion which would reduce unit costs and prepare the firm to meet export demand in the Latin American Free Trade Area, private textile interests raised such a hue and cry that Ayotla suspended its plans. When Altos Hornos tried to buy up a steel pipe manufacturing firm in Monterrey — a purchase which its financial resources certainly would have allowed and which its power position as supplier of steel plate might easily have forced — the private sector's defense included political pressures through the office of the President of the Republic, and the publicly owned steel firm contented itself with a minority share.

The illustrations just given indicate that traditional theories of business-firm behavior are not very helpful for an understanding of Mexican conditions. Oligopoly theory, always an awkward part of the theory of the firm, is here of very limited applicability. True, many Mexican markets are "oligopolies" in the sense of a few sellers, but they are not simple structures in which profit maximization can be taken as a meaningful guide. True, as in oligopolies everywhere, the actions of any major producer are important to the total market, and the fear of retaliation is always present. But the participants are special breeds of economic animal. Public-sector firms are expected to behave in part like private enterprise, with an eye on costs and profits. Their position through interlocking directorates and public control often makes it possible to coordinate output with customers and suppliers in a way which their private competitors could not; yet their behavior must reflect the general concern of the Mexican government for preserving alternative producers, for maintaining employment in various geographical regions, and for retaining the support of the private sector by demonstrating that the party and the administration are not dedicated to the proposition of public in preference to private ownership.[8]

Private firms, for their part, can conduct a running campaign of criticism against public competitors, while at the same time resting secure in the knowledge that the same public powers which ultimately determine the behavior of the competitors are also solicitous of the well-being of private enterprise and are eager to offer public help in the form of credits, technical assistance, tax exemption, or other measures. In major tests of strength, the private sector knows from past experience that restraining influences can be brought to bear through political channels.

The Mexican oligopoly game is not played under the watchful eye of some regulatory commission or assistant attorney general intent upon "preserving competition," but rather under the watchful eye of a President of the Republic intent upon preserving employment, promoting growth, and holding the general loyalty of major economic interest groups. From his office are appointed cabinet officials and other functionaries who are responsible for the allocation of public credit, the control of the private banking system, the determination of policy for many public-sector firms, and administrative rulings on licenses, permits, and procedures which help to determine the conditions under which any business firm operates. In a good many industries this system produces much the same results as private-enterprise oligopolies do in other countries: regular pressures for technical change and increased plant size from the larger firms, tempered by "gentlemen's agreements" on markets and prices.

Nacional Financiera has no choice but to play the game in a fashion which restrains its behavior very much indeed. As a consequence, its entrepreneurial role can be characterized with reasonable accuracy as a rather passive one. One frequently hears the criticism, both inside and outside NAFIN, that the institution has never really taken the initiative in promoting economic growth. It has been most often a banker rather than a principal entrepreneur, and the spark of initiative has typically been struck by some agent other than Nacional Financiera.

The government itself, acting through ministries and agencies responsible to the chief executive, has been the prime mover in Nacional Financiera's investments in infrastructure and in the manufacture of railroad cars, automobiles, coke, chemicals, and fertilizers. Private enterprise has conceived and initiated most of the other projects, including a few in which NAFIN is now principal stockholder. Though Nacional Financiera has aided and abetted the development process, and though its feasibility studies have been important in the selection of projects, it has usually found itself merely screening proposals and financing what it deemed to be the better ones.

It could hardly have been otherwise. In the realm of the infrastructure, decisions about irrigation works, electrical energy, road building, and railroad transportation clearly belong to the total executive establishment, including many decentralized agencies of the Mexican government. In the industrial sphere, NAFIN has had to contend with a private sector requiring repeated assurance that public entities would not encroach too much upon its domain. Even in the field of development financing, NAFIN has shared its function with a dozen or so public institutions in Mexico.[9]

Because the Mexican government has tried to avoid financing through the printing press, NAFIN has been forced to rely increasingly on foreign funds. Lenders have been willing to come in only when return seemed assured by obvious market potential or by governmental guarantee. With foreign loans usually available only on a project-by-project basis and with the lender exercising the power of veto, Nacional Financiera's ability to act as a risk-taking entrepreneur, spreading investments over a wide range of new and uncertain industries, has been severely restricted.

The very development of the Mexican securities market, too, has mitigated against Nacional Financiera's assumption of a more active role in the promotion process. The predilection of Mexican investors for fixed-income securities, and Nacional Financiera's accommodation to that fact, have reduced the frequency of NAFIN's moves into and out of business ventures through purchases and sales of stock.

Under the combined restraints imposed by the hostility of the private sector, the diffusion of public development decision-making, an anti-inflationary policy, a reliance upon conservative foreign lending, a poor internal market for risky equity shares, a fear of concentrated stock ownership, and a conformity to the fixed-income securities market, Nacional Financiera has had relatively little freedom to act as a bold entrepreneurial agent.

Chapter 4

The Future of Nacional Financiera

NACIONAL Financiera's future status as an established and reputable institution in Mexico is a matter of foregone conclusion. As an old and experienced hand, just nine years the junior of the central bank, and as one of the four original pillars of the "Revolutionary" financial structure, it has durability and functionality that are not open to question. What is open to speculative inquiry, however, is the character of its future role.

Now, predicting the future is hardly the forte of the economist, least of all the present writer. And it is hardly polite for an uninvited outside observer to offer gratuitous prescriptions of policy. Nevertheless, a study of NAFIN's past leaves a genuine curiosity about its future, especially for someone interested in the relative roles of private and public initiative in the development process.

Mexico's future administrations will of necessity be preoccupied with the problems of promoting continued economic expansion. Precisely where the impetus is to come from is not a matter easily deduced from either Mexico's recent history or its revolutionary philosophy. The experimental and pragmatic approach to development which has characterized four decades of Mexican behavior suggests that the future, like the past, does not pose some simple alternative of excessive statism or unbridled private enterprise. Each administration will be hard put to decide upon the emphases which it can give successfully to the public and the private sectors.

It is quite possible, however, that development stimuli can be had in such fashion that the "public versus private" issue will remain in its present state of quiescent simmer rather than boiling over to disrupt the growth process. There are combinations of emphases which fit this recipe: e.g., increased public investments in the rural areas (particularly in electricity and in farm-to-market and access roads), increased aid to private enterprise in a range of new import-replacing industries, and financial help to both public and private firms for the development of exports to the Latin American Free Trade Area and to the United States.[1] Any such "mixed" program would leave the present character of Nacional Financiera's activity largely unchanged.

The López Mateos administration began in 1962 to prod the private sector by issuing a publication containing a long list of industrial products which the administration felt ought to be manufactured by Mexican enterprises in substitution for prevailing imports.[2] Both the publication itself and President López Mateos' speech to the Congress on the same theme specified private industry; and the chief executive appealed to the "patriotic enthusiasms" of private citizens. Private enterprise has been assured that NAFIN will consider giving financial assistance in the industries listed, judging each individual case on its merits.[3] Should the private sector respond on a grand scale, Nacional Financiera would likely continue in its passive role of screening and financing proposals. But if the response is not satisfactory to future administrations, NAFIN could be made the active promoter of many of the ventures, with or without participation on the part of private investors.

There is at least one other context in which NAFIN's promotional role could take on a more active character, without representing any major ideological shift within Mexico. One can imagine a vigorous NAFIN — responding to the policy and the personality of some future Mexican president, and guided by the discoveries of investment needs turned up in its own division of industrial programming — initiating a broad range of enterprises, selling them off at an early stage, and moving on to new promotions. Increased public initiative would not necessarily lead to increased public ownership.

To make NAFIN's future so different from its past, however, would require significant changes in monetary and fiscal policy, important modifications in the equity securities market, and a diminution of the mutual suspicions harbored by public and private decision-makers. It would also require a President of the Republic who would be willing to risk offending some segments of his political apparatus by stimulating other segments to action.

PROTECTIONISM IN MEXICO

by
Rafael Izquierdo

Chapter **I**

Imports and Import Controls

P ROTECTIONISM in modern Mexico begins in earnest with the Second World War. Previous protectionist policy had been by no means negligible; but, because industrial diversification had not gone very far, decisions had been limited to a few specific activities, such as the manufacture of textiles. During the war years the supply of goods from foreign countries dwindled and the market for domestic production grew rapidly. Both the government and private industry became keenly aware of the advantages to be gained, when peace came, by restricting imports of goods that could be produced locally and at the same time facilitating imports of capital goods.

Since then, protectionism has come a long way. What attitudes have government and private enterprise taken? How have relations between them evolved? To what extent has protectionism adapted to the complex, changing needs of the industrialization process? This study takes up those questions. It is a study of protectionism for manufacturing; we do not attempt to analyze the other important aspect of Mexican protectionism, which has for its purpose the promotion of agriculture. Our purpose is to trace the evolution since 1940 of Mexican import policy with respect to industrial growth; to describe the shifting positions of private businessmen toward that policy; and, finally, to draw conclusions about Mexico's experience with protectionism which may serve as a guide for future decisions in Mexico — and also in other countries to the extent that analogous situations exist.

In the study of protectionism the Mexican experience is especially valuable. The years since 1940 have been marked by a variety of economic situations, including rapid economic growth followed by relative inactivity; high export revenues and their subsequent decline; and major changes in the composition of imports. All this has taken place in a period in which political and social stability has prevailed, so that the application of various kinds of economic policy has been possible in response to changing circumstances.

In one respect, this study bypasses the issue which is central to most analyses of protectionism. We do not propose to compare the merits of free trade and protectionism in a developing economy. We take it as "given" (1) that industrial diversification is essential to achieve such national goals as providing jobs for the fast-growing population and attaining adequate rates of growth of real per capita income, and (2) that appropriate measures of protection are usually an indispensable, albeit insufficient, corollary of the process of industrialization. Attention is therefore centered on the internal factors that determine the specific form of protectionism.

These internal factors are complex. In the implementation of a policy of protection there is continual conflict over goals and motives. Different public goals are often at odds with one another, each demanding a different approach to import policy. The government's interest in social welfare is often at loggerheads with the interests of private enterprise. Moreover the interests of the various sectors of private enterprise frequently conflict. Disagreements arise between importers and producers; and disputes develop among the producers themselves as production is diversified and the composition of imports changes.

All this must be analyzed in terms of the Mexican experience, but first it is necessary to show briefly the significance of imports to the economy and government of present-day Mexico.

THE CONTRIBUTION OF IMPORTS

Imports play a critical role in Mexico's economic development. As Table 1 shows, they complement the domestic supply of goods to an important degree; in 1960, purchases from abroad constituted more than one fourth of the value of domestic production.

IZQUIERDO, TABLE 1

Share of officially registered imports in the supply of goods and in capital formation in Mexico, 1940–1960

(value figures in millions of constant pesos, adjusted to reflect 1950 prices)

	1940	1945	1950	1955	1960
SUPPLY OF GOODS					
Value of all kinds of imports	1,932	3,959	4,807	6,286	7,273
Value of domestic production[a]	9,445	12,685	17,406	21,990	28,410
Imports as a percentage of domestic production	20.5%	31.2%	27.6%	28.9%	25.6%
CAPITAL FORMATION					
Value of imports of capital goods[b]	508	1,293	1,710	2,165	2,455
Value of gross fixed investment	2,270	4,699	6,122	7,182	9,080
Imports of capital goods as a percentage of investment	22.4%	27.5%	27.9%	30.1%	27.0%

[a] Includes aggregate value of agriculture and stockraising, mining, petroleum, and manufacturing.

[b] Machinery and equipment for manufacturing, mining, agriculture, transportation, and construction; does not include raw materials.

Sources: Compiled from the following: Enrique Pérez López, "El producto nacional," in *México, 50 años de revolución: La economía* (Mexico, D.F.: Fondo de Cultura Económica, 1960), table 4, p. 589; data assembled by Economic Commission for Latin America; annual reports of Nacional Financiera; data provided by Dirección de Inversiones Públicas of the Secretaría de la Presidencia.

The characteristics of the imports tell us even more about their importance in the Mexican economy. Table 2 shows that by 1960 more than 83 per cent of the value of the nation's imports consisted of goods for use in connection with production, rather than goods for consumption. The percentage would be even higher if fuel imports, here treated as a small separate category, could be accurately divided between production and consumption goods. According to the table, 44 per cent of Mexico's recorded imports in 1960 was raw materials and 39 per cent was capital goods such as machinery and trucks. For the most part these capital goods are not produced in Mexico and therefore the imports are indispensable to the maintenance and expansion of productive capacity. Since some of the technology of capital-exporting countries is embodied in these imports, their importance to Mexico is greater than their money value suggests.

At the same time, however, the importance of imports is also an indication of the vulnerability of Mexico. Referring to Latin American countries, Dr. Raúl Prebisch observed recently: "It remains a paradox that industrialization, instead of helping greatly to soften

IZQUIERDO, TABLE 2

Composition of Mexico's officially registered imports by groups of products, 1940–1960

(percentages, based upon value figures which were adjusted to reflect 1955 prices)

Groups of products	1940	1945	1950	1955	1960[a]
Total registered imports	100.0	100.0	100.0	100.0	100.0
Consumer goods	23.9	21.7	15.8	15.4	12.1
Nondurable	13.8	11.4	8.3	7.0	6.6
Durable	10.1	10.3	7.5	8.4	5.5
Fuel[b]	2.6	2.7	4.1	7.9	4.1
Raw materials	42.0	38.3	39.4	37.2	44.4
Metallic	12.0	9.8	10.5	10.4	11.4
Nonmetallic	30.0	28.5	28.9	26.8	33.0
Capital goods[c]	30.6	36.8	40.0	39.3	39.1
Construction materials	6.3	5.7	7.8	5.9	4.4
Other goods for agriculture	3.4	3.5	4.6	5.0	3.2
Other goods for manufacturing and mining	13.8	23.7	23.1	22.7	24.0
Other goods for transportation	7.1	3.9	4.5	5.7	7.5

Note: Detail does not add exactly to 100 per cent, mainly because an "unclassified" category of less than 1 per cent is here omitted.

[a] Preliminary figures.

[b] The imported fuel, most of which is petroleum products, may be considered part consumer goods and part production goods, the exact proportions being undetermined.

[c] The data on capital goods underlying the figures in Table 2 differ from those in Table 1, because of the use of different price deflator series.

So urce: Economic Commission for Latin America.

the internal impact of external fluctuations, is bringing us to a new and unknown type of external vulnerability." [1] Mexico's present situation confirms this opinion. Since purchases of industrial raw materials and capital goods constitute so huge a proportion of total imports, any general measures to restrict imports could have the effect of cutting off critical supplies to certain sectors of the economy. Accordingly, Mexico's vulnerability to a decline in foreign-exchange earnings is very great.

Table 3 dramatizes this vulnerability. It shows, for example, that in 1960, Mexico's foreign expenditures exceeded her receipts from the export of goods and services by 174 million United States dollars. And in that same year the nation's officially registered imports (which, as we have seen, were mainly production goods) accounted for 70 per cent of her foreign expenditures. Moreover, this is not the whole story, for Table 3 shows also that if incoming shipments classified as "border trade" are added to registered imports, the sum represents not 70 but almost 86 per cent of Mexico's foreign expenditures.

Border trade is a peculiar and an important phenomenon. Up to now, we have used the terms "imports" and "exports" without qualification, implicitly accepting the definitions employed in Mexico's official statistics. In order to interpret the foreign-trade statistics of Mexico accurately, however, one has to know a little about the conditions on Mexico's northern border. The Mexican–United States border extends nearly two thousand miles. Since it is practically impossible to patrol the border effectively, Mexico has established border areas in which import and export controls are not applied. For control purposes the Mexican economy begins on the southern edge of those areas.

Generally speaking, goods taken out of these border areas to the United States are not classified as exports; they are regarded as tourist revenue for Mexico. Indeed, most of what is classified as tourist revenue in the Mexican balance of payments — nearly 80 per cent of the total — consists of purchases by United States residents of goods and services in these Mexican border areas; some

IZQUIERDO, TABLE 3

Principal elements in the current account of
Mexico's balance of payments, 1940–1960

	1940	1945	1950	1955	1960
CURRENT ACCOUNT					
(in millions of U.S. dollars)					
Receipts	$214.0	$500.8	$832.7	$1,280.3	$1,520.3
Expenditures	186.9	499.4	780.1	1,190.4	1,694.3
Balance	27.1	1.4	52.6	89.9	−174.0
COMPOSITION OF RECEIPTS (in percentages)					
Total	100.0	100.0	100.0	100.0	100.0
Exports of merchandise	44.1	54.2	59.3	57.7	48.6
Tourist trade in Mexico	23.5	22.1	28.7	34.8	44.1
Others[a]	32.4	23.7	12.0	7.5	7.3
COMPOSITION OF EXPENDITURES (in percentages)					
Total	100.0	100.0	100.0	100.0	100.0
Registered imports of merchandise, plus border trade	70.8	74.6	86.3	88.5	85.8
Registered imports	n.a.	n.a.	76.4	74.2	70.0
Border trade	n.a.	n.a.	9.9	14.3	15.8
Tourist expenditures abroad	15.0	12.0	0.9	1.0	1.7
Service on direct foreign investment	11.2	10.0	8.5	6.7	8.4
Others	3.0	3.4	4.3	3.8	4.1

n.a. = not available.
a The bulk of this category is exports of gold and silver and dollar remittances from Mexican agricultural workers in the U.S.
Source: Banco de México.

part of these purchases, in other circumstances, would certainly be classified as Mexican exports.

Likewise, goods brought into the border areas from outside Mexico are not registered as imports; they are regarded as Mexico's "tourist expenditure" abroad. The largest part of Mexico's "tourist expenditure" abroad consists of purchases by residents of these border areas in the neighboring territory of the United States.

Over the years, these imports of goods into the border areas have grown faster than other Mexican imports. One reason is that the border region has enjoyed a higher increase in per capita income than the average for the rest of the country, primarily because of the expansion of the cotton and tourist industries. Another reason is that there is large immigration to the region. But the expansion may also be due in part to an increase in smuggling. For example, the amount of chocolate imported into the border region is more than enough to satiate the inhabitants, whereas the recorded imports of chocolate into the rest of Mexico are meager. And when import quotas and tariff increases have been applied to machinery and parts, disproportionate increases in imports into the border areas have suggested the existence of smuggling in these categories as well.

In Table 4 we have regrouped Mexican import statistics to include the imports of the border areas. This table shows the growing importance of the border areas in Mexico's imports. By 1960, 17 per cent of Mexico's total imports was going into these areas, apparently either for consumption or for smuggling into the interior. In addition, another 7.9 per cent was being imported into the so-called free zones, an ambiguously defined group of areas (some-

IZQUIERDO, TABLE 4

Distribution of Mexico's imports by destination, including imports to the border areas and free zones, 1950–1960

(in percentages of total value)

Types of import	1950	1955	1960[a]
Total imports including those to border areas and free zones	100.0	100.0	100.0
To the interior (officially registered imports)	81.8	77.1	75.1
To border areas ("border trade")	11.3	14.8	17.0
To free zones[b]	6.9	8.0	7.9

Note: Because of rounding, detail does not necessarily add to 100.0.
[a] Preliminary figures.
[b] The products destined for the so-called "free zones" are largely materials and equipment consigned to certain areas for transshipment abroad or to specific industrial establishments in the interior which only pay duty on their imports when processed products are shipped from the plant into the Mexican market. There are obviously some problems in double counting here. Wherever products imported into the free zones are processed for legal shipment into the interior, they may be counted twice in the "total" figures on which this table is based.
Sources: Economic Commission for Latin America and Banco de México.

times including individual plants or warehouses) with free-import privileges. This means that in the same year only 75 per cent of *total* imports was subject directly to the controls implicit in protectionist policy. It means also that imports of consumer goods into Mexico had a much greater relative importance than is generally assumed, because the goods imported into the border areas are principally consumer goods.

Mexico's lack of elbow room in the formulation of import policy is illustrated in other ways as well. About one fourth of the government's total revenue is supplied by duties on foreign trade, and import duties are the major source of this kind of government revenue. (See Table 5.) Furthermore the public sector itself is a

IZQUIERDO, TABLE 5

Taxes on foreign trade as a percentage of total fiscal revenue of Mexican federal government, 1940–1960

	1940	1945	1950	1955	1956	1957	1958	1959	1960
Total taxes on foreign trade	27.0	21.1	29.5	32.5	27.9	24.7	25.6	27.4	24.8
Taxes on imports	17.8	11.6	14.1	12.5	12.2	12.3	14.7	17.2	16.2
Taxes on exports	9.2	9.5	15.4	20.0	15.7	12.4	10.9	10.2	8.6

Source: Secretaría de Hacienda y Crédito Público.

heavy generator of import needs, relying on foreign goods both for current use and for capital investment. (See Table 6.) The Mexican government owns enterprises engaged in certain basic economic activities (oil, railroads, and electric power); it owns or controls a few enterprises in a diversity of other fields (including steel, paper, and fertilizer); and it operates extensively through government agencies in a variety of other activities (for example, irrigation and road building) which require the importation of goods. As a whole, these public activities generate about 19 per cent of the total value of the nation's imports; in fact, the figure might be even higher if one could take account of the government's purchases

IZQUIERDO, TABLE 6

*Imports by Mexico's public and private sectors,
by groups of products, 1955–1960*

(in percentages of total value)

	1955	1956	1957	1958	1959	1960
Total imports	100.0	100.0	100.0	100.0	100.0	100.0
Public sector	16.0	18.3	22.2	19.5	12.6	18.5
Private sector	84.0	81.7	77.8	80.5	87.4	81.5
Consumer goods	100.0	100.0	100.0	100.0	100.0	100.0
Public sector	3.2	15.6	27.1	20.5	8.4	n.a.
Private sector	96.8	84.4	72.9	79.5	91.6	n.a.
Raw materials[a]	100.0	100.0	100.0	100.0	100.0	100.0
Public sector	15.1	13.9	16.6	11.6	8.9	n.a.
Private sector	84.9	86.1	83.4	88.4	91.1	n.a.
Capital goods	100.0	100.0	100.0	100.0	100.0	100.0
Public sector	22.3	24.5	27.1	27.8	18.2	n.a.
Private sector	77.7	75.5	72.9	72.2	81.8	n.a.

n.a. = not available.
[a] For the purposes of this table, fuel imports are included in raw materials, but see our Table 2 note b.
Sources: Economic Commission for Latin America and Comité de Importaciones del Sector Público.

of foreign products previously imported into Mexico by the private sector.

INSTRUMENTS OF IMPORT CONTROL

The critical role of imports in Mexico's economic life has made the question of import policy a central public issue. In shaping that policy, the Mexican government in recent years has had a free hand as far as international commitments are concerned. For until recently Mexico has remained aloof from any international commitments which might restrict her freedom to make unilateral decisions.

Mexico was not always free in this respect. In 1943, a trade agreement with the United States was put in force, committing both parties, among other things, not to increase certain tariff rates.

By 1951, the agreement was terminated by mutual consent, in view of Mexico's desire to be free of such commitments. It was not until 1960 that Mexico decided on a sharp departure from its no-agreements policy and entered into an agreement with eight other Latin American countries to create a free trade area.[2] The ratification of this treaty by the Mexican Senate on November 3, 1960, may be symptomatic of a new outlook on trade policy and may herald more active participation by Mexico in international trade groups. Nevertheless, during most of the period under consideration in this study, the policy was to avoid international trade agreements.

Not only has Mexico's president been free of international commitments during recent years, but also, in sharp contrast to executives in other countries, he has had a free hand in relation to Mexico's Congress. The function of the Congress in the field of trade policy has been largely formal; in effect, it has simply given approval to decisions already made by the president.[3]

Inside the executive branch, the president has assigned the responsibility for administering tariff policy to the Secretaría de Hacienda (finance ministry), and quantitative controls have been administered by the Secretaría de Industria y Comercio. These two kinds of control are the basic instruments of Mexico's import policy. Unlike many other Latin American countries, Mexico has not resorted to exchange controls and differential exchange rates.

The need for closer coordination in the use of tariffs and quantitative restrictions has only recently been recognized. One manifestation of this recognition has been the fact that the government reorganization act of 1959 made the Secretaría de Industria y Comercio responsible for "studying, planning, and establishing tariffs and specifying the restrictions on imports and exports, in conjunction with the Secretaría de Hacienda . . ."[4] If this provision were enforced, the ministry of industry and commerce would become the dominant agency in all forms of import-control policy. But, at this writing, the provision has not been put into practice; the finance ministry continues in charge of tariffs. One must conclude that the finance ministry was unwilling to relinquish its control over an important source of revenue.

Still another kind of coordination was attempted in 1959. A Comité de Importaciones del Sector Público (committee on imports by the public sector) was set up inside the executive branch for the purpose of establishing effective control over government imports. The constituting decree acknowledges that "the strengthening of the nation's economy requires better organization and greater responsibility on the part of the government as well as greater cooperation by private elements."

The machinery of the Mexican government in the field of import policy includes not only a series of channels for coordination inside the government but also a variety of means for coordination with the private sector. Under Mexican law, for instance, tariff policy is supposed to be formulated jointly by government and private enterprise through a mixed Comisión General de Aranceles (general tariff commission). But this is only theory. Many years have passed since this commission functioned effectively. First, the government, guarding its freedom to take swift and decisive action in this critical field, has been unwilling to curtail that freedom by giving status to "suggestions" coming from national representatives of the private sector. Second, the frictions and conflicts within the private sector made it highly unlikely that private enterprise would be in a position to speak with one voice in the provision of such advice. And finally, the government's willingness to approve petitions of individual businessmen for tariff increases has generally left the private sector with little cause for complaint over the level of tariff rates.

There has been discord between the finance ministry and business groups, but not usually over tariff rates. Complaints are commonly lodged against troublesome bureaucratic procedures and red tape, especially in connection with the time lapse between the filing of an application for a tariff increase and the resolution of the matter. The bitter tone of the complaints ought perhaps to be attributed to the natural tendency of entrepreneurs to consider their own problems the most acute and the most urgently in need of solution. On the other hand, it is true that public officials have not always been as efficient as one might wish, though progress has been made in this respect.

In fixing individual tariff rates, the Secretaría de Hacienda has no specific norms or uniform criteria. Each application for the alteration of a rate is dealt with individually. Once the government has decided to approve a particular application for protection, little attention is given to determining the exact rate of duty. The tariff rates suggested by the businessmen are generally adopted, unless they are unusually high. The basic guiding principle is to provide a duty which will guarantee the market for the national product. At present the average duty on raw materials is 5 per cent, on capital goods 10–15 per cent, on consumer goods 50 per cent, and on articles considered luxury goods 100 per cent.

Although the granting of applications is fairly cut and dried as regards consumer products, the problem becomes a little more complicated in the case of raw materials and intermediate goods. Here the amount of duty is important not only to the domestic manufacturer of the product but also to those who use the product for further processing. Sometimes applications for tariff increases in these products have led to the imposition of two rates: a high duty for a time sufficient to ensure that the domestic production of the article has been sold, then a low duty thereafter.

When we turn from tariff policy to quantitative controls, the ties between the government and the private sector are seen to be entirely different. The tariff is a general instrument of import control which is applied equally to all importers. The amount of duty on any particular item is a matter of public record, which anyone may look up. On the contrary, quantitative controls must be administered case by case, and therefore private businessmen are deeply and continuously involved.

Quantitative controls are administered through an import-licensing system. Import licenses are required for about three fourths of the items imported into Mexico. For certain of these products, including automobiles, cigarettes, whiskey, cheese, and ham, there are annual quotas, which are allocated to importers in proportion to the amounts they previously imported. For other products, having no quotas, licenses are granted in accordance with the circumstances, and the government has great latitude in regulating the volume of imports.

The involvement of the private sector goes not so much to the question of determining the basic list of items subject to import license as to the issue of determining whether licenses should in fact be granted. The list itself is the product of a continual process, responsive to two main pressures: balance-of-payments crises and the desires of private producers to obtain protection as an inducement to production. No matter why a product is placed on the licensing list, however, once it gets there it is rarely removed. For example, when balance-of-payments difficulties are responsible for adding items to the list, the tendency is to maintain the formal requirement for an import license for all those goods even after the crisis has passed and they have once more been allowed to enter the country freely. Thus the stand-by authority that exists is slowly but steadily widened.

Though the list changes slowly, the policies on granting licenses are much more mercurial. The government, especially when there is no annual quota, may reduce the number of licenses without prior notice, suspend licensing altogether, and grant licenses to some importers and not to others. Decisions of the government approving or rejecting applications are not a matter of public record. And when licenses are issued, they are not transferable. These characteristics of the system account for the eagerness of all groups in the private sector to participate actively in the decisions.

In contrast to the operations of the Comisión General de Aranceles in the field of tariffs, advisory committees on import licensing are very active. At the end of 1958 twenty-one committees were functioning, and by mid-1961 there were twenty-seven.[5] Their activity is indicated by the fact that the committee on chemical products was meeting three times a week.

Each committee consists of an official of the Secretaría de Industria y Comercio, acting as chairman, and representatives of the organizations of private industry and commerce. Other appropriate government agencies also take part. For example, a representative of the public health ministry sits with the chemical products committee, and a representative of the agriculture ministry with the oils and fats committee. Each committee has its own staff, which prepares reports on the applications for licenses which the Secretaría de Industria y Comercio has submitted to the committee for consideration.

The committee, by majority vote, recommends either granting or denying the license. The standards of the committees in considering these applications are based on regulations issued in 1956. Under these regulations, there is a presumption against granting an import license. Licenses are to be issued "when the national product is obtainable only under conditions which compare unfavorably with the foreign product, as far as quality and time of delivery are concerned." They also may be issued when (a) no domestic substitute is available; (b) local production is insufficient to supply the internal market; (c) temporary scarcity occurs; and (d) a reserve of raw materials or manufactured goods has to be built up.[6]

One omission is self-evident. The price element, which might seem critical in the abstract, in fact is not usually taken into consideration in individual decisions. Superficial appearances might seem to indicate the contrary; whenever a public statement is made about the need to protect industry, for instance, it also mentions that the protection must not be allowed to raise the consumer's prices excessively. But in practice the government follows the basic conviction that industrialization and the creation of employment through import restriction are worth the costs that must be paid in the transition period. In a few exceptional cases, it is true, price considerations have been allowed to play a part in shaping import policy. For example, companies that import materials from abroad and yet sell their finished products at excessively high prices have been told by the government that unless they reduced prices, competitive finished products would be admitted from abroad. The price element has also been important in certain periods, such as 1955–1958, when the government embarked on a definite anti-inflationary policy. But, by and large, price considerations have been insignificant.

The role of private enterprise in the granting of import licenses, it will be noted, is purely advisory. Representatives of the private sector on the committees mentioned earlier have no guarantee that all applications for import permits will be submitted to them for consideration, nor are they notified of the ultimate fate of the applications on which they have recommended. In 1960 the Cámara Nacional de la Industria de Transformación (CNIT), one of the two main organizations of industrialists in Mexico, suggested a change in the regulations which govern the committees. It proposed that "the President should announce the government's revisions of the committees' recommendations, in every instance, and explain the reasons for the revisions, in order to guide the organizations represented on the committees, and for statistical purposes." [7] The suggestion was unheeded.

The consideration which the government has given to the committees' recommendations has varied according to the shifts in over-all import policy. It is difficult to verify the extent to which such recommendations were adopted. At times, such as the period between 1955 and 1958, they were apparently adopted on very few occasions. In 1957 the CNIT declared: "In many instances import controls have provided inadequate protection for national manufacturers partly because of the lack of a unified approach to the question of licenses. This lack has resulted in cases where the government has approved licenses which were not recommended for approval by the committees, and then failed to notify the committees that the licenses had been approved. In view of the more favorable [i.e., more restrictive] attitude of high officials of the Secretaría de Hacienda at present, it is suggested that a more adequate system of protection be provided for cases of this type." [8]

If an importer's application for a license is denied, the importer may appeal to the government for reconsideration. The government may then either take a decision independently or resubmit the matter to the appropriate committee. Generally, applicants accept a refusal without resorting to formal appeals. The refusal of a license does not necessarily mean that another application will be refused in the future. Besides, the entrepreneur prefers to avoid conflicts with public officials whose good will is of such importance to him.

The concept of the functions of these committees in 1956 cast them in a larger role. The regulations issued that year not only gave them an advisory function on individual applications but also (in Article VIII) provided that they make recommendations periodically "for purposes of planning." In practice, however, the role of the committees in policy-making has been minimal. The government has not encouraged this sort of activity; and private enterprise — interested primarily in specific cases, ignorant of the ultimate resolution of problems, and overwhelmed by the chore of studying thousands of applications — has not been eager for policy-making responsibility.

In 1960 the government did begin to use the committees for larger objectives, albeit in a fashion not originally contemplated when the committees were created. The government has used the committee discussions of applications for import licenses as a means of obtaining increased information on the state of domestic manufacturing and the possibilities of import replacement in specific fields. This information, in turn, has been used in efforts to channel investment into enterprises which promote Mexico's industrial integration. The government has used its accumulated information to suggest investment opportunities to private entrepreneurs.[9] One tangible result has been to unite the different producers of synthetic fibers in the formation of a new company to manufacture the raw materials for nylon in Mexico.

Operating in a system of this sort, the private sector exercises influence at two levels: at the institutional level, through committees and organizations; and at the individual level, through personal contacts in the executive branch.

At the institutional level the private sector's bargaining position is limited by the diversity of its interests and its consequent inability to present a unified front in the agencies charged with the administration of policy. Each entrepreneur is concerned with imposing his own point of view and resolving his own problems. Differences of outlook are aired before government authorities. Regardless of what the final decision may be, there is almost always at least one private group or individual entrepreneur willing to approve it. The situation is further complicated by the fact that the administration of protectionist measures is not centralized in a single agency of the executive branch. A businessman who does not get the protection he wants through tariffs may attempt to get it through quantitative controls. On the other hand, he has no guarantee that the protection he obtains through quantitative controls will not be nullified by tariff reductions.

All these circumstances combine to increase the importance of direct contacts between individual entrepreneurs and government officials. These contacts determine the strength of the individual businessman's position in relation to both the government and rival entrepreneurs. Many facets of these personal contacts are extremely subtle. The entrepreneur gains a certain advantage from the fact that he knows exactly what he wants and can exert appropriate pressure to get it. On the other hand, the public officials in charge of administering controls — despite the existence of general regulations — have no clear-cut policy to guide them.

Government technicians — *técnicos* — find themselves in a difficult position; they must maintain a certain equilibrium between conflicting interests. They may be praised by their superiors for a decision taken in certain circumstances only to be censured for a similar decision made in altered circumstances. It is no exaggeration to say that in Mexico the *técnico* must be able to transform himself, when conditions require it, into a *político,* that is, into a person who can make decisions on the basis of his judgment of the forces involved. The only way to escape this need is to shun administrative responsibilities.

Nevertheless, even though the prevailing atmosphere of regulation is one of *ad hoc* decisions and individual pressures, there have been a number of changes in the general direction of government policy which have altered the framework in which these decisions are made.

Chapter 2

Evolution of Import Policy

THE significant shifts in Mexico's import policy since 1940 have largely mirrored the changes that have taken place in the Mexican economy. There was a period of wartime shortage, followed by one in which the satisfaction of pent-up demands was dominant. Then followed the boom conditions of the Korean War, only to be succeeded by a sharp slump in external demand in 1953 and devaluation of the peso in 1954. Thereafter, the fall-off in the demand for Mexico's goods seemed to take on longer-term characteristics, leading to the most recent period of slower and less certain growth. The country's economic performance during these periods is shown in Table 7.*

THE SECOND WORLD WAR

The events of the Second World War contributed to a big expansion of the internal market of Mexico; the gross domestic product of the country during the war years increased 54 per cent. In the early years of the war, an attempt was made to alleviate to some extent the scarcity of foreign goods. The undertakings to bind various tariffs, embodied in the reciprocal trade agreement which was negotiated with the United States during 1942, were intended in part to contribute to this end. However, it was not long

---

* Most of the figures given in the text of this chapter are based on Table 7.

IZQUIERDO, TABLE 7 · Indicators of Mexican economic activity, 1940–1960

| Period | Years | Gross domestic product[a] | Imports[a] | Indices (1950 = 100) | | Gross fixed investment[a] | | | Annual per cent change in wholesale price index | Millions of current U.S. dollars | |
| | | | | Buying power of exports[b] | | | | | | | |
				Total	Goods	Total	Public	Private		Balance on current account	Foreign public credit[e]
Second World War	1940	49.9	40.2	41.0	46.5	37.2	32.9	40.9	4.0	27.1	n.a.
	1945	77.0	82.4	65.8	71.2	77.1	65.8	8.9	11.3	1.4	8.3
Deferred demand for imports	1946	82.1	109.7	69.3	71.6	95.2	64.7	121.5	12.1	−174.1	37.4
	1947	83.2	117.6	69.7	80.5	111.1	79.1	138.7	8.8	−167.1	31.7
	1948	86.9	95.0	79.6	80.9	102.3	78.0	123.2	7.3	−59.9	18.7
	1949	90.7	n.a.	76.8	78.0	86.3	73.3	97.6	9.5	49.3	31.8
	1950	100.0	100.0	100.0	100.0	100.0	100.0	100.0	9.3	52.6	28.6
Korea to devaluation of 1954	1951	107.2	130.3	107.0	113.3	110.7	91.6	127.1	24.0	−199.1	35.5
	1952	108.4	127.2	107.2	111.4	106.6	94.9	116.7	−3.6	−103.2	63.2
	1953	107.0	123.4	101.2	95.6	96.9	82.9	109.0	−1.0	−91.3	51.9
	1954	115.2	122.8	112.8	105.4	103.4	96.2	109.5	9.4	−24.3	78.7
Decline of buying power of exports[b]	1955	126.5	130.8	135.4	124.3	118.1	93.1	139.6	13.6	89.9	101.8
	1956	134.9	154.3	142.5	123.6	123.8	89.1	153.5	4.6	−35.6	114.7
	1957	139.8	160.9	143.8	108.5	130.1	97.9	157.8	4.3	−199.0	158.2
	1958	146.0	154.0	134.3	107.1	133.0	102.2	159.4	4.4	−181.6	238.9
	1959	152.8	142.5	154.5	113.6	137.0	106.8	162.9	1.2	−31.7	221.0
	1960	161.5	151.3	149.4	107.7	149.0	127.4	167.6	4.9	−174.0	332.8

n.a. = not available.

[a] Calculated on constant values at 1960 prices.

[b] That is, the capacity of exports of goods and services (including tourist trade in Mexico) to pay for imports. Figures are obtained by dividing the current value of these exports for each year by the index of the prices of imports.

[c] Includes gross proceeds from long-term credits. Excludes foreign private investment.

Sources: Based on Enrique Pérez López, "El producto nacional," in México, 50 años de revolución: La economía (Mexico, D.F.: Fondo de Cultura Económica, 1960), table 4, p. 589; Economic Commission for Latin America; annual reports of Nacional Financiera; data provided by Dirección de Inversiones Públicas of the Secretaría de la Presidencia and Banco de México.

before a new outlook, oriented toward industrial expansion and diversification, became apparent.

Conditions favored industrial undertakings. A rise in effective internal demand and the absence of foreign competition caused an increase in prices. Even when established plants were fully utilized, output proved insufficient. To a certain extent, considerations of price and quality were relegated to second place.

The profits earned in industry attracted a greater inflow of capital resources. These profits had been augmented by the increase of exports, which had grown even faster than the gross product. Nevertheless, the latent opportunities of the period could not be fully exploited because of a scarcity of production goods, that is, of machinery, equipment, repair parts, and raw materials. It was thus that government and private industry recognized the benefits that might be derived at the war's end from a policy of maintaining restrictions on the importation of goods which were or could be produced locally for an expanded internal market, and of simultaneously facilitating the purchase abroad of production goods.

The industrial growth of the years preceding the war supported an optimistic view of the future, and the optimism proved to be justified. During the war and immediately after, important investments were made in the steel industry (Altos Hornos, Compañía Fundidora de Fierro y Acero de Monterrey, La Consolidada), fertilizers (Guanos y Fertilizantes), and copper manufacturing (Cobre de México). Companies producing cement, steel furniture, glass, tires, and many other products also expanded. Between 1936 and 1946, Mexico acquired more than four hundred new manufacturing plants, with a capital of 300 million pesos.[1]

Though the shortage of foreign goods was acute in 1942 and 1943, foreign supply conditions eased a little as the war went on. As a result, the intensity of the deferred demand for imports began to be registered in rising imports. As a reaction to growing import demand, in 1944 an import-licensing system was instituted to deal with the increase in purchases of foreign goods. In time, this mechanism was destined to be the most effective instrument for controlling and channeling Mexico's imports; but it was not immediately put into effect. And in 1945 the value of imports (in constant prices) was more than double that of 1940.

THE DEFERRED DEMAND FOR IMPORTS

The period from 1946 to 1950 was especially important in the formulation of a general import policy. Events took place which left an enduring mark on Mexico's commercial policy. The trade agreement with the United States played an important part in these events.

Several months after the trade agreement had gone into effect in January 1943 the Mexican government had issued a decree providing for substantial increases in the customs duties on many products. Although the increases did not affect any of the articles regulated by the trade agreement, the United States government protested on the ground that the spirit of the agreement forbade such measures, and the decree was not put in force. Opposition in Mexico to international trade agreements began at that time. The opposition increased in intensity at the end of the Second World War. Under the agreement the binding of duties prevented not only tariff increases but also the imposition of quantitative controls on the same products.

At the Inter-American Conference on Problems of War and Peace held in Mexico in 1945 (known as the Chapultepec Conference), the United States proposed a general approach to international trade problems, embracing free trade in the broadest sense. But Mexico and other Latin American countries maintained a firm opposition to this. In 1947 the controversy was reopened at the Havana Conference, which led to the creation of the General Agreement on Tariffs and Trade (GATT). This agreement provides that the signatory countries grant reciprocal commitments on tariff rates and undertake to conform with certain general commercial principles. The Mexican government decided not to participate in the GATT, and important sectors of private industry supported the government's decision.

As the underlying difference in philosophy between Mexico and the United States grew clear, the trade agreement between the United States and Mexico was looked upon with increasing disfavor by Mexican businessmen, politicians, and economists. In 1948 the government began negotiations to revise the agreement, but these soon came to a standstill. The United States delegation naturally sought compensation for the changes suggested by the Mexican delegation. The Mexicans, on their part, were unwilling to jeopardize the flexibility of their import policy; they wanted to be free to adjust it to new circumstances as these arose. The deadlock continued until in 1951 the two countries finally agreed to renounce the agreement.

Throughout this period of policy reorientation, Mexico's trade patterns were undergoing major changes. In 1946, the current account of Mexico's balance of payments, which had been positive from 1942 to 1945, showed a deficit of 174 millions of United States dollars. Foreign-exchange reserves, which had increased from 54 to 344 million dollars in the four preceding years, went down in 1946 by more than 40 per cent. In 1947, imports were still rising rapidly.

Until July 1947, the import-licensing system set up in 1944 had not been applied. But in that month, a drastic step was taken. A group of articles considered luxury items, which had accounted for 18 per cent of the total value of imports in 1946, was made subject to import licenses and prevented from entering the country. The restrictive effect of these prohibitions was mitigated in many cases by the importation of the raw materials and intermediate goods needed to produce the final product. For example, the ban on the import of finished automobiles was accompanied by annual quotas on imports of assembly parts. Between 1946 and 1948 the number of automobiles assembled in Mexico increased from 10,460 to 21,597. This marks one of the early appearances of a type of import replacement which was to become a well-defined trend in subsequent years.

The action of July 1947 was only one step in the policy of

introducing import licensing as an effective technique. A year later the government's intention to continue the technique was signaled by the decision to empower the Secretaría de Economía Nacional (now known as the Secretaría de Industria y Comercio), without further authorization, to amend the list of products requiring import licenses. The Secretaría de Hacienda (finance ministry), under the new decree, had to be consulted in cases where national revenue might be affected.

The policy changes of this period were not confined to import licensing. In November 1947 a significant change was made in the tariff system. Up to that time, Mexico's tariff rates were expressed largely in specific form, that is, at the rate of so much per physical unit. Increases in the prices of imported goods had greatly reduced the protective impact of the tariff. To re-establish protection for some industries and to provide it anew for others, major changes were initiated. Thenceforth, duties were to be levied by a system of compound rates (specific and ad valorem), and official prices were to be used as the basis for valuation of goods.[2] Those two features were to have important effects upon the efficiency of the tariff as an instrument of protection as well as a source of revenue.

These changes came too late to have much effect in 1947. The balance on current account for the year showed a deficit of 167 million dollars, and foreign-exchange reserves fell another 50 million dollars. Devaluation appeared necessary in order to restore external equilibrium. On June 22, 1948, the exchange rate of 4.86 pesos to the dollar was abandoned. For several months the rate was maintained between 6.85 and 6.89, but in February 1949 it was allowed to fluctuate more widely. Finally on June 17, 1949, a new exchange rate of 8.65 to the dollar was established.

The devaluation prejudiced the interests of those domestic manufacturers who still depended upon a supply of materials from abroad, and it put new pressures on the internal price level. Responding to these problems, the government decided to reduce import duties on a wide range of raw materials and intermediate goods. Classification practices that had impeded the importation of machinery were improved.

In the same year (1949) the Comisión General de Aranceles was reorganized. The commission had been set up in 1927 for the purpose of studying tariff policy and recommending suitable changes to the Secretaría de Hacienda. It consisted of twelve members: eight from various ministries and the remaining four representing the national organizations of industrialists, merchants, farmers, and labor.

In the years after its founding the commission — and the private sector — gradually lost authority in the formulation of tariff policy. As early as 1934 it was announced that the representatives of the private sector had a voice but no vote in the commission. But the changes of 1949 pushed the private sector even further into the background. A new Comisión Ejecutiva de Aranceles (executive tariff commission), composed mainly of representatives of government agencies, was created to take over some of the functions of the Comisión General de Aranceles. The general commission would study and make general proposals but could no longer concern itself with specific cases.

The general assembly of the Confederación de Cámaras Industriales (CONCAMIN) declared in 1953:

> From the outset the representatives of industry have pointed out that the provisions of this law [that of 1949] could not satisfy the needs of the representatives of private enterprise in the Comisión de Aranceles. In fact, although these representatives had won the right to active participation in the study of cases brought before the Commission, they were nevertheless excluded. Their right to supervise the study and solution of problems which concerned them was nullified and their function within the Commission was minimized. Everything was left in the hands of a bureaucratic group which operates in exactly the same way as analogous groups in other agencies; that is, behind closed doors, without the participation of the representatives of private institutions.[3]

And so matters were destined to stand in the field of tariffs from that time on. Despite sporadic attempts by the private sector to recapture some measure of participation in tariff-making policy in the years that followed, the function thereafter remained firmly in governmental hands.

The objectives of import policy during these crucial postwar years — that is, to reduce imports and encourage domestic production — were accomplished. As a result of devaluations and restrictive measures, imports fell by almost 18 per cent between 1947 and 1950. The trend was most conspicuous in durable consumer goods (refrigerators, washing machines, radios, automobiles, etc.), where heavy domestic investment was leading to a rapid displacement of imports. By 1950, imports of durable consumer goods constituted only 7 per cent of total imports, as compared with 11 per cent in 1947. During these same years, economic growth was accelerated; between 1945 and 1950 the country's gross product increased at an average annual rate of 5.5 per cent, while the buying power of its exports expanded 8.8 per cent annually. (The "buying power of exports," given in Table 7, is the value of exports of goods and services, adjusted to reflect changes in their purchasing power with respect to imports.)

The above figures are a pale reflection of the euphoria of "growth" which Mexico enjoyed at the end of the forties. The government championed industrialization and appeared to have found the formula for sustained and accelerated growth. Requests for protection from foreign competition were willingly considered, without careful attention to the type of product or the extent to which national materials were employed in its manufacture. After all, there was enough to pay for imports of needed capital goods. Besides, the establishment of industries would produce substantial profits and these in turn would make it possible to increase domestic investment. Economic growth seemed limited only by the degree of imagination and audacity shown by government and private enterprise. The Korean war prolonged the euphoria. In 1950, the buying power of exports rose 30 per cent over the prior year; between 1950 and 1951 it rose 7 per cent. But the period of euphoria was soon to be brought to an abrupt end by the termination of the abnormal conditions which the Korean war had generated.

FROM KOREA TO THE DEVALUATION OF 1954

The Korean conflict created expectations for a period of scarcity of foreign goods, and induced in 1951 a large increase in imports. The government did not wish to create unnecessary delays in imports, and thus the strict controls of previous years were eased. In January 1951 the import bans of 1947 and 1948 were revoked and various products were exempted from the import-license requirement. Protection was carefully continued on articles which had already begun to be manufactured locally; but such protection was not extended to industries still in prospect.

When the international situation returned to normal, a decline in internal demand tended to curb imports. The gross product, which had been in uninterrupted ascent since 1940, remained nearly constant in 1952 and in the next year actually fell a little.

Early in 1954, as a result of measures to stimulate the economy, imports picked up and a large deficit in the balance on current account led to efforts to stimulate exports. Export duties were lowered at this time, a policy which has been maintained almost continuously ever since. Simultaneously, an across-the-board increase of 25 per cent in import duties was authorized, to compensate for the decrease in export revenue.

In April of that same year a new devaluation was ordered, mainly to promote exports and curb imports. The exchange rate of 8.65 pesos to the dollar was superseded by the rate of 12.50 which is still in effect today. But the increase in imports was not greatly slowed. Consequently, import duties were raised again for certain goods, but at the same time, in order to reduce the pressure on internal prices, the 25 per cent increase mentioned earlier was abolished for imports of raw materials, intermediate products, and capital goods. Most of the articles which had been removed from the licensing control list in 1951 were returned to it, and many new items were added for the first time.

Despite the devaluation of 1954, and in contrast to the situation which had followed the devaluation of 1948–1949, imports of all categories of products except nondurable consumer goods continued to rise between 1954 and 1955. This may have been due in part to the growing inelasticity of demand for imports — inelasticity resulting from the change in the structure of imports from consumer goods to production goods. The demand for production goods is much less responsive to increases in the prices of imports.

Although import policy was not yet used directly as a general device to further industrial integration through greater use of domestic production goods, the dependence of Mexican industry on such imports was recognized as a national problem. In January 1955 the national law granting tax exemptions to "new or necessary industries" was revised with a view to checking the indiscriminate establishment of assembly plants in the country. Thenceforth, the benefits of the law were available only to businesses in which at least 60 per cent of the prime cost of production (including labor and depreciation as elements of "prime cost") was domestic in origin.[4] Subsequently attempts were made to push industrial integration by granting larger tax benefits to those industries which reported the highest degree of integration. To date, however, the system seems to have had only limited success.

THE DECLINE OF THE BUYING POWER OF EXPORTS

During the four years from 1955 to 1958 inclusive, the government tended on the whole to reduce its reliance on import restrictions as a device of national policy. In that period its approach was to concentrate on two objectives: (1) to avoid increasing prices to consumers, and (2) to avoid discouraging foreign investment.

The orientation of protectionist policy since 1947 had led to the increasingly inelastic demand for imports, mentioned above. This presented no immediate problem as long as foreign-exchange earnings were adequate; but the growth in those earnings began to slow up in 1955. Between 1955 and 1960 there was an increase of only 10 per cent in the buying power of exports, as compared with an increase of 35 per cent between 1950 and 1955. The performance of 1955 to 1960 would have been even worse if Mexico had not been favored with a growing revenue from tourism and had been forced to rely primarily on sales of goods to increase her export earnings. The portion of the buying power of exports represented by exports of goods fell 13 per cent between 1955 and 1960, as compared with an increase of 24 per cent in the preceding five-year period.

The increase in imports and the rise in their average prices resulted in heavy deficits in the balance on current account. These were particularly high in 1957, 1958, and 1960; in those three years the deficits were 199 million, 182 million, and 174 million United States dollars, respectively.

Confronted with this drain, the government had two major alternatives. One was to concentrate on industrial integration through persuasion or compulsion. The other was to concentrate on expanding the flow of foreign capital, public and private, into the country irrespective of its use. The second course presented fewer problems and was a more effective measure in the short run.

To be sure, the government continued during these years to make some changes in the national tariff. But none of the changes was aimed at broadening protection to domestic industries. The measures adopted were important principally from a technical point of view. In 1956 a new tariff classification system went into effect. In spite of innumerable modifications during the preceding years, the existing tariff classifications no longer reflected the composition of imports. Before 1956, when duties were increased for fiscal purposes, precise differentiations between the various raw materials and intermediate products were required in order to minimize the effect upon internal costs. Measures of this sort were applied, but without any intent or desire to expand protection.

Official statements on import policy during this period were meager and timid. The protectionist impetus of previous years seemed lost. The absence of specific references to industrial integration was especially conspicuous.

Why was the government unwilling to extend the protectionist policy of earlier years? The answer to our question is a matter of conjecture.

One reason, apparently, was a desire to avoid price increases. In 1953, the government of Adolfo Ruiz Cortines had undertaken to maintain stable prices. The 1954 devaluation had made this impossible; domestic wholesale prices rose 9.4 per cent in 1954 and 14 per cent in 1955. Thereafter, the Ruiz Cortines government seemed more than ever determined to hold the line on prices, even at the risk of reducing the possibilities of growth.

Another factor was the desire to attract foreign investment, including direct foreign investment in manufacturing. In the period from 1955 to 1958, Mexico had all the requisite attractions for foreign investment — traditional absence of exchange controls, high profits in industry, and political stability. And the government at that time was trying to create a still more favorable climate for foreign investment, particularly for investment in joint ventures of Mexicans and foreigners.

Under some conditions, import restrictions can accelerate the flow of foreign investment in manufactures. Investment in assembly plants, for instance, is readily stimulated by prohibitions on the import of consumer goods, provided the investors are permitted to import intermediate materials and machinery without difficulty. In the period from 1955 to 1958, however, the restrictions on the import of consumer goods were already quite extensive. Any further restrictions would have begun to cut into the sensitive area of intermediate materials and machinery. Government officials may well have concluded that these further measures, on balance, would discourage foreign direct investment and would therefore defeat the administration's efforts to increase foreign-exchange reserves.

We shall never know precisely what motivated the government action of this period. The conjecture above is just that — an interpretation based upon numerous interviews with public officials and businessmen. Official declarations of policy at the time neither support nor deny the conclusion; they are simply barren of any indication of motive. As a working hypothesis, the conclusion seems to fit the facts better than any other.

RECENT DEVELOPMENTS

Although it is perhaps too soon to judge, the measures taken in Mexico since 1959 would appear to indicate that protectionist policy is being adapted to the objective of accelerating the integration of manufacturing. The government, in contrast to its relatively passive attitude in the years just preceding, took a stronger position on import replacement. The government no longer acted only in response to the requests of private enterprise for protection. Measures designed to achieve a higher level of industrial integration, either by persuasion or compulsion, as the case required, were adopted.

The federal executive branch, in its determination to restrict imports further, has been obliged to win over the public sector itself. Until 1959 when the Comité de Importaciones del Sector Público was set up, the government had no control over its own imports. The railroads, the petroleum industry, the national electric power company, and other government entities had a comparatively free hand in deciding where to buy. The regulations on government purchasing provided merely that "when a choice must be made between national and foreign products of the same type and quality, preference will be given to the domestic article, so long as its price is no more than ten per cent higher than the normal foreign price plus import duties and charges." [5]

In 1953 the second congress of the Cámara Nacional de la Industria de Transformación (CNIT) declared: "It would be useless for the government to oblige the Mexican people, by means of tariffs and other protectionist devices, to consume domestic products while the government itself purchased abroad; for this would curtail the market for Mexican industry . . . It is therefore of vital importance to national industry that the government be required by law to purchase domestic goods whenever possible and that this requirement be strictly enforced." [6]

The establishment of the committee on the imports of government agencies has given a boost to "Buy Mexican" policies inside the public sector. Lists of domestic suppliers have been drawn up and domestic products are given preference wherever possible.

The reorientation of public buying has not been easy, however. Government agencies are just as readily attracted to foreign supplies as private entrepreneurs are. Lower prices, proven reliability, and more dependable delivery dates permit the agency to argue that it is using its funds to better advantage by buying foreign goods than it could with domestic goods. Thus it has been necessary to resort to drastic measures. Prior authorization by the committee has been required for all imports by government agencies, as well as for local purchases of imported goods. Customs officials have been directed not to process the importation of any foreign product until the agency involved presents proof of authorization for the import.

As far as the private sector is concerned, the government's expanded emphasis on the integration of domestic manufacture has been manifested in several ways.

In the first place, if the prices of domestic products with a heavy import content are substantially higher than international levels, manufacturers have been notified that competitive imports would be permitted unless production were gradually integrated or prices considerably reduced. Powerful businesses have been affected by measures such as this, which reflect the government's new outlook. A report by President Adolfo López Mateos on September 1, 1961, pointed out that "it was decided to reduce tariffs and abolish import controls in the case of certain industrial products and basic raw materials whose local prices were manifestly and unjustifiably higher than the international prices. The government is determined to apply this policy whenever abuses by manufacturers and merchants tend to reduce purchasing power." [7]

The government holds that the level of integration of domestic materials in a given industry is the prime consideration in justifying higher local prices. If integration is well-advanced and the industry in question contributes to economic growth, creates employment, utilizes technological advances, and creates markets for other products, then the government feels that the difference in price between the domestic and the imported product is justified. But in the absence of these conditions, protection is regarded as self-defeating.

In addition, firms which have not advanced very far on the road to national industrial integration have been required to present plans for furthering import substitution either by producing their own intermediate materials or by purchasing them from Mexican suppliers. Written rather than oral commitments are required, because oral assurances were rarely fulfilled in the past. The flexibility of the import licensing system permits the government to withhold licenses from enterprises which do not follow through on their commitments for gradual integration, while granting licenses to businesses which fulfill their commitments.

There is another way in which the recent emphasis on integration has been applied — an approach which may play an increasing role as the Latin American Free Trade Association develops. In the absence of direct investment controls, the Mexican government in the early 1960's began using import restrictions as a means of preventing foreign investors from establishing or expanding a Mexican enterprise as a base for exporting to the rest of Latin America inside the free trade area — especially in cases in which indigenous Mexican investors promise to be able to supply those markets through their own enterprises in Mexico. But this line of policy is still in its infancy; how it will develop remains to be seen.

What this exposition demonstrates more than anything else is the complexity and the changing character of the objectives which government has sought to achieve through import policy. The simple protectionist concept of "import replacement" at different times has been the rival of other objectives — notably maximizing government revenue, easing government procurement, encouraging foreign direct investment, holding down internal prices.

This complexity on the public side has been more than matched by conflicts among interests inside the private sector as they sought to influence the policy of import restriction. These conflicts are the subject of the next chapter.

Chapter 3

The Positions of Private Enterprise

P RIVATE enterprise as a group has no common interests with regard to protectionist policy. Conflicts arise continually between importers and domestic manufacturers. Still more important are the conflicts which arise among the different groups of manufacturers themselves, for these conflicts increase in severity as imports grow more varied. This is an important point to remember; it accounts in good part for the lack of unity among the different elements of private enterprise in dealing with the government. And this lack of unity limits the influence of the private sector.

DIVERSE INTERESTS IN THE PRIVATE SECTOR

The Mexican industrialist takes an eclectic position toward protectionist policy: absolute protection for his product and free importation of the goods he requires to manufacture it.

Clashes occur when a new group of industrialists invests in the domestic manufacture of products which another group is importing. If the product is manufactured out of imported rather than domestic raw materials, then the new manufacturers demand free importation of these raw materials at the same time that they request protection for their finished product. Thus, the development of conflicting interests among producers is a cumulative and self-perpetuating process.

The desire of manufacturers to be able to buy from the cheapest source while selling in protected markets is not unique to Mexico.

But it is of special importance in a country that is in Mexico's stage of development, because there is a very heavy burden on the manufacture of intermediate products. To a certain extent the initial orientation of protectionist policy, beginning with the protection of consumer goods, is responsible for the added burden. Measures protecting the assembly of consumer goods, such as radios, affect all brands and models equally. If the traditional foreign suppliers want to retain the market they must establish assembly plants. This is not a difficult step to take, since the economies of scale associated with the mere *assembly* of radios (as of many other products) are not very great; so fairly small plants will do. As a result, in Mexico, where aggregate personal income is less than 10 billion United States dollars per annum and where the per capita income is about 300 dollars, there is as great a variety of brands of locally assembled durable consumer goods as one finds in countries with very much larger and more affluent internal markets. Therefore domestic producers of intermediate goods would have to supply a very diversified demand on the part of assemblers — with the consequent costs involved in short runs and frequent changes.

The assemblers, whether foreign-owned or indigenous, resist pressures to shift to higher-cost domestic sources not only because of price but because of other considerations. Shifting to a domestic source means, in the short run, confronting new uncertainties in the field of quality control, in the scheduling of deliveries, in the acquisition of technological information, and so on. Burdens of this sort previously assumed by the foreign supplier are shifted onto the shoulders of the assembler. In the opinion of many of the entrepreneurs we interviewed, this is a factor of considerable importance in explaining the resistance to purchasing domestic products.

Price and quality differences between domestic and imported articles are not the only cause for conflict between industrialists. Technological advances in the industrialized countries are forever producing new articles which complete, in one way or another, with existing products. When an import replacement is made in an underdeveloped country, that country acquires the corresponding technological skill. However, it cannot thereafter absorb advances in this technology which are developed in the industrialized countries. There is a continual flow into the market of new articles for which the consumer is willing to pay a higher price. An illustration is nylon cord for tires. Today there is a strong competition in the United States between producers of nylon and rayon cord; tomorrow, the competition may be between nylon and some newer substitute. Mexico has achieved complete replacement of the old cotton cord with rayon cord and produces it in adequate amounts to supply her tire producers. But the tire producers in Mexico want to import nylon cord in order to sell their tires at a higher price, while the manufacturers of rayon cord oppose imports of the nylon product. The controversy has been resolved by permitting the importation of a given amount of nylon cord in return for the purchase of a given amount of the Mexican-manufactured rayon cord.

Like the family quarrels that go on inside the public sector, those within the private sector are almost never publicly aired. This may be due to the fact that each entrepreneur wants protection for his own products. If he wishes to import machinery or materials and argues that national products are more expensive, he may be obliged to admit that his own product is expensive. If he complains of the quality of a national product that he does not wish to buy, he may be reminded that his own product was once inferior as well.

The foregoing paragraphs have emphasized certain matters that are important to the study of relations within the private sector. Now let us review the actual events.

INTRAMURAL RELATIONS IN THE PRIVATE SECTOR

Immediately after the Second World War, the conflicts among manufacturers in Mexico over import policy were not acute. It is true that the established industrialists who already enjoyed adequate protection were less enthusiastic for the widening of protection than were the new industrialists. But the principal differences at that time were between manufacturers as a class and merchants as a class.[1] In 1945, the Cámara Nacional de la Industria de

Transformación (CNIT), at its first national congress, used strong words against the importing merchants, declaring that "the people in Mexico who support free trade only seek unlimited profits through imports and speculations, regardless of the effect of such a policy on national industry. Generally they represent the groups which are indifferent or opposed to Mexican industrialization." [2]

From the outset, the national will to industrialize, together with the need to adopt measures to conserve exchange, tipped the scales in favor of industrial rather than commercial interests. Then, as industry expanded and grew more diverse, the conflicts within the industrial world became ascendant.

In Mexico private industrial enterprise is grouped in two large organizations: the Confederación de Cámaras Industriales (CONCAMIN) and the aforementioned Cámara Nacional de la Industria de Transformación (CNIT). Legally the CNIT is a component part of the CONCAMIN, but in practice the two groups represent opposing viewpoints on all the central issues of industrialization policy, and most especially on the question of the role of direct foreign investment in the country's industrial growth. [3]

The spokesmen of the CNIT express the viewpoint of small and medium-sized enterprises. In general, such enterprises have neither the credit nor the connections to rely upon imported intermediate products, and tend to concentrate upon manufactures that are produced from readily available domestic components. In general, they think of their interests as being furthered by a greater use of domestic components.

The CONCAMIN, on the other hand, is the spokesman for the large industrial firms, including foreign-owned subsidiaries. These larger firms, whether domestic or foreign, have been in a superior position to obtain and import foreign materials. The foreign-owned subsidiaries in particular have had a special incentive to use foreign materials. In many cases, these subsidiaries were originally created as a response to restrictions which blocked off a lucrative export business by the foreign parent firm. The subsidiaries were a means of overleaping an import barrier; hence, their original method of operation was to import components from the parent for assembly in Mexico. Accordingly, the justification for the investment seen through the eyes of the foreign investor has rested in part upon the ability of a parent company to continue to sell components from its home location.[4] In addition, foreign-owned subsidiaries have had the greatest concern about maintaining standardized products, since they have been the firms with international trade names and brands. For these reasons and others, the foreign-owned subsidiaries have had the largest stake in fighting the policy of integration and in maintaining some degree of access to imported materials and components.

The CNIT has had a great deal to say on the subject of import policy, entirely in support of the greatest possible restrictions. But it has chosen to justify its support for import restrictions not so much on the need for integration as upon its more general policy of opposition to the unrestricted growth of direct foreign investment. The second congress of the CNIT, in 1953, stated: "It has been observed that many foreign industrial undertakings are unwilling to utilize national products or materials in their manufacturing processes. This attitude does not stimulate expansion of the internal market or domestic capital formation." [5] The same worry has been expressed repeatedly since that time.

The CONCAMIN has given little attention to the problem of import policy. Nor has it concerned itself with the problems of industrial integration, either in its annual reports or at its national congresses. However, on many occasions it has expressed concern over the use of the tariff for revenue purposes and over the scant importance the government gives the Comisión General de Aranceles, the mixed group that theoretically contributes to the formulation of tariff policy.

Although there is no overt public expression of divergent interests on import policy within private industry, the *sub rosa* conflict takes shape subtly around the administration of quantitative controls. We observed earlier that, unlike the demand for consumer goods, the demand for raw materials, intermediate goods, equipment and machinery is relatively inelastic. Adjustments in tariff rates tend to have little effect on the amount of goods imported. Therefore, as the composition of imports changes, the relative importance of tariff policy declines and quantitative controls become increasingly important as effective instruments of protection. In these circumstances, quantitative restrictions can be fatal to the existing patterns of operation and procurement.

This is probably why the CONCAMIN, which includes the major assemblers dependent on imported products, has found it difficult to endorse the use of quantitative restrictions and has insisted — as it did at its fourth congress in 1957 — that "restrictions on imports should not be used to benefit a few enterprises and prejudice others which are more firmly established and more important. Protectionist measures will impede industrialization instead of facilitating it, if these considerations are overlooked." [6]

The CNIT, on the other hand, has had no objection at all to quantitative controls, including import licensing. That same year the CNIT president, departing from the usual reluctance to criticize in public, sharply attacked the CONCAMIN, saying: "One of the most helpful instruments in solving these problems is the system of import controls designed to protect those industries which have operated satisfactorily, using methods that are consistent with the country's circumstances and economic interests. The fourth Congreso de Industriales is indulging in nonsense when it calls for the revision of a policy that, generally speaking, has been positive and has favored the industrialization of the country." [7]

The recent policy shift whereby the government stopped being only an acquiescent partner in providing protection and became an active protagonist in encouraging integration has had mixed effects on the private sector. It has irritated certain entrepreneurs, aroused strong and determined opposition in some, and caused satisfaction in others. This variety of attitudes is the inevitable result of the conflicting interests within the private sector which we mentioned earlier. The reaction of private enterprise to the government's decision to accelerate the process of industrial integration is illustrated by developments in two industries — automobile assembly and electronics.

Automobile assembly plants were originally established in Mexico to supply the center and south of the country. Unassembled parts could be transported more cheaply than finished units, and thus it was more advantageous to assemble cars near these markets. In 1930 the trend was strengthened by very high import duties on finished vehicles, which forced the principal United States producers to set up their own assembly plants to supply all parts of Mexico.

In order to conserve foreign exchange, the importation of assembled vehicles was prohibited in 1947 and two new types of control were established: (1) annual assembly quotas and (2) import bans on parts that were manufactured locally — at that time mainly tires and inner tubes. The total quota was distributed among the assembly plants in proportion to their volume of production, without restrictions on types or models. In 1951, a price-control system was established for low-priced cars and all types of trucks. In 1954, import quotas for assembly plants were made contingent upon the export of an equivalent amount of cotton, to compensate for the outlay of foreign exchange. And in 1959, in order to obtain more units for the same amount of dollars, the government granted import licenses on small finished cars — models with a maximum official price of 40,000 pesos — a step which had the effect of reducing internal prices considerably.

None of these measures seemed to have had the precise motive of establishing an integrated automobile industry. The low degree of integration in that industry is therefore not surprising. It is true that by the early 1960's some parts were Mexican-made, as a result of import prohibitions; these included tires and inner tubes, upholstery, batteries, seat cushions, battery wires, seat springs and certain other springs, plate glass, tools, shock absorbers, radios, and paints. But these parts still represented only an estimated 20 to 25 per cent of the cost of the vehicles. Furthermore, it should be noted that many of these articles are not completely national products. For example, the rubber in tires is imported; so are the ingredients of paint, and, until recently, a high proportion of radio parts.

Neither did any of these measures deal with one of the fundamental obstacles to the development of a national automobile industry, namely, the excessive number of models. According to experts in the field, the Mexican market of the early 1960's was only big enough to support five or six models if most of the advantages of large-scale production were to be exploited. Despite that fact, in 1959 a great increase in the number of models was permitted; buyers were allowed to choose among more than forty brands and one hundred models. In 1961 some of the highest-priced cars were eliminated but there were still close to thirty brands and seventy models on the market. Since that time the government has attempted further reductions in the number of brands and models.

There is no doubt that the government now intends to press for the integration of the automobile industry and that the reduction in the number of models is a preliminary step in that direction. In the 1960's there was a change in policy on shifting the procurement of major parts from foreign to domestic sources of supply. The government began exerting continuous pressure in that direction. Illustrative of the pressure is a decree issued in August 1962 requiring assembly plants to submit integration programs which would lead to the local production of motors and mechanical units by 1964. This should lead to an accelerated process of integration. The point to be stressed once again is that a firm governmental decision was required in order to induce the private sector on the path of integration. Market forces, in the peculiar circumstances of a country in Mexico's situation, will not bring such integration about.

The electronics industry is an important example of the progress that is possible when the government's position is firm and the problems of import substitution less formidable. For many years the government attempted to promote integration by persuasion. All of the companies produced what was easiest — cabinets and consoles — and imported the rest. In thirteen or fourteen years the Mexican-made parts came to represent no more than 20 per cent of the cost of materials. The resistance of the private sector was not overcome until the government announced unequivocally that import licenses would only be granted to enterprises which had really gone along with national integration. The results were soon apparent. In approximately three years between 1959 and 1962, another 60 per cent of the cost of materials was being bought from domestic sources. The firms were obliged to find and encourage domestic suppliers, and production was begun on certain types of tubes which in 1959 had cost 44 million pesos in imports.

The explanation why progress toward integration was greater in the electronics industry than in the automobile industry can be found primarily in economic and technical considerations. In the final analysis the basic problem is product differentiation and the size of the market. If manufacturers can be persuaded to standardize technical specifications, mass production does not present important difficulties. But if there is resistance to standardization, the possibilities of efficient domestic production are more limited. The degree of resistance to standardization, in turn, depends on the type of competition in the market. Where product differentiation is of prime importance and price competition is secondary, the resistance to standardization is greatest.

In Mexico, automobile assembly plants compete with one another in the pattern established in the United States or Europe. "Subtle differentiations" are indispensable. This accounts for the resistance of the assembly plants to buying standardized, uniform products. In the case of radios and television sets, on the other hand, product differentiation is less important and the price element is a more serious consideration. No single brand, hence no single entrepreneur, enjoys an assured market. Consequently, the producer who does not participate in integration from the outset runs the risk of having to close his plant.

Does the Mexican experience of the last twenty years suggest a pattern for protectionist policy in the future?

Chapter 4

A New Direction

THE considerations that enter into formulating a comprehensive import policy are extraordinarily complex. Questions of government revenue, issues of inflation, problems of foreign confidence, and efforts to affect income distribution are intermingled with the usual issues of protection and industrialization. Here, however, we concentrate on the role of protectionism as the focal point of our study.

In the 1940's in Mexico, when industrial experience was still meager, the country's policy of protection was directed principally at consumer goods. At that stage, the policy of protection promoted economic growth and industrial diversification simply by limiting foreign competition. It reduced the risks and increased the profits for investors in the private sector and helped to change traditional patterns of investment.

For several years, the benefits of protection were apparent in the returns on investment, the level of employment in industry, and the sense of technological progress in the country. But, before long, the policy had reached the end of the line. Further import replacement could only take place in conjunction with national industrial integration. But such integration was difficult. It ran contrary to the interests of important groups in the private sector; it was hampered by limitations in markets for domestic production; and it was restrained by problems of technology and skill.

The Mexican experience demonstrates that the formula of industrialization through protection is not self-perpetuating. At various stages, further protection will generate new resistances in the private sector, as businessmen are forced to give up the privilege of buying raw materials cheaply while they sell finished goods at high prices in protected markets. To overcome their resistance is not an easy task, even for a resolute and stable government.

In Mexico, much of the import replacement which the private sector has undertaken has been a by-product of import prohibitions and quotas used to handle balance-of-payments difficulties, of tariffs levied for revenue purposes, and of devaluations. Though the government has almost always given favorable replies to requests for protection, it has done so without due consideration of the type of product or its proportion of imported inputs, and without demanding the fulfillment of progressive integration programs. What might be called the "natural" theory of import replacement was widely accepted. If the internal market were protected, "invisible" forces would inevitably appear on the scene to profit from the opportunities the government had created.

There were many difficulties with the government's policy. For one thing, it did not take account of the special problems involved in moving demand from final products to intermediate goods. For another, it did not take account of the considerable lag which sometimes occurs between the appearance of a potential market for an import replacement and the decision of the private sector to supply that market.

For Mexico, it has been particularly important that progress in import replacement should be rapid. The buying power of exports has been declining, and it has become increasingly necessary to resort to foreign credits to finance imports. Besides, a high proportion of exchange earnings is committed to pay for raw materials and intermediate products, and is not available for domestic capital formation. The rise in national output per capita has stalled; yet political and social conditions have made it imperative to avoid a new devaluation.

Expansion of domestic production cannot be accomplished, as it was in the past, by the simple expedient of closing the border. The formula for import replacement — ample effective demand and restricted foreign competition — has lost its magic powers. Today, there is no alternative but to take a more decisive role with respect to private investment. This is true for two reasons. First, it is illogical to expect that entrepreneurs will, of their own volition, take steps toward industrial integration which seem contrary to their interests. Second, the indiscriminate use of import restrictions today — unlike the situation of the late 1940's — would simply cut off supplies to existing industry, thus cutting down production, reducing payrolls, and ultimately impairing internal demand.

Though the Mexican government now seems interested in encouraging integration, its principal regulatory device still seems to be that of import restrictions. But the efficiency of that device is limited. Protection is by nature coercive: "the importation of this or that part is prohibited"; "lower the domestic price or imports will be allowed." Protection alone cannot be considered an adequate instrument for ensuring the social utility of investments.

Worried by the pressure of imports on the balance of payments, the government has been resorting to general restrictive measures, and these measures have been leading to a nonselective integration of sorts. But this kind of integration has led to cumulative increases in costs and prices. It has generated intermediate goods which must be purchased locally at prices a good deal higher than those prevailing in the international market. And these high prices for intermediate products have snowballed into even higher prices for the finished goods.

The subordination of import policy to an over-all plan for investment in industry cannot be delayed. This is the only way to avoid the abuses which inevitably arise when instruments of protection operate independently, unrelated to any long-range objectives.

A nonselective program for integration, of the sort which, until recently, government policies were encouraging, cannot go very far. Capital investment tends to be high in the production of intermediate goods, and technological problems tend to grow increasingly complex. The government's decision to allow free imports of certain hitherto protected, incompletely integrated raw materials, when their price is appreciably higher than the world market price, is an important step encouraging selective integration of a more economic type. Still, in the absence of a long-range program of economic development, which would establish an order of priorities and encourage private investment, protectionist policies will continue to function autonomously, inadequate to the task of furthering import replacement efficiently. The character of protectionism will continue to be determined by the most pressing transitory needs, and requests for protection will continue to be examined in the light of their immediate repercussions.

Mexico has traveled a long way on the road to industrialization. Protectionism, in spite of all its shortcomings, has unquestionably been beneficial, even indispensable. But its usefulness as a separate, isolated measure has long since ended. The policy should be reevaluated in terms of the present level of development. It is especially important to improve the competitive position of Mexico's products in relation to imports. Continued evasion of these questions means running the risk of squandering scarce resources, despite the substantial profits they may be producing for private entrepreneurs. The time has come to reflect upon Ragnar Nurkse's observation that nothing is gained by doing a great deal with wavering energy in many fields.

NOTES
AND
INDEX

Notes

MIGUEL S. WIONCZEK, ELECTRIC POWER

Chapter 1: Origins of the Industry

1. For background on the introduction of electricity to Latin America, see J. Fred Rippy, *Latin America and the Industrial Age* (New York: G. P. Putnam's Sons, 1944), pp. 208–217; and James S. Carson, "The Power Industry," in *Industrialization of Latin America*, ed. Lloyd J. Hughlett (New York: McGraw-Hill, 1946), pp. 319–345.

2. For U.S. investment data, see Melville J. Ulmer, *Capital in Transportation, Communications, and Public Utilities: Its Formation and Financing*, a study by the National Bureau of Economic Research (Princeton, N.J.: Princeton University Press, 1960), p. 548. The figures on Mexico are my estimates based upon a variety of sources.

3. Based upon estimates made in a forthcoming volume on economic conditions during the Porfirio Díaz era, in the series *Historia Moderna de México*, directed by Daniel Cosío Villegas and published in Mexico, D.F., by Hermes.

4. See the extremely illuminating Pearson biography, written by his subordinate and friend, J. A. Spender, *Weetman Pearson, First Viscount Cowdray, 1856–1927* (London: Cassell & Co., 1930).

5. Ernesto Galarza, *La industria eléctrica en México* (Mexico, D.F.: Fondo de Cultura Económica, 1942), p. 74. Galarza was the first Mexican historian of the electric power industry.

6. Alfred Tischendorf, *Great Britain and Mexico in the Era of Porfirio Díaz* (Durham, N.C.: Duke University Press, 1961), pp. 111–127.

7. J. Fred Rippy, *British Investment in Latin America, 1822–1949* (Minneapolis: University of Minnesota Press, 1959), p. 97. It is interesting to note that the same author in an earlier study when appraising the over-all financial performance of foreign public utilities in Latin America between 1900 and 1940 wrote that their services to the countries concerned were "enormous," but that "in some cases their profits have been too large." *Latin America and the Industrial Age*, already cited, p. 217.

8. According to Weetman Pearson's biographer, J. A. Spender (already cited), Pearson's electric power enterprises "were prosperous until the outbreak of the Revolution." The semiofficial history of the Mexican Light & Power Company and its subsidiaries, part of an undated volume (1952?) published by the Banco de México, *Generación y distribución de energía eléctrica en México, 1939–49,* dwells in detail upon the company's financial difficulties after 1912 but has nothing to say about its problems before that date. This leads to the conclusion that the company's financial performance under Díaz was considered at least satisfactory.

9. In a series of articles published in *El Economista Mexicano* during the winter of 1905–06.

10. See Raymond Vernon, *The Dilemma of Mexico's Development* (Cambridge, Mass.: Harvard University Press, 1963), esp. p. 40.

Chapter 2: From Revolution to Depression

1. See Ernesto Galarza, *La industria eléctrica en México* (Mexico, D.F.: Fondo de Cultura Económica, 1942), p. 86.

2. José Herrera y Lasso, *La fuerza motriz en México* (Mexico, D.F., 1927), p. 228. In Mexico, this was the first officially sponsored study of all aspects of the industry; it was prepared in 1925–1926 under the auspices of what was then called the Secretaría de Industria, Comercio y Trabajo.

3. *Comisión Nacional de Fuerza Motriz: Su organización, labores y tendencias,* a pamphlet published by that commission in 1924.

4. *Ibid.,* pp. 35–37, printing a document of May 1923 entitled "Programa general de las labores de la Comisión Nacional de Fuerza Motriz."

5. José Herrera y Lasso, who was a member of the commission, later cited as an example of the relative success of this agency the fact that one of the companies gave the commission access to its books for the purpose of discussing the rate structure. See his *La industria eléctrica lo que al público interesa saber* (Mexico, D.F.: Editorial Cultura, 1933), p. 269.

6. See one of Calles' electoral campaign speeches in Morelia, in May 1924, included in *Méjico ante el mundo: Ideología del Presidente Plutarco Elías Calles* (Barcelona, 1927), pp. 72–73: "Those who oppose my candidacy — the capitalists and conservatives of the country — say that I am in favor of change through unrest and upheaval. This is untrue. My colleague who has just addressed us has painted with true strokes the situation currently facing the Mexican proletariat. He has spoken of the need of the working people of the Republic for the establishment of factories and industries, and the innumerable instances of development of natural resources that progress demands

in order to increase the nation's wealth . . . In effect, we need capital to come in and establish itself in our country; we need industrial capital to enter in order to give life to our existing industries and to establish new ones. *I am not an enemy of capital; quite the contrary. I want it to come in to develop our natural wealth* . . . and ultimately not only to bring the greatest profit for the owner thereof, but collective benefit as well." (Italics are in the Spanish text.)

7. José Herrera y Lasso, "Los antecedentes de la ley de 30 de abril de 1926," *El Universal,* March 12, 1931, reprinted in his book *La industria eléctrica* (note 5, above), pp. 124–129.

8. Herrera y Lasso, *La industria eléctrica,* pp. 130–131.

9. *Ibid.,* p. 132.

10. According to Cristobal Lara Beautell, *La industria de energía eléctrica* (Mexico, D.F.: Fondo de Cultura Económica, 1953), p. 174, ". . . all the economies achieved in generation and distribution during that period [between 1900 and 1932], which were not unappreciable, exclusively benefited the stockholders and at no time were passed along to the consumer to any degree whatsoever."

11. *El Comercio* (Puebla), July 18, 1928.

12. Robert Peter Wolfangel, "The History and Development of Private Electric Power Interests in Mexico," unpub. M.A. thesis at Mexico City College, June 1961, p. 142.

Chapter 3: The Conflict

1. Ernesto Galarza, *La industria eléctrica en México* (Mexico, D.F.: Fondo de Cultura Económica, 1942), pp. 86–90.

2. Describing the progressive development of government participation in the electric power industry in the U.S., the monumental study by the Twentieth Century Fund, *Electric Power and Government Policy: A Survey of Relations Between the Government and the Electric Power Industry* (New York, 1948), p. 42, had this to say about the attitudes of U.S. public opinion toward the private companies at the beginning of the Great Depression: "In 1929 it became evident that many utility systems had taken full advantage of the opportunity [for uncontrolled exploitation]. The collapse of many utility holding company stocks was interpreted as evidence of exploitation. Unintentionally the industry offered itself as a scapegoat for the sins, real and imagined, of the business world, and its offer was accepted by a public in no mood for a just and careful allocation of praise and blame."

3. *Luz y Justicia,* a periodical edited by the Tampico consumer league, Oct. 13, 1932.

4. Not all the *técnicos* were satisfied with the new legislation. Considering it an obstacle to Mexican electrification, José Herrera y Lasso

commented in March 1931: "The new law appears to be fearful of the hoarding of water resources by large utilities, who necessarily operate with foreign capital . . . From the standpoint of strict nationalism it would be very desirable for all the country's natural resources to be developed by the Mexican financial community. However, such financial facilities are not available in the necessary proportions, nor does our capital show very much interest in investments of that nature . . . Water resources may indeed be cornered . . . [but] they are not properties such as mines or oil deposits whose exploitation exhausts them progressively until they finally disappear completely. Waterfalls are resources that are not consumed with use, I insist, and are of no value for electricity if not utilized. Said utilization should therefore be encouraged by making it feasible for those who have the necessary means." Article from *El Universal*, reprinted in Herrera y Lasso's book *La industria eléctrica lo que al público interesa saber* (Mexico, D.F.: Editorial Cultura, 1933), pp. 148–149.

5. See the leading Mexico City dailies of June and July 1933.

6. *Memorandum de la Confederación Nacional Defensora al Gen. don Plutarco Elías Calles*, reproduced in *El Economista*, July 20, 1933.

7. Daniels was the U.S. ambassador in Mexico from 1933 to 1942. On his attitudes toward big business, including public utilities in the U.S. and abroad, see his memoirs, *Shirt-Sleeve Diplomat* (Chapel Hill: University of North Carolina Press, 1947), and E. David Cronon, *Josephus Daniels in Mexico* (Madison: University of Wisconsin Press, 1960), particularly chap. i, "Shades of Veracruz," and chap. v, "Dollars and Diplomacy."

8. *Plan Sexenal del Partido Nacional Revolucionario, 1934–1939*, quoted in Rolfo Ortega Mata, *Problemas económicos de la industria eléctrica* (Mexico, D.F., 1939), pp. 135–136.

9. "Decreto que autoriza al Ejecutivo Federal para constituir la Comisión Federal de Electricidad," published in *Diario Oficial*, Jan. 20, 1934.

Chapter 4: Enter the Government

1. Oscar R. Enríquez, "Informe preliminar sobre la mobilización de obras e instalaciones eléctricas existentes en México," the first document in a mimeographed report made on behalf of the bureau of electricity in the Secretaría de Economía Nacional, November 1946, p. 10.

2. The power companies believed that Cárdenas' hostility extended to all foreign interests in Mexico. "Cárdenas felt toward foreign electric companies just as deeply as he did in the case of the oil companies," wrote a power company official, Robert Peter Wolfangel, in 1961. See his "The History and Development of Private Electric Power

Interests in Mexico," unpub. M.A. thesis at Mexico City College, June 1961, p. 48.

3. E. David Cronon, *Josephus Daniels in Mexico* (Madison: University of Wisconsin Press, 1960), pp. 122, 124. Cronon says Cárdenas intimated to U.S. Ambassador Daniels that he needed the law also to deal if necessary with some illegally enriched members of Calles' group.

4. A Mexican expert hostile to the private firms hinted broadly in 1939 that the companies had used their influence on the lower echelons of the Secretaría de Economía Nacional to make the draft more palatable. Rolfo Ortega Mata, *Problemas económicos de la industria eléctrica* (Mexico, D.F., 1939), p. 127.

5. The railroad expropriation created some concern among foreign investors in Mexico, but did not give rise to any open hostility, since "the position of the minority stockholders and bondholders [given the firm's chronic state of near bankruptcy] could hardly be worsened by the government's assuming full ownership of an enterprise that had long since ceased to attract risk capital." Cronon, p. 127.

6. Article 5 of the presidential decree, which was entitled "Ley que crea la Comisión Federal de Electricidad" and was published in *Diario Oficial*, Aug. 24, 1937.

7. Press statement of Secretaría de Economía Nacional, Oct. 11, 1938, as quoted by the Comité para el Estudio de la Industria Eléctrica Mexicana (CEE-MEX), *Desarrollo de la industria eléctrica mexicana*, Mexico, D.F., mimeo. [1957], p. 295.

8. Josephus Daniels, Mexico City, to Sumner Welles, Nov. 7, 1938. *Papers of Josephus Daniels*, Library of Congress, Washington, quoted by Cronon, p. 122.

9. Wolfangel (our note 2, above) said on his p. 51 that "on the surface, the law appeared to be what the companies had long awaited. The law and its regulations were very sound in principle."

10. This résumé takes into account the original law of 1938 as revised in 1940 and the pertinent *reglamentos* issued in 1940 and 1945. See "Ley de la industria eléctrica" of Dec. 31, 1938 (published in the *Diario Oficial*, Feb. 11, 1939); the amendatory decree of Dec. 31, 1940 (*Diario Oficial*, Jan. 14, 1941); "Reglamento de la ley de la industria eléctrica" (*Diario Oficial*, Aug. 28, 1940); and "Nuevo reglamento de la ley de la industria eléctrica" (*Diario Oficial*, Oct. 4, 1945).

11. Annual Report (1939) of the Puebla Tramway, Light & Power Company.

12. Ample documentation on this case was published in 1944 in a pamphlet edited by two leaders of the electrical union who successfully fought the battle against rate increases in this period.

See Francisco J. Macin and José Zavala Ruiz, *La electrificación de México* (Mexico, D.F., 1944), p. 120.

13. Letter of the minister of national economy, Efraín Buenrostro, to G. R. Convay, president of Mexlight, dated Nov. 12, 1940, reproduced in Macin and Zavala Ruiz, pp. 25–26.

14. Wolfangel, p. 80.

15. That this description of the prevailing attitudes is not exaggerated is demonstrated by the following rather pathetic complaint: "It was hard to believe how public opinion had turned on the electric companies, especially the larger ones. In the beginning these companies held the highest prestige in the community; they were the forerunners of progress and civilization . . . And yet when the systems consolidated and adequate service given, these same companies were despised and hated because of what they stood for." Wolfangel, p. 38.

16. See the plan as quoted in Rolfo Ortega Mata, *Los problemas económicos de la industria eléctrica* (Mexico, D.F., 1949), pp. 147–149. This book should not be confused with his earlier book of almost the same title, cited in our note 4, above.

17. See Carlos Ramírez Ulloa, "Estado actual de la industria eléctrica," in the periodical *Revista Mexicana de Ingeniería y Arquitectura*, October 1939; and Hector Martínez D'Meza, "Los problemas de la industria eléctrica en México" in the same review, February 1940. Both authors played a decisive role in the establishment and functioning of the CFE in the 1940's and early 1950's.

18. Wolfangel, p. 118.

19. Enríquez (note 1, above), pp. 11–12.

20. See "The Light and Power Industry: New Capital Is Urgently Needed to Expand Capacity to Fill Demands," one of the articles in a special supplement on Mexico and her relation to the American defense effort, published in *The Journal of Commerce and Commercial* (New York), Aug. 27, 1940, second section, p. 27, and reproduced in Spanish in the Mexico City monthly *El Economista*, Dec. 1, 1940. This Mexican magazine, issued since the late thirties and sponsored by business interests, has no connection with another *El Economista*, run by a group of leftist intellectuals in the thirties.

21. See James C. Bonbright, *Principles of Public Utility Rates* (New York: Columbia University Press, 1961), p. viii.

Chapter 5: Beginning of the End

1. The investment figures are my estimates, painfully built up from a variety of published and unpublished sources. The preceding figures on the growth of capacity are from the annual surveys of Dirección General de Electricidad, Secretaría de Industria y Comercio, and the annual reports of the CFE and the private companies.

2. Comité para el Estudio de la Industria Eléctrica Mexicana (CEE-MEX), *Desarrollo de la industria eléctrica mexicana,* Mexico, D.F., mimeo. [1957].

3. *Ibid.,* p. 860.

4. Robert Peter Wolfangel, "The History and Development of Private Electric Power Interests in Mexico," unpub. M.A. thesis at Mexico City College, June 1961, p. 62.

5. See records of the CNIT's second annual congress held in mid-1953 in Mexico City, and of subsequent annual meetings of the same organization; also a series of CNIT-sponsored studies, especially Hector Cassaigne *et al., Energética: Notas y estudios para su planeación en México* (Mexico, D.F.: EDIAPSA, 1953); José Domingo Lavín, *Inversiones extranjeras: Análisis, experiencias y orientaciones para la conducta mexicana* (Mexico, D.F.: EDIAPSA, 1954); and Antonio Carrillo Flores *et al., Notas sobre la industria básica* (Mexico, D.F.: EDIAPSA, 1953).

6. On this point see José Domingo Lavín, just cited, p. 249.

7. Describing the early postwar difficulties of the companies, Wolfangel noted that in the latter part of the forties "cultivation of key friends within the agencies seemed to be a method of attack by several companies. Elegant parties, paid 'business trips,' gifts, etc., were part of the campaign by the companies to get the bureaucrats to render favorable resolutions, especially related to rate matters. Everybody went through the motions of being very congenial, but it soon became obvious to the companies that the rate situation was not improving to the extent that they had been led to believe that it could." Consequently, these practices were discontinued, though they reappeared for a short time in the mid-fifties when again the hope of a better deal arose. Wolfangel, p. 64.

8. See Mexico City press reports on annual meetings of Cámara Nacional de Electricidad, and specifically the organization's mimeographed collection of documents entitled *Reunión previa y XXI Asamblea de Asociados* (meetings held in Mexico City, April 27–28, 1958).

9. Wolfangel, p. 68.

Chapter 6: The Final Act

1. American & Foreign Power Company, Inc., *36th Annual Report, 1959* (New York, 1960), p. 22.

2. *Journal of Commerce* (New York), June 3, 1960.

3. Robert Peter Wolfangel, "The History and Development of Private Electric Power Interests in Mexico," unpub. M.A. thesis at Mexico City College, June 1961, p. 68.

4. Herbert Bratter, "Latin American Utilities' Nationalization Proceeds Inexorably," *Public Utilities Fortnightly* (Washington), July 7, 1960, pp. 1–15.

5. See *La campaña electoral de 1957–1958* (*Documentos — Programas — Plataformas*), vol. 4 of *Problemas de México*, ed. Manuel Marcué Pardiñas (Mexico, D.F., 1959), pp. viii, 320; and Adolfo López Mateos, *Pensamiento y Programa* (Mexico, D.F.: Editorial la Justicia, 1961), a collection of the president's speeches during the electoral campaign in 1957–1958.

6. Wolfangel, p. 69. In the words of the same author, "the sellout was made under very agreeable conditions, both to the Mexican Government as well as to American & Foreign Power. From private industry's viewpoint, the company showed signs of brilliancy in successfully completing the sale of property" (p. 70).

7. The explanation of this evolution in the attitudes of the various business groups toward foreign investment in the late fifties can be found in Raymond Vernon, *The Dilemma of Mexico's Development* (Cambridge, Mass.: Harvard University Press, 1963), chap. vi, "Leadership Ideology in the Private Sector since 1940."

8. See the text of the speech of the finance minister, Antonio Ortiz Mena, in his capacity as new chairman of the board of the former Mexlight, on Sept. 27, 1960, published in full in Mexico City dailies on the following day.

9. A long time before the nationalization the absence of interconnection among the principal generating systems was considered the main obstacle to the country's electrification. See Cristobal Lara Beautell, *La industria de energía eléctrica* (Mexico, D.F.: Fondo de Cultura Económica, 1953), pp. 121 ff.

10. These viewpoints were expressed in innumerable public meetings, lectures, and pamphlets during the winter of 1960–61. See, specifically, press reports on lectures given by various experts at the Colegio Nacional de Ingenieros Mecánicos y Electricistas in Mexico City in November 1960; Enrique Vilar, *Meditaciones sobre el tema de la nacionalización de la industria eléctrica* (Mexico, D.F., March 1961); Luis Yañez Pérez, "La nacionalización de la industria eléctrica en México," *Actividad Económica en América Latina*, March 15, 1961, pp. 11–33; and Comisión Federal de Electricidad, *La nacionalización de la industria eléctrica en México* (mimeo., Mexico, D.F., July 1961), paper presented to the ECLA Seminar on Electric Energy in Latin America (Doc. ST/ECLA/Conf.7/L.1.05a).

11. Jorge Davo Lozano, "Problemas conexos a la nacionalización de la industria eléctrica de México," *Excelsior*, Sept. 8, 1960.

12. "Sabotaje en la Cía. de Luz — La empresa no platicará en tanto exista coerción," *Novedades*, Dec. 8, 1961.

13. See statements by the president of the Confederación de

Cámaras Industriales, Manuel Fernandez Landero, and a leader of the CFE trade union, Francisco Pérez Ríos, among others, published in Mexico City on Jan. 20, 1962, and comments by *Panorama Económico,* the monthly organ of the Banco de Comercio, Mexico's second biggest private bank (January 1962 issue). *Panorama Económico* stressed that "even with new increases, Mexico will still be a country with cheap electric power."

DAVID H. SHELTON, THE BANKING SYSTEM

Chapter 1: Mexican Finance Today

1. The most recent and complete description of Mexican financial institutions is that contained in O. Ernest Moore, *Evolución de las instituciones financieras en México* (Mexico, D.F.: Centro de Estudios Monetarios Latinoaméricanos, 1963).

2. Banco de México, *Informe anual, 1962* (pub. 1963), pp. 90–93. This publication is the annual report of the Banco de México and is extensively cited hereinafter. Until recent years its title was given as the number of the annual stockholders' meeting to which the report corresponded. For convenience, the publication, even for the earlier years, will be referred to in notes as *Informe anual.* A change in the method of dating the report must also be noted. Before 1960, the date on the cover was the year of publication; thus the *Informe anual, 1957* described the events of 1956. In 1960 this procedure was changed to that of giving the report the date of the year whose events were described. This resulted in there being two reports whose covers bear the date 1959. The first, published in 1959, describes the events of 1958. The second, published in 1960 and designated *Informe anual correspondiente al año 1959,* describes 1959.

The asset figures in the text — and all those used in this study with the possible exception of very old data — exclude so-called *cuentas de orden.* Mexican financial institutions customarily carry *cuentas de orden* on both sides of their balance sheets; these items are sometimes larger than the total of all the items in the balance sheet proper. *Cuentas de orden* appear to represent no actual flow of funds through the financial institutions; their principal components in most cases are contingent liabilities arising out of guarantees given by the financial institution (together with the assets which secure these liabilities) and the liabilities and assets which arise when institutions accept securities or other property for management or safekeeping (but not in trust). Identical totals for *cuentas de orden* are always carried on both sides of the balance sheet.

3. Statistics in last three paragraphs are computed from peso figures in Banco de México, *Informe anual, 1962* (pub. 1963), pp. 94–95; Comisión Nacional de Valores, *Boletín Mensual,* May 1963.

4. Comisión Nacional de Valores, *Memoria anual, 1962* (pub. 1963), pp. 103, 104, 112.

5. The changes in banking legislation are described in *El Mercado de Valores,* Dec. 31, 1962, pp. 788–789, and Jan. 7, 1963, pp. 3–14.

6. At the end of 1962, private enterprises and individuals held only 8.4 million pesos of a total of 7,513.2 million pesos in directly issued federal government securities outstanding. By contrast, the same group held 786.5 million pesos of 839.1 million pesos outstanding in Patronato del Ahorro Nacional securities, and they held 1,543.6 million pesos of a total of 4,208.7 million pesos in outstanding Nacional Financiera fixed-income securities. Figures are from Banco de México, *Informe anual, 1962* (pub. 1963), pp. 120–121.

7. In this estimate, "liquid assets" include cash and demand deposits, various minor items considered the equivalent of cash, time deposits, savings deposits, and holdings of most fixed-income securities. The major financial assets excluded are hoarded gold, holdings of funds and securities abroad, and variable-income securities. Figures are from Banco de México, *Informe anual, 1959* (pub. 1959), p. 123; and *Informe anual, 1962* (pub. 1963), pp. 69, 116. Percentages computed.

Chapter 2: Background of the Modern System

1. Particularly valuable sources of information on early banking in Mexico are Ernesto Lobato López, *El crédito en México* (Mexico, D.F.: Fondo de Cultura Económica, 1945); Gilberto Moreno Castañeda, *La moneda y la banca en México* (Guadalajara: Imprenta Universitaria, 1955); and Walter F. McCaleb, *Present and Past Banking in Mexico* (New York: Harper & Brothers, 1920).

2. Enrique Martínez Sobral, *Estudios elementales de legislación bancaria,* quoted in Lobato López, *El crédito,* p. 191.

3. McCaleb, *Present and Past Banking,* pp. 180–189.

4. *Legislación bancaria* (Secretaría de Hacienda y Crédito Público, Dirección General de Crédito, 1957), I, 113.

5. Antonio Manero, *La revolución bancaria en México* (Mexico, D.F.: Talleres Gráficos de la Nación, 1957), p. 32.

6. The limited number of banks was not a wholly pernicious characteristic. Though it did reduce competition and place the borrower at a disadvantage, the fewness of banks also imparted stability to the system. Mexico, in part because of its concentrated banking system, had nothing resembling the waves of bank failures which plagued the United States. If the public paid the cost of semi-monopoly when it borrowed, a substantial refund was received in the form of funds not lost because banks did not fail. A sympathetic account of the Díaz banking system is given by McCaleb, *Present and Past Banking,* esp.

pp. 99–143. Lobato López, *El Crédito,* gives quite a different interpretation; see esp. pp. 210–223.

7. Antonio Manero, *La reforma bancaria en la revolución constitucionalista* (Mexico, D.F.: Talleres Gráficos de la Nación, 1958), esp. pp. 89–134. This work contains a detailed description of the destruction and later reconstruction of the banks.

8. *Ibid.,* p. 323. (The quotation is from Carranza's "Informe del Primer Jefe a la XXVII legislatura.")

9. *Ibid.,* p. 88.

10. For steps leading to the new legislation, see *Legislación bancaria,* II, 20–25.

11. Text of the creating document, "Ley que crea el Banco de México (25 de agosto de 1925)," is found in *Legislación sobre el Banco de México* (Secretaría de Hacienda y Crédito Público, Dirección General de Crédito, 1958), pp. 57–105.

12. *Legislación bancaria,* II, 28.

13. Statistical sources are: Banco de México, *Informe anual, 1926* (pub. 1926); Comisión Nacional Bancaria, *Boletín Mensual,* December 1941, pp. 2–3; Joaquín Loredo Goytortúa, "Producción y productividad agrícolas," in *México, 50 años de revolución: La economía* (Mexico, D.F.: Fondo de Cultura Económica, 1960), p. 112; Manero, *La revolución bancaria* (our note 5, above), p. 32. In the per capita computation, Mexico's population was taken as 16 million in 1925.

14. Virgil M. Bett, *Central Banking in Mexico* (Ann Arbor: Bureau of Business Research, University of Michigan, 1957), pp. 33–39.

15. The 1925–1930 figures are from Comisión Nacional Bancaria, *Boletín Estadístico,* January-February 1961, pp. 6–7, and Banco de México, *Informe anual,* 1926 and 1931.

16. Bett, *Central Banking,* pp. 47–49.

17. Comisión Nacional Bancaria, *Boletín Estadístico,* January-February 1961, pp. 6–7.

18. This period is described in Alberto J. Pani, *El problema supremo de México* (Mexico, D.F.: Inversiones A.R.P.A., 1955), esp. pp. 49–86, and in Víctor Urquidi, "Tres lustros de experiencia monetaria en México: Algunas enseñanzas," in *Memoria del Segundo Congreso Mexicano de Ciencias Sociales,* vol. II (Mexico, D.F.: Artes Gráficas del Estado, 1946), esp. pp. 429–433.

19. Pani, *El problema supremo,* pp. 63–67.

20. Texts of the 1932 laws are found in *Legislación sobre el Banco de México,* pp. 151–172, and *Legislación bancaria,* III, 9–144.

21. Bett, *Central Banking,* pp. 66–68.

22. Comisión Nacional Bancaria, *Boletín Mensual,* various issues, 1933–1937. Computed percentage is based on asset figures from this source, gross national product estimates from Enrique Pérez López, "El producto nacional" in *México, 50 años de revolución: La economía*

(Mexico, D.F.: Fondo de Cultura Económica, 1960), pp. 587–589, and the index of wholesale prices contained in Secretaría de Economía, *Memoria, 1957* (pub. 1957), p. 191.

23. *Discursos pronunciados por los Cc. Secretarios de Hacienda y Crédito Público en las convenciones bancarias celebradas del año 1934 a 1958* (Secretaría de Hacienda y Crédito Público, Dirección General de Prensa, Memoria, Bibliotecas, y Publicaciones, 1958), p. 22.

24. Bett, *Central Banking,* p. 112, gives the amount of government securities held by the Banco de México (excluding short-term loans) as 293 million pesos at the end of 1940. Most of this was in excess of legal limitations on the holding of government paper by the Bank.

25. *Boletín Mensual,* January-February 1941.

26. Bett, *Central Banking,* p. 114; *Boletín Mensual,* January-February 1941.

27. *Boletín Mensual,* December 1941.

28. Heliodoro Duenes, *Los bancos y la Revolución* (Mexico, D.F., 1945), p. 223.

29. Bett, *Central Banking,* p. 114; Pérez López (see note 22, above), pp. 587–589. For an index of wholesale prices, see Secretaría de Economía, *Memoria, 1957* (pub. 1957), p. 191.

Chapter 3: Emergence of the Modern System

1. "Decreto que reforma la ley general de instituciones de crédito (21 de marzo de 1935)," in *Legislación bancaria* (Secretaría de Hacienda y Crédito Público, Dirección General de Crédito, 1957), III, 237.

2. *Discursos pronunciados por los Cc. Secretarios de Hacienda y Crédito Público en las convenciones bancarias celebradas del año 1934 a 1958* (Secretaría de Hacienda y Crédito Público, Dirección General de Prensa, Memoria, Bibliotecas, y Publicaciones, 1958), p. 21.

3. See "Ley orgánica del Banco de México (26 de abril de 1941)" and "Decreto que modifica la ley orgánica del Banco de México (31 de diciembre de 1941)," in *Legislación sobre el Banco de México* (Secretaría de Hacienda y Crédito Público, Dirección General de Crédito, 1958), pp. 331–366.

4. See "Ley general de instituciones de crédito y organizaciones auxiliares (3 de mayo de 1941)," in *Legislación bancaria,* IV, 9–128. Important further steps in the same direction were taken with the "Decreto que reforma la ley general de instituciones de crédito y organizaciones auxiliares (11 de febrero de 1949)," *Legislación bancaria,* IV, 217-272.

5. *Legislación bancaria,* IV, 42.

6. The exact amount of the inflow is uncertain, but its magnitude

and effects are suggested by these facts: In 1940, the total assets of the Banco de México were about 733 million pesos; at the end of 1945 (after some outflow had begun), the Bank's gold, silver, and foreign-exchange account alone totaled some 1,800 million pesos, while its total assets exceeded 3,400 million pesos. Banco de México, *Informe anual, 1941* (pub. 1941), balance sheet; *Informe anual, 1947* (pub. 1947), table 25.

7. *Discursos,* appendix table; and Comisión Nacional de Valores, *Memoria anual, 1958* (pub. 1959), p. 85. Percentages computed.

8. Nacional Financiera and private institutions themselves are often the supporters or repurchasers of their liabilities. Formal repurchase agreements were included in the terms of many securities until the early 1950's. These have been largely discontinued, but the support of liquidity continues as a strongly established policy. Whether followed by Nacional Financiera or by a private institution, this policy could not withstand any substantial attempt by the public to liquidate securities without the background support of the Banco de México. For a discussion of wartime and early postwar policy, see Eduardo Villaseñor, "La estructura bancaria y el desarrollo económico de México," *El Trimestre Económico,* April-June 1953, pp. 199–230.

9. On these and other wartime control measures, see Raúl Martínez Ostos, "Algunos aspectos de la política monetaria del Banco de México," *El Trimestre Económico,* July-September 1944, pp. 209–229; and Banco de México, *Informe anual,* 1942 to 1946.

10. This total does not include discounts for national credit institutions or credits to business-type enterprises in the public sector since these are not identified in Banco de México accounts. Statistics are from Banco de México, *Informe anual, 1941* (pub. 1941), balance sheet, and *Informe anual, 1947* (pub. 1947), table 25.

11. Comisión Nacional Bancaria, *Boletín Mensual,* January-February 1941, pp. 8–9; Banco de México, *Informe anual, 1941* (pub. 1941), balance sheet; *Informe anual, 1947* (pub. 1947), table 25; *Informe anual, 1961* (pub. 1962), p. 59. Percentages computed.

12. Percentages computed from Banco de México, *Informe anual, 1947* (pub. 1947), table 25.

13. Banco de México, *Informe anual,* 1947 to 1961.

14. See, for example, the discussion in Raúl Martínez Ostos, "Algunos aspectos"; and speeches by Aníbal de Iturbide and Juan Sánchez Navarro in Asociación de Banqueros de México, *Carta Mensual,* no. 60 (1951), pp. 583–589, and in *Revista Bancaria,* March 1962, pp. 134–136.

15. Roberto Dávila Gómez Palacio, "Concentración financiera privada en México," *Investigación Económica,* vol. 15 (1955), pp. 249–261.

16. Banco de México, *Informe anual, 1947* (pub. 1947), table 25, and *Informe anual, 1949* (pub. 1949), table 24.

17. Average annual turnover of peso demand deposits jumped from 23.9 in 1945 to 33.2 in 1947, indicating a large increase in transactions velocity; this was accompanied by a sharp rise in the ratio of gross national product in current pesos to the money supply, indicating a growth of income velocity. Banco de México, *Informe anual*, 1947 and 1949.

18. Banco de México, *Informe anual, 1949* (pub. 1949), table 24, *Informe anual, 1951* (pub. 1951), table 15; and my table 1.

19. Comisión Nacional de Valores, *Memoria anual, 1958* (pub. 1959), p. 85.

20. It must be emphasized that the ordinary budgetary revenues of the federal government exceeded expenditures for current purposes during 1948–1952. Small deficits in 1948 and 1952 were more than offset by surpluses in 1949, 1950, and 1951. Moreover, the share of federal budgetary receipts in the gross national product increased from 6.1 per cent in 1948 to 8.3 per cent in 1952. The surplus in the federal budget did not offset the deficit of the rest of the public sector. Much of the total public program of capital expenditures was outside the federal budget and was financed through special-purpose federal borrowing, through borrowing by the national credit institutions, and through borrowing by government-controlled enterprises. For budget figures see *Discursos,* appendix table.

21. From 1948 through the end of 1950 the Banco de México was able to offset part of an expansion in its gold, silver, and foreign-exchange account, though the extent of this offset was slight. From 2,619 million pesos at the end of 1948, the Bank's loans and investments slid to 2,385 million at the close of 1950. Over the same period the foreign account increased from 839 million pesos to 2,846 million pesos. Between 1950 and 1952, however, the situation was reversed. Gold, silver, and foreign-exchange holdings of the Bank fell, while its loans and investments mounted rapidly. Banco de México, *Informe anual,* 1950 to 1954.

22. The requirements cited were summarized from Banco de México, "Recopilación e instructivo de las disposiciones contenidas en las diversas circulares expedidas por el Banco de México, S.A., en relación con el depósito obligatorio," 1950, mimeo., pp. 1–8.

23. Nacional Financiera, *Informe anual,* 1956 to 1962.

24. Comisión Nacional de Valores, *Memoria anual, 1962* (pub. 1963), p. 105.

Chapter 4: Banking Policy and Economic Growth

1. Ramón Beteta, *Pensamiento y dinámica de la Revolución mexicana* (Mexico, D.F.: Editorial México Nuevo, 1950), pp. 81–82. The passage is from a speech delivered in 1930.

2. *El Mercado de Valores,* Nov. 27, 1961, p. 604.
3. *Revista Bancaria,* March-April 1961, p. 141.
4. The modifications are described in *El Mercado de Valores,* Dec. 31, 1962, pp. 788–789, and Jan. 7, 1963, pp. 3–14.
5. The famous study mentioned is Raúl Ortiz Mena *et al., El desarrollo económico de México y su capacidad para absorber capital del exterior* (Mexico, D.F.: Nacional Financiera, 1953). Other studies are Barry N. Siegel, *Inflación y desarrollo* (Mexico, D.F.: Centro de Estudios Monetarios Latinoaméricanos, 1960), and Ifigenia M. de Navarrete, *La distribución del ingreso y el desarrollo económico de México* (Mexico, D.F.: Instituto de Investigaciones Económicas, Escuela Nacional de Economía, Universidad Nacional Autónoma de México, 1960).

Calvin P. Blair, NACIONAL FINANCIERA

Chapter 1: The Nature of Nacional Financiera

1. José Hernández Delgado (president and general manager of Nacional Financiera), *The Contribution of Nacional Financiera to the Industrialization of Mexico,* address at luncheon of Mexico City Rotary Club, Aug. 1, 1961, pamphlet (Nacional Financiera, 1961), p. 14; Nacional Financiera, *Informe de actividades 1961* (report to stockholders for fiscal year, July 1, 1960, to June 30, 1961), p. 12.
2. The estimates were made with data from Nacional Financiera, *Informe anual* for 1958 (pub. 1959), table 14, pp. 114–115, and from Dirección General de Estadística, *Censo industrial 1956 (Información censal 1955), Resumen General Tomo I,* table VI, pp. 34–45. Estimates of invested capital as of a moment of time appear only in the industrial census, the latest of which (taken in 1961 with data for 1960) is not yet available at this writing.
3. The organic law, its subsequent amendments, and NAFIN's by-laws are reprinted in Nacional Financiera, *Ley orgánica y estatutos sociales,* pamphlet, 1963.
4. Hernández Delgado, *Contribution,* p. 7.
5. Nacional Financiera, *Informe anual* for 1961 (pub. 1962), table 3, p. 107.
6. See, for example, Nacional Financiera, *Tercera asamblea general de accionistas* (annual report for 1936, pub. 1937), p. 18; *Cuarta asamblea general de accionistas* (annual report for 1937, pub. 1938), p. 14; and *Quinta asamblea general de accionistas* (annual report for 1938, pub. 1939), p. 14. These are the agency's first three annual reports. Beginning with the annual report pertaining to the events of 1952 (pub. 1953), the title *Informe anual* is used on the cover. These calendar-year annual reports are distinct from the fiscal-year reports

to stockholders which NAFIN began to publish in 1960 as *Informe de actividades* (e.g., note 1, above).

7. Hernández Delgado, *Contribution*, p. 10. For an earlier statement of the same theme, see Nacional Financiera, *Sexta asamblea general de accionistas* (annual report for 1939, pub. 1940), p. 27.

8. Nacional Financiera, *Informe de actividades 1962*, p. 9. Data on "resources channeled by Nacional Financiera, S.A., to different economic activities" have been published only for years beginning with 1953. See Nacional Financiera, *Informe anual* for 1958 (pub. 1959), table 10, p. 44; *Informe anual* for 1960 (pub. 1961), table 10, p. 44; and *Informe anual* for 1961 (pub. 1962), table 9, p. 49. These data are given for 1953, 1958, and mid-1961 in Table 4 in our next chapter. Data for NAFIN's "own resources" plus the additional resources derived from trust funds and guarantees should add up to the "resources channeled by Nacional Financiera, S.A., to different economic activities." However, there is an unexplained discrepancy in the data in all of the years for which the two series, "own resources" and "resources channeled," are both available. The discrepancy is due apparently to different treatment of some of the liability items in NAFIN's balance sheet. Nacional Financiera ceased publishing the series on its "own resources" in 1957 (but it is easily computed for later years as the sum of liabilities and capital, plus the value of *certificados de participación* in circulation). These data on NAFIN's "own resources" are those which William Diamond gives as "investment resources of the Nacional Financiera" in his book, *Development Banks* (Baltimore: Johns Hopkins University Press, 1957), p. 121.

Chapter 2: The Record of Nacional Financiera

1. "Ley que autoriza a la Secretaría de Hacienda y Crédito Público para la fundación de una sociedad financiera, con carácter de institución nacional," *Diario Oficial,* Aug. 31, 1933.

2. "Ley que modifica la que autorizó a la Secretaría de Hacienda y Crédito Público para la fundación de una sociedad financiera, y que crea la 'Nacional Financiera,' S.A., con el carácter de institución nacional de crédito," *Diario Oficial,* April 30, 1934.

3. Nacional Financiera, *Quince años de vida, 1934–1949,* pamphlet (August 1949), p. 6.

4. José Hernández Delgado, "Nacional Financiera, S.A., Symbolizes Mexico's Industrialization," in Adolfo López Mateos, *The Economic Development of Mexico during a Quarter of a Century (1934–1959),* pamphlet (Nacional Financiera, 1959), p. 18.

5. Nacional Financiera, *Tercera asamblea general de accionistas*

(annual report for 1936, pub. 1937), p. 17. The Compañía Productora e Importadora de Papel, S.A., used the NAFIN loan to rediscount notes given by small printers in payment for supplies of paper. Critics from the private sector have argued that this activity, together with direct loans and investments by NAFIN in printing companies, is a possible indirect form of control of the press. They argue that publishers too critical of the government might not get supplies and credit, while those with "correct" editorial policies will. The charge is difficult to substantiate.

6. Nacional Financiera, *Cuarta asamblea general de accionistas* (annual report for 1937, pub. 1938), pp. 23, 25–27.

7. Nacional Financiera, *Sexta asamblea general de accionistas* (annual report for 1939, pub. 1940), pp. 21–22.

8. José Hernández Delgado, *The Contribution of Nacional Financiera to the Industrialization of Mexico,* address at luncheon of Mexico City Rotary Club, Aug. 1, 1961, pamphlet (Nacional Financiera, 1961), p. 7.

9. Secretaría de Gobernacíon, *Seis años de gobierno al servicio de México, 1934–1940* (1940). See, esp., pp. 65–78.

10. "Ley orgánica de la institución nacional de crédito denominada 'Nacional Financiera,' S.A.," *Diario Oficial,* Dec. 31, 1940. This law, its subsequent amendments, and NAFIN's by-laws are reprinted in the pamphlet cited in our next note.

11. Nacional Financiera, *Ley orgánica y estatutos sociales,* pamphlet, 1963, p. 13.

12. *Ibid.,* p. 15.

13. Nacional Financiera, *Informe anual* for 1960 (pub. 1961), pp. 90–93, and the same agency's *Quince años de vida, 1934–1949,* p. 29.

14. Nacional Financiera, *Duodécima asamblea general ordinaria de accionistas* (annual report for 1945, pub. 1946), p. 52 and annex table 2.

15. *Ibid.,* annex table 1; *Décimatercera asamblea general ordinaria de accionistas* (annual report for 1946, pub. 1947), annex table 1.

16. Joaquín Loredo Goytortúa, "Producción y productividad agrícolas," in *México, 50 años de revolución: La economía* (Mexico, D.F.: Fondo de Cultura Económica, 1960), p. 162.

17. Nacional Financiera, *Décimaséptima asamblea general ordinaria de accionistas* (annual report for 1950, pub. 1951), p. 121. The relatively small magnitude of this output can be appreciated by comparing it with the 66,000-tons-per-year capacity of a single plant built later at Cuautitlán, in the State of Mexico.

18. International Bank for Reconstruction and Development, Combined Mexican Working Party, *The Economic Development of Mexico* (Baltimore: Johns Hopkins University Press, 1953), p. 242.

19. Nacional Financiera, *Octava asamblea general de accionistas* (annual report for 1941, pub. 1942), p. 29.

20. Nacional Financiera, *Duodécima asamblea general ordinaria de accionistas* (annual report for 1945, pub. 1946), pp. 31-32.

21. *Ibid.,* p. 33.

22. *Ibid.,* p. 28.

23. Four of the major firms promoted by NAFIN (in steel, paper, cement, and copper) failed to conform to the proposed ideal of capital structure; each had preferred shares considerably in excess of common as of the end of 1945. *Ibid.,* annex table 2. In the one firm of the four in which NAFIN became majority owner (Altos Hornos de México, S.A.), the proportions were later changed to all common stock and no preferred.

24. *Ibid.,* p. 20.

25. "Ley reformatoria de la orgánica de la Nacional Financiera, S.A.," *Diario Oficial,* Dec. 31, 1947.

26. Quoted in Nacional Financiera, *Ley orgánica y estatutos sociales,* p. 40.

27. Nacional Financiera, *Ley orgánica y estatutos sociales,* p. 43.

28. See Sanford Mosk, *Industrial Revolution in Mexico* (Berkeley: University of California Press, 1950), p. 247.

29. See Nacional Financiera, *Informe anual* for 1960 (pub. 1961), table 12, p. 101.

30. In 1960, imports of paper and paper products were valued at 310 million pesos. One fifth of the cellulosic pastes consumed in Mexico were imported. Domestic production of newsprint was less than one sixth of the quantity imported in that year. See Banco Nacional de México, S.A., Departamento de Valores, "Prontuario de análisis de empresas y valores" (mimeo. loose-leaf sheets, May 1961), sheets 166–21 through 166–25.

31. NAFIN's notion as to what constitutes "basic" industries has varied. The classification of "basic industry" which appears in our Table 4 was adopted in 1959; in 1962 it was modified to include non-ferrous metals, in addition to the categories shown in Table 4. Earlier, NAFIN had referred to "basic industries" as comprising electricity, transportation & communication, iron & steel, and petroleum; the first two are now classified in the "infrastructure." Especially arbitrary is the classification of one major energy source (electricity) in the "infrastructure" and others (petroleum and coal) in "basic industries." See Nacional Financiera, *Décimasexta asamblea general ordinaria de accionistas* (annual report for 1949, pub. 1950), p. 68; *Informe anual* for 1958 (pub. 1959), p. 45; and *Informe anual* for 1961 (pub. 1962), p. 51.

32. See Nacional Financiera, *Informe anual* for 1960 (pub. 1961), table 12, pp. 99–102, and the analogous table in other annual reports.

33. Nacional Financiera, *Informe anual* for 1959 (pub. 1960), tables 12 and 13, pp. 103–109.

34. See Nacional Financiera, *Informe anual* for 1960 (pub. 1961), table 14, pp. 106–111.

Chapter 3: The Character of Nacional Financiera's Entrepreneurial Role

1. Francisco Sarabia Dueñas, "La política de promoción industrial de la Nacional Financiera, S.A.," unpub. thesis, Universidad Nacional Autónoma de México, Escuela Nacional de Economía, 1959, p. 44.

2. The stocks of eight of these thirteen firms accounted for almost two thirds of NAFIN's equity holdings in industry at the end of 1959.

3. Few data are available on the amounts paid in honoraria, but one of NAFIN's more successful firms reported in 1955 that it paid 25,920 pesos to each director and 7,000 pesos to each alternate director (the equivalent of $2,073.60 and $560.00, respectively).

4. "Ley que modifica la que autorizó a la Secretaría de Hacienda y Crédito Público para la fundación de una sociedad financiera, y que crea la 'Nacional Financiera,' S.A., con el carácter de institución nacional de crédito," *Diario Oficial,* April 30, 1934.

5. See Nacional Financiera, *Ley orgánica y estatutos sociales,* pamphlet, 1963, pp. 26–32.

6. See, for example, Práxedes Reina Hermosillo (a NAFIN official at the time), "The Role of Nacional Financiera in the Development of Industry in Northern Mexico," in University of Texas, Institute of Latin-American Studies, *Basic Industries in Texas and Northern Mexico,* Latin-American Studies, IX (Austin: University of Texas Press, 1950), p. 9.

7. José Hernández Delgado, *The Contribution of Nacional Financiera to the Industrialization of Mexico,* address at luncheon of Mexico City Rotary Club, Aug. 1, 1961, pamphlet (Nacional Financiera, 1961), p. 15.

8. See Hernández Delgado, *Contribution,* pp. 16–18. It is reported by Merle Kling that one major firm owned by NAFIN even makes a monthly contribution to the Instituto de Investigaciones Sociales y Económicas, a right-wing Mexican business group which devotes much of its budget to publishing denunciations of government enterprise. See Kling's *A Mexican Interest Group in Action* (Englewood Cliffs, N.J.: Prentice-Hall, 1961), p. 27.

9. For an interesting study of Mexico's development banking policies and institutions, see Charles W. Anderson, "Bankers as Revolutionaries," one of the two studies in William P. Glade, Jr., and Anderson, *The Political Economy of Mexico* (Madison: University of Wisconsin Press, 1963).

Chapter 4: The Future of Nacional Financiera

1. A qualitative appraisal of some of the opportunities for export to the United States appears in a talk by Calvin P. Blair, "United States Economic Growth and Markets for Mexican Exports," before the Second Annual United States–Mexico Trade and Investment Institute, San Antonio, Tex., mimeo., Oct. 21, 1960.

2. Secretaría de Industria y Comercio, Dirección General de Industria, *Posibilidades para la promoción industrial privada en México,* pamphlet, 1962.

3. See Alfredo Navarrete, "Nacional Financiera: políticas y prácticas en el campo de la promoción industrial," *El Mercado de Valores,* Sept. 17, 1962, p. 563. The article summarizes a speech which Dr. Navarrete, a vice-president of NAFIN, made to the American Club of Mexico City, Aug. 28, 1962.

RAFAEL IZQUIERDO, PROTECTIONISM IN MEXICO

Chapter 1: Imports and Import Controls

1. Raúl Prebisch, "Economic Development or Monetary Stability: The False Dilemma," *Economic Bulletin for Latin America* (U.N. Economic Commission for Latin America, Santiago, Chile), vol. VI, no. 1, March 1961, p. 5.

2. This treaty was signed by Mexico, Brazil, Argentina, Uruguay, Peru, Ecuador, Colombia, Chile, and Paraguay. The U.N. Economic Commission for Latin America had promoted the idea and had prepared numerous studies demonstrating the need for such an arrangement. See Víctor L. Urquidi, *Free Trade and Economic Integration in Latin America* (Berkeley: University of California Press, 1962).

3. The "Ley de ingresos de la federación" (federal revenue law) of 1959 provides a clear illustration of the scope of the executive's powers: "The executive is empowered, during the year 1959, to increase, decrease, or eliminate the export and import tariffs levied on products, goods, or articles which require increase, decrease, or elimination; to restrict or prohibit imports and exports which affect the nation's economy unfavorably. The general tariff schedules for exports and imports in effect in 1958 are approved. The executive will report to Congress on the use he may make of these powers when he submits the annual budget for 1960" (*Diario Oficial,* Dec. 29, 1959). These powers were broadened in 1960 to empower the executive to set up a budget for the total foreign exchange available for imports; but no such budget had been set up by 1963.

4. "Ley de secretarías de estado" of 1959, *Diario Oficial*, Dec. 24, 1958.

5. These committees covered the following product groups: (1) paper and related products; (2) oils, fats, and oleaginous seeds; (3) construction materials; (4) iron and steel industry and railroads; (5) fertilizers and insecticides; (6) wires and nails; (7) spare parts for automobiles; (8) copper products; (9) tin plate and sheet metal; (10) tubular products and fittings; (11) electrical appliances; (12) motors for electrical appliances; (13) food products and beverages; (14) valves; (15) iron and steel; (16) electric lamps; (17) motorcycles and bicycles; (18) chemical products; (19) wool; (20) hides and skins; (21) shoes; (22) textiles and clothing; (23) ceramics, crystal, crockery, and porcelain; (24) laminated plastics and plastic articles; (25) refrigerators, washing machines, and other household equipment; (26) pens, watches, and jewelry; (27) machinery.

6. Secretaría de Industria y Comercio, "Reglamento para la expedición de permisos de importación y exportación mercancías sujetos a restricción" (1956), article II, paragraph IV.

7. Mimeographed document of CNIT, without title or date, presented to the Secretaría de Industria y Comercio early in 1960.

8. *Informe que presenta el Dr. e Ing. Santos Amaro, Presidente de la Cámara Nacional de la Industria de Transformación, a la XVII Asamblea General Ordinaria* (Mexico, D.F.: Editorial Cultura, 1957), p. 62.

9. In June 1962, the Secretaría de Industria y Comercio published a pamphlet for industrialists entitled *Posibilidades para la promoción industrial privada en México* (possibilities for private industrial promotion in Mexico).

Chapter 2: Evolution of Import Policy

1. Speech of Finance Minister Eduardo Suárez on March 21, 1946, at the twelfth Convención Nacional Bancaria, printed in *Discursos* (a collection of speeches published by the finance ministry in 1958), p. 84.

2. Official prices must be used as the basis for valuation except when invoice prices are higher. Official prices are set in accordance with the wholesale price of the article in the principal supplying country. If the foreign wholesale price is very much lower than that of similar domestic articles the official price may be set in accordance with local wholesale prices or local costs of production. Actually there is a discrepancy between the prices of legal transactions (those in which no attempt is made to undervalue the imported articles) and official prices.

3. Confederación de Cámaras Industriales, *Asamblea General Ordinaria de 1953: Ponencias* (Mexico, D.F., 1953), pp. 5–6.

4. Unfortunately, import statistics which differentiate products according to the degree of processing are not available, nor has it been possible to prepare them. Studies such as those prepared in Europe by the Organization for European Economic Cooperation (OEEC), showing the origin of products in a free trade area, would be extremely helpful in obtaining a clear idea of the process of import replacement. Technical specifications which clearly delimit the processes of assembly, at least in certain basic industries, could be established so that it would be possible to determine the stage of manufacturing at which protection might be applied to advantage.

5. Secretaría de Hacienda y Crédito Público, *Tarifa del impuesto general de importación: Disposiciones generales* (1956).

6. Cámara Nacional de la Industria de Transformación, *Memorias y documentos,* a collection of papers from this organization's second national congress (Mexico, D.F.: EDIAPSA, 1953), p. 245.

7. *Excelsior,* Sept. 2, 1961, p. 3.

Chapter 3: The Positions of Private Enterprise

1. Sanford A. Mosk's *Industrial Revolution in Mexico* (Berkeley: University of California Press, 1950) contains references to protectionist policy at the end of the Second World War. The Mexican journal *Problemas Agrícolas e Industriales,* vol. III, no. 2 (1951), published the Mosk book in translation together with comments on it by various Mexican economists. These commentaries also contain some discussion of protectionism.

2. Cámara Nacional de la Industria de Transformación, "Protección a la industria," p. 14. This paper is found in the CNIT's "Memoria del Primer Congreso de la CNIT" (mimeo., 1945).

3. The policies of these two organizations are analyzed in Raymond Vernon, *The Dilemma of Mexico's Development* (Cambridge, Mass.: Harvard University Press, 1963), esp. pp. 167–175.

4. Riversdale Garland Stone, "La situación económica y comercial de México," *Problemas Agrícolas e Industriales de México,* vol. X, nos. 3–4 (1958), p. 232.

5. Cámara Nacional de la Industria de Transformación, *Memorias y documentos,* a collection of papers from this organization's second national congress (Mexico, D.F.: EDIAPSA, 1953), p. 190.

6. Confederación de Cámaras Industriales, *Memoria del IV Congreso Nacional de Industriales,* vol. II (Mexico, D.F., 1957), p. 703.

7. *Informe que presenta el Dr. e Ing. Santos Amaro, Presidente de la Cámara Nacional de la Industria de Transformación, a la XVII Asamblea General Ordinaria* (Mexico, D.F.: Editorial Cultura, 1957), p. 43.

Index

BOOKS PREPARED UNDER THE AUSPICES OF THE CENTER FOR INTERNATIONAL AFFAIRS, HARVARD UNIVERSITY

PUBLISHED BY HARVARD UNIVERSITY PRESS

The Soviet Bloc, by Zbigniew K. Brzezinski, 1960 (sponsored jointly with the Russian Research Center).

Rift and Revolt in Hungary, by Ferenc A. Váli, 1961.

The Economy of Cyprus, by A. J. Meyer, with Simos Vassiliou, 1962 (jointly with the Center for Middle Eastern Studies).

Entrepreneurs of Lebanon, by Yusif A. Sayigh, 1962 (jointly with the Center for Middle Eastern Studies).

Communist China 1955–1959: Policy Documents with Analysis, with a Foreword by Robert R. Bowie and John K. Fairbank, 1962 (jointly with the East Asian Research Center).

In Search of France, by Stanley Hoffmann, Charles P. Kindleberger, Laurence Wylie, Jesse R. Pitts, Jean-Baptiste Duroselle, and François Goguel, 1963.

Somali Nationalism, by Saadia Touval, 1963.

The Dilemma of Mexico's Development, by Raymond Vernon, 1963.

The Arms Debate, by Robert A. Levine, 1963.

Africans on the Land, by Montague Yudelman, 1964.

Public Policy and Private Enterprise in Mexico, ed. Raymond Vernon, essays by Miguel S. Wionczek, David H. Shelton, Calvin P. Blair, and Rafael Izquierdo.

AVAILABLE FROM OTHER PUBLISHERS

The Necessity for Choice, by Henry A. Kissinger, 1961. Harper & Bros.

Strategy and Arms Control, by Thomas C. Schelling and Morton H. Halperin, 1961. Twentieth Century Fund.

United States Manufacturing Investment in Brazil, by Lincoln Gordon and Engelbert L. Grommers, 1962. Harvard Business School.

Limited War in the Nuclear Age, by Morton H. Halperin, 1963. John Wiley & Sons.

Counterinsurgency Warfare, by David Galula, 1964. Frederick A. Praeger.

People and Policy in the Middle East, by Max Weston Thornburg, 1964. W. W. Norton & Co.

Shaping the Future, by Robert R. Bowie, 1964. Columbia University Press.

Foreign Aid and Foreign Trade, by Edward S. Mason, 1964 (jointly with the Council on Foreign Relations). Harper & Row.